10/11

VISIONS OF GHOST ARMIES

Visions of Ghost Armies

Real-Life Encounters with War-Torn Spirits

From the Files of FATE Magazine

BARNES
& NOBLE
BOOKS

NEW YORK

2003 Barnes & Noble Books

ISBN 0-7607-3954-4

Text design by Kevin McGuinness

Printed and bound in the United States of America

04   05   06   07   08   09   M   9   8   7   6   5   4   3   2

BVG

CONTENTS

PHANTOM MARCHERS OF CRETE   1

LEGION OF THE DAMNED   8

PHANTOM ARMIES ROAM HAWAII   12

THE WHITE CAVALRY   14

ETERNAL SOLDIER   20

GHOST ARMY OF FONTAINEBLEAU   23

SEVENTEENTH-CENTURY BRITISH BATTLE REVISITED   24

THE MYSTERIOUS SAVIOR OF HADLEY   27

DEVIL RIDER OF CHISHOLM HOLLOW   30

THE CAPTAIN WHO CAME TO TEA   36

WHERE IS YESTERDAY?   38

PHANTOM RIDERS ON SOUTER-FELL   42

THE GHOST OF COLONEL WALLACE   51

THE GHOST ARMY OF CHIMNEY ROCK PASS   55

THE UNEASY DEAD AT FORT MIMS   57

THE GHOST OF GOLIAD   65

PHANTOM TROOPERS   67

THE PHANTOM ARMY OF THE CIVIL WAR   70

GHOST OF WAR 74

SOLDIER AT THE DOOR 77

GHOST WATCH AT WEST POINT 79

GHOST ARMY OF JOHNSON'S ISLAND 86

THEY'VE BEEN WAITING 88

OUR CONFEDERATE GHOST 97

GHOST ARMY OF THE CIVIL WAR 100

THE RETURN OF PRIVATE DUPOY 102

KINDRED SPIRITS 105

THE GHOSTS OF TUNNEL HILL 113

CIVIL WAR GHOST 118

THE MOST HAUNTED BATTLEFIELD OF THE CIVIL WAR 120

A MYSTERIOUS GUIDE AND PHANTOM TROOPS 122

CUSTER'S LAST STAND? 125

GHOST OF THE CIBECUE CREEK MASSACRE 126

SILENT SENTRY IN VIETNAM 130

I WRESTLED A GHOST 134

THE UNKNOWN SOLDIER 136

THE EARTHBOUND SOLDIER 138

CAPTAIN CROCKETT'S MESSAGE 145

PHANTOM FLIERS 147

THE FLYING COFFIN 154

THE HAUNTED SUBMARINE 156

GHOSTLY SOLDIER SAVES FRIEND 163

THE PHANTOM OF THE CRUISE 165

Brother Against Brother   169

Tale of Two Ghosts   171

Vision of World War I   175

Ghost Soldier in Our Attic   177

The Phantom Barrage   182

Steve Came Home   184

The Phantom Soldier   186

The Smirking Airman   188

The Officer Who Returned   190

Ghosts of the Battlefield   194

Ghost Plane of World War II   196

Cursed Airport   198

Fifty Yards from Death   199

Haunted Airport of England   200

A Perfect Ghost Story   202

Dead Man's Landing   204

Corregidor's Ghostly Troops   205

Reliving the Dieppe Raid   207

Keith's Visit with Grandpa   214

The Phantom at Pleskau Airfield   216

Strange Vision   220

Unofficial Notification   222

Light in the Night   223

D-Day Echoes in England   225

Her Soldier Came Back   227

THE SIGN OF THE FLAMING HEATHER 229

THE GALLOPING COLONEL 234

MY SOLDIER RETURNED 236

DEAD SOLDIER ON SENTRY DUTY? 238

MESSAGE IN VERSE 242

RETURN FROM LOVE HILL 244

MOTHER'S DAY 245

KEEP MOVING 247

WE ALL "COME HOME" 249

THE HAUNTED AIR BASE 251

GHOST ARMY OF THE RISING SUN 252

THE RESTLESS DEAD OF LONDON 254

I THINK THERE'S A GHOST HERE THAT LIKES ME 256

THE GHOST THAT HATED HITLER 259

THE LEGEND OF SCREAMING CHARLIE 267

OLD SOLDIERS DON'T FADE AWAY 273

GHOST ON THE HIGH SEAS 279

THE PHANTOM NON-COM 281

DAVID CAME HOME 282

MY LIFE WAS SAVED BY A DEAD SOLDIER 285

A SOLDIER RETURNS 288

THE DISAPPEARING HERO 290

SOLDIER'S RETURN 291

WITH HIS HEAD TUCKED UNDERNEATH HIS ARM 293

SAY GOOD-BYE 297

JIMMY, IS THAT YOU?   298

LAST PLANE OUT   300

MISSING IN ACTION   303

"I WAS KILLED INSTANTLY . . ."   305

A BROTHER'S LOVE   307

JOHN'S GI GUARDIAN   309

PHANTOM MARCHERS OF CRETE

Harold J. Wilkins

ROWNING OVER THE LONELY BEACH OF FRANCOKASTELLI (CAS-
tle of the Franks), towards Cape Krio in Crete, is a ruined
castle built in the late Middle Ages by the old Doges of
Venice. Its gray walls and weathered turrets tower into the clear
blue sky, and its foundations are washed by the sparkling waters of
the Mediterranean. Inland from the beach is a desolate plain, but-
tressed by a wild range of mountains. Across this eerie plain,
marching in procession after sunset or just before sunrise, a phantom army marches from the shadows of the mountains towards the
ruined castle.

The tall and spectral figures are always seen between the middle of
May and the first week in June. They march, aureoled with mystic
light, from east to west, down to the lonely beach where they vanish
into the air or the sea. The place is remote and far out of the track of
tourists who do not brave the wild and dangerous mountain trails to
reach it from Knossos.

Some eyewitnesses say the figures appear to be soldiers of some
very ancient time. They wear antique armor and helmets, carry
spears and short swords, and bear shields that appear older than
those of the days of Homer. Peasants and even administrators of
Crete who have seen them say they are very tall men, almost giants,
and they pass like an army of the dead towards the shadows of the

old castle of the Doges. Yet it is evident that this old castle is not their mysterious bourne.

When the old Turks of Constantinople ruled Crete in the 1860s and 1870s, the soldiers of the garrison at Francokastelli saw them and were scared almost out of their lives by these soundless marchers. Attention was first drawn to them, outside Crete, by a well-known British M.P., Sir Ernest Bennett, at one time Postmaster General in the British government, who was war correspondent of the *London Times* during the rebellion of the Greeks of old Crete against the Turks in 1897. He tells how, in 1927, an Englishman named Baker, who had lived for many years in the Levant and had an intimate knowledge of the mentality of the Cretan peasants, whose tongue he spoke, was travelling in the Ida mountains with muleteers, when they came to a solitary village called Sphakia Kora. It is about 12 miles from Francokastelli.

Said Baker's head muleteer, "This is the month of May, the time of the year when people come from all over Crete to see the Men of the Shadows."

"What 'Men of the Shadows'?" asked the surprised Englishman.

"Shadows of strange big men in armor, who are seen at this very time coming across the plain from the shadows of the mountains, in the dim light before dawn. They march in uncanny procession, making no sound, towards the old ruined castle on the beach of Francokastelli. I am surprised, Master, that you who know Crete have never heard of them. We call them, as have our forefathers before us, the 'Dew Men,' or 'Drousolites,' because they are seen always when the dew is on the ground and the sun has not yet risen."

"Tell me more of this," said Baker.

"My father and my grandfather have seen these Men of the Shadows, and so have many of the people of the village of Francokastelli. Every year, in mid-May and early June, they assemble on the beach before dawn to watch for their coming. . . . Here is Petro. Ask him about the Dew Men."

Baker turned to Petro, another muleteer, who told a queer story.

"I was engaged by some Germans, about 10 years ago, to help in some archaeological work near where they are seen. And it was while I was there that I and many other local people saw these Men of the Shadows. It was after sunset and dark when we saw this strange army of phantoms coming across the plain towards the beach where we stood. They uttered no sound. They seemed to be in armor. Some wore strange helmets. All carried weapons, shields, short swords, and spears.

"They were very tall men. As we looked, they seemed to vanish into the air as suddenly as they had come. Holy Virgin, how frightened we were! We were rendered dumb till the dawn came. Who can say what these Shadow Men are? I have heard a foreign scientist in the ruins of Hajia Triada which lies not many miles away, say an old Roman garrison might have been wiped out here in the days of the old Roman Emperors. But who knows?"

Hajia Triada, it may be noted, is like the famous Knossos, also one of the old cities of the Minoans. These uncanny shadows of men do *not* look like old Roman legionnaries. Petro added that an Italian scientist told him they might be men of some archaic race of old Crete.

Reports of this weird spectacle drifted across the Sea of Candia and the Aegean to Athens in old Greece, which is some 220 miles north, as the crow flies. Here is what a Cretan wine merchant, G. S. Naxakis, wrote to one of the leading newspapers in Athens:

"I know that a former Greek governor of Crete has seen these strange Dew Men. His secretary, M. Psyllakis, saw them in the dim light before dawn and the rising of the sun. But they have also been seen in the dusk, after sunset. Never are they seen when the sun shines, or in daylight."

Sir Ernest Bennett, who is a classical graduate of Hertford College, Oxford University, was in Athens and read these newspaper reports. He knew Crete and its people, and he determined to go to the island in the last week of May, in 1928, and visit the lonely beach and ruined castle where the Dew Men of the Shadows are seen. He intended to question the local eyewitnesses.

On May 17, 1928, Sir Ernest camped out on the beach, a few yards from the gray and badly weathered ruins of the old Venetian castle, towards whose main gate the phantoms are seen to march in the pale light from the still starry pre-dawn sky over brooding Mount Ida. He interviewed villagers who testified that they had seen the Dew Men. A peasant named Delyanis said:

"I saw them moving like shimmering lights. This army of men who make no sound seemed to advance and retreat for about 15 minutes. Then they seemed to vanish into the sea."

Another villager, Petrides, said:

"I and others standing on this beach saw the Dew Men about a third of a mile away, near the mountains, yonder. Three other men saw them in 1924, when they were advancing on a line from east to west. We could not see their legs, but they had the heads of men. About them shone a strange light."

Another eyewitness said:

"The Dew Men moved along like water pictures until the sun rose, when they vanished." One woman was seen to be actually standing right in the midst of those moving phantoms, yet she herself did not see them!

In a cottage close to the ruined castle of Francokastelli, in 1928, lived an abbot. He told Sir Ernest:

"I have seen the phantoms twice. They were like an army on the march, going from east to west. The Archbishop of Crete, M. Eumenios, was with me at one of those times, and we saw them very early in the morning. All staying in my house came out to see them. They appeared beyond the belt of trees towards the mountains of Ida, and we could see them better when we stooped. They were marching in a column about a quarter of a mile away. The phenomenon lasted 15 minutes."

The secretary of the governor, M. Psyllakis, saw them in the last week of May 1906, from a hamlet some distance from the beach. He told Sir Ernest:

"I saw them about 220 yards away. I had gone especially to witness the phenomenon. It was 10 minutes before the sun rose and the stars were still in the sky. It was then that I saw a host of moving shadows, like those cast by people on the blinds of a lighted house in the dark. They were men of various shapes, but I do not recall seeing horses or spears among them."

Sir Ernest waited, camped on the beach, until the end of May, but he did not see the Dew Men. He left for Candia, and the following week he had a letter from a general of the Cretan army, M. Hadjimichalis, who wrote:

"I went there to unveil a memorial to my grandfather, a general killed in action with the Turks at Francokastelli. After you had gone, and on 4, 5 and 7 of June 1928, the phantom Dew Men appeared. A woman harvester, not a native of the place, was out in the fields when the ghostly band appeared. She thought they were laborers, come to seek work in the harvest. 'What brings all these hundreds of men here?' she asked another woman. 'There is not work for all of them.' The other woman told her they were the Dew Men. On each day they marched, in a procession from east to west, from the foot of the mountains across the dark plain towards the ruined castle. Sometimes they were massed in formation; at other times the columns were thin and dispersed. It must be some strange natural phenomenon."

But Sir Ernest, on the weight of the evidence, does not believe it is a natural phenomenon but something supernormal and mystic.

If it is urged that the Dew Men are just mirages, it must be remembered that mirages are refracted images, with a maximum range of about 40 miles, and visible only when the sun has risen, and in the light of clear day. As one has commented, the phantoms are seen only in pre-dawn light and in a limited period of weeks between mid-May and early June.

Further, all around the lone, wide beach are only the ruins of the old castle and a very few houses, from which, or from the few scattered hamlets lying out on the plain between the foot of the Ida range and the shore, no host of such men like these could possibly come. And if it were just an image refracted from some place 40 miles or more away, it is extremely unlikely that so many living men would be about in the hour before dawn.

Who and what are these Dew Men? Whence do they come? Why do they appear only at a certain time? What object are they serving?

It appears certain that the Dew Men are in no way linked with the history of the old Venetian castle. The Italian savant who suggested that these Men of the Shadows belong to the archaic past of Crete may have been close to the truth. Eyewitnesses have described the phantom marchers as wearing helmets and armor and carrying spears and shields, like some archaic company out of Homer's *Iliad* or *Odyssey*. And all eyewitnesses seem agreed that the phantoms are very tall men.

The mountains from whose shadows the Dew Men appear to begin their march were the home of the priests dedicated to the cult of the Great Earth Goddess-Mother of Jupiter. In a very remote age she was an androgyne or bisexual diety, a god combining the attributes of both father and mother. It thus appears that mysterious rites of some sort were celebrated by the Dew Men in life, several millennia ago, when they marched on the east-west line between the middle of May and early June toward the lone beach at Francokastelli.

Some say, as did Diodorus Siculus, about 35 B.C., that old Crete was the very ancient residence of Zeus, the Atlantean, who with others went from there and founded Eastern Atlantis, whose long-vanished continental island was the mysterious Panchaea located far out in the Indian Ocean between Ceylon and Madagascar. Diodorus drew on the libraries of ancient Carthage, which the barbarous Romans destroyed. Suppose, then, that some ancient, long since drowned land lay beyond what is now the desolate beach of Francokastelli. Can it be religious rites connected with the traditions of this lost land and taking place on the beach, which bring the phantom marchers here?

LEGION OF THE DAMNED

A. C. McKerracher

I USED TO HAVE DOUBTS ABOUT THE PARANORMAL. AFTER ALL, ONE person's psychic experience is difficult to prove or disprove. I even dismissed my own uncanny encounter as a trick of the imagination until it was unexpectedly verified in October 1984. Now I am certain I heard the ghosts of a doomed Roman legion marching to its fate 2,000 years ago.

In 1974 I moved to a new housing estate on a hill above the small country town of Dunblane in Perthshire, Scotland. Shortly after arriving I was working late one September night when I went outside for some fresh air. It was a clear frosty night with not a sound to be heard anywhere. Most of my neighbors were in bed and down below the town was covered in mist.

As I turned to go back indoors, I suddenly heard the strangest noise coming across the fields to the south. It sounded like a large number of people on the move with faint voices rising and falling. I listened in puzzlement, then decided my imagination was playing tricks and went inside. But I couldn't get the curious matter off my mind, and 20 minutes later I went outside again.

To my horror, the noise was now much louder. I say, "to my horror" because it was now passing immediately behind the houses on the other side of the street. For the first time in my life I felt the skin rise from my scalp and my hair bristle. I could now make out individual voices but couldn't understand what they were saying. But quite clearly I heard the tramp of marching feet and the jingle of what sounded like weapons and armor.

I stood rooted to the spot as the unearthly, unseen cavalcade passed by. The marchers must have numbered in the thousands, for the noise went on and on. Suddenly snapping out of the spell, I turned inside and went straight to bed. I was convinced I had been overworking and for this reason did not mention the episode to my family in the morning.

I put the experience from my mind until a week later when I called on an elderly couple, Major and Mrs. Chapman, who had moved in farther up the street. I was telling them about our Residents' Association when their German shepherd dog rose up to stretch. "Sit down!" its mistress commanded. "You're seeing things again."

"What things?" I asked.

"Well, the strangest thing happened last week," she replied. "We were sitting up reading about 1:00 A.M. when the cat and dog suddenly woke up. They stood bolt upright with all their hair bristling up their backs and seemed to watch something crossing the lounge for about 20 minutes. They were terrified."

When I questioned the Chapmans further, I was astonished to learn this strange episode had taken place on the same night and at precisely the same time I had heard the invisible army pass by.

Out of curiosity I began to research local history. I learned that the housing estate was built on the site of two large Roman marching camps,* the first having been built in A.D. 83, when General Agricola

---

*"Whenever a Roman army was on the march, especially in enemy territory, it always built an entrenched camp for the night, where the men slept in leather tents within the safety of the earthworks and palisades. Since the camp layout was standardized, each man knew exactly where his quarter lay and the camp could be set up in quick time and in good order."—K. H. Scullard, *Roman Britain* (1979).

invaded Scotland to extend the Roman Empire to the very tip of Britain. I located some old aerial photographs which clearly showed the outlines of the camps. They also showed the line of the Roman road which ran north directly behind the houses on the other side of my street.

I also began to study the paranormal. I found that some modern researchers speculate that "ghosts" are not literally spirits of the dead but are formed by a strong emotional or violent event which registers itself in the earth's magnetic field—a bit like a magnetic video recording. For some reason this can be picked up by receptive persons at particular times. This was an idea I felt I could accept. But what event had been so terrible that its occurrence on that Roman road had been recorded for eternity?

When I searched the Roman history of Britain, I learned that in A.D. 117 the Caledonian tribes in Scotland had risen in revolt and destroyed the small Roman garrisons. The Emperor Hadrian ordered the elite IX Hispana Legion, stationed at York, to march north to subdue the tribes. This unit had been known as the Unlucky Ninth ever since A.D. 60, when it had flogged Queen Boadicea of the southern English Iceni tribe and raped her daughters. Boadicea had cursed the legion to eternity and it was cut to pieces when she led all the tribes in a bloody revolt.

The IX Legion had been reformed although it never prospered. But it was still an elite unit of 4,000 battle-hardened legionnaires when it marched into Scotland in the autumn of 117. It was last heard of marching along the Roman road which now lies behind the modern housing estate of Dunblane, Perthshire—and from there it disappeared from the face of the earth. Not a trace of the finest fighting unit in the Roman army has ever been found—not a body, not a coin, not a weapon. Four thousand soldiers simply vanished into the mist.

I never heard the noise again and I later moved to the older part of

Dunblane. I had forgotten all about the incident until October 1984, when I was giving a lecture on local history to a ladies' club. Cecilia Moore, one of the members, came up afterwards to say how interested she had been. "I never knew the Romans came as far north as this," she said. Then she astounded me by adding with a laugh, "I wonder if that was the ghost of a Roman army I heard."

When I asked her what she meant, she said she had moved into a house on the other side of the street from my old property. "You won't believe this," she said, "but I was putting the cat out one night when I heard what sounded like an army passing right through my back garden. It was fascinating but when I told my family they just laughed." It turned out that she had heard this at 1:00 A.M. on exactly the same date in September that I had heard the sound 10 years earlier.

I am convinced that what she and I heard—and what my neighbors' animals saw—was the doomed Ninth Legion marching to its terrible unknown fate nearly 2,000 years ago.

Phantom Armies Roam Hawaii

Vincent H. Gaddis

O CCASIONALLY FROM THE AWESOME DEPTHS OF TIME AND space, from the ethereal history of humankind, come the ancient warriors of Hawaii. Led by their chiefs, carrying torches and beating drums, they frighten the modern natives. Anyone caught in their line of march is left dead. So when the living hear or see the approach of these bands, they flee or hide at a safe distance until the marchers have passed.

The Japanese attack on Pearl Harbor took place on the morning of December 7, 1941. The night before, just hours before the attack, two warrior armies marched. The report appears in *Paradise of the Pacific* magazine, published in Honolulu (December 1943 issue). Were these appearances harbingers of the tragic assault about to begin?

Near the village of Maluhonua, not far from Pearl Harbor, the residents were awakened by the sounds of marching men shortly before midnight. Some went to the doors and looked outside. They could not see, but could only hear the grim tramping. It was coming from the *heiau* (ruins of an ancient temple platform) at the head of the valley. Then it passed through the village and outward to the sea.

A scream of mortal agony was heard during the march in the valley above the settlement. The next morning the lifeless body of a young man of the village was found on the trail. It showed no marks of violence.

At about the same time, there was a similar march in the Lumahai Valley on the island of Kauai. This time witnesses could not only hear the sound of the march, but they could also see apparitions of the warriors. The body of an elderly Japanese man was found in the path of the marchers.

THE WHITE CAVALRY

Captain C. W. Haywood

LATE WINTER OF 1917 AND EARLY SPRING OF 1918 WERE TRYING times for Great Britain and her Allies, owing to the fact that her troops were fighting on so many different fronts in various parts of the world, and that the U-boat menace had severely affected her shipping.

Although the British Dominions had sent troops to her help and the United States was doing likewise, there were several sectors on the Western Front where tired British troops had to fight on without relief until reinforcements were available.

At that time I was intelligence officer on the First Army Front with headquarters in the bright little town of Bethune on the LaBassee Front; so the occurrence now related is from personal experience.

Portugal had entered the war on the side of Great Britain and one of their detachments was sent to relieve the men on the First Army Front and to take over a sector of trenches from the British Forces. I was advised that they would pass through Bethune, and my instructions were to the effect that two German spies would be amongst them disguised as Portuguese soldiers and that I was to arrest them.

In the meantime the German Forces opposite the British First Army had been strongly reinforced by troops withdrawn from the

Russian Front, where fighting had ceased owing to the collapse of the Russian Empire and the breakup of the Russian Army.

When the Portuguese detachment passed through Bethune the men were allowed a short halt for refreshments and poured into a couple of *estaminets* to order their drinks before going forward.

Since the national drink in Portugal is wine and the national drink in Germany is beer, I instructed some of my men to look out for anyone who ordered the latter drink and to arrest them. This order was carried out very effectively.

Thus we were able to catch the spies and to find out from them that numbers of heavy artillery had been trained on the trenches the Portuguese were to take over. When that unfortunate detachment relieved the British they were literally blotted out by the concentrated mass of bursting shells which rained upon them. The few left abandoned the trenches and came fleeing through Bethune, absolutely panic-stricken and demoralized.

This meant that our front line had a big gap and it became necessary for the whole of the British Forces on our left and right to retreat in order to prevent being enfiladed and destroyed. They came pouring through Bethune and the town itself was subjected to heavy enemy shell fire which brought many houses crashing to the ground in ruins. There was considerable loss of life to the civil population, all of which had to be evacuated by the British, who commandeered any available transport—whether lorries, buses or private cars—in order to get them out of the danger zone. This was finally accomplished under numerous difficulties, not the least being the reluctance of the women, especially, to leave their homes.

In order to keep back the advancing enemy, whose long lines of gray-coated infantry could clearly be seen from the borders of the ruined town, British gunners took up their positions on our side of the LaBassee Canal, occupying shell holes and putting up a very effective machine-gun barrage, thus checking the Germans and help-ing to cover the retreat of our troops until they were enabled to dig themselves into a strong line of trenches some miles further back.

In England as well as in the United States, national prayer went up once more to God in this new "time of trouble."

At Bethune, the terrific shelling to which we had been subjected for a considerable period suddenly lifted and began to burst on open ground beyond the town, although it was absolutely bare of houses, trees, or human beings. Yet the shell fire increased in intensity and was followed by heavy bursts of concentrated machine-gun fire. We stood looking in amazement.

"Fritz has gone barmy, sir," said a sergeant standing close to me. "What in the world can he be peppering that open ground for?"

"I can't think of any reason," I replied, "but get along down to the canal and see what is happening there."

Shortly afterwards I followed him and, arriving at the outskirts of Bethune, I walked across a small patch of grass as I made my way to the canal. As I did so, a lark arose from near my feet and soared up and up into the blue sunlit sky on quivering wings, then, poised on the soft breeze, sent down a lovely song of thankfulness and praise to God. Heartened and inspired, I went forward again through the intervening mud and, on arriving near the canal, I saw my men stand-ing on the edge of a shell hole waving their "tin helmets" and shout-ing out:

"Fritz is retiring! Fritz is retiring!"

The heavy artillery and machine-gun fire had ceased and as we watched with wonder-struck eyes we saw the whole of the appar-ently victorious German Army break up into a disorganized rabble of men fleeing in panic, throwing away their rifles and kit in order to run the faster.

"Get out after them!" I shouted. "Bring back prisoners, officers if possible. I must find out the meaning of this sudden retreat."

With a rousing cheer our men crossed the pontoons still spanning the canal and dashed after the disorganized enemy, whom they had to follow for a considerable distance before they were able to take any prisoners.

When they did return, I noticed that each Tommy had anywhere from two to four or more prisoners, all of them following like sheep. Their faces had a curious strained look, as if they had seen something which had been terrifying and unusual.

During the following days I examined many prisoners, both officers and men, and though their accounts differed in small details, in the main they tallied and can be summarized in the words of a Prussian officer who gave me this version:

"We were advancing at the head of our troops, all of whom were in excellent spirits, singing as they swung along, thinking that the British were now defeated and all that remained was to go forward without much opposition and capture Paris, where we would have a fine time—plenty of drinks and all else we desired.

"By my side was my lieutenant, Fritz, and he suddenly seized hold of my arm, saying: 'Look! *Herr Kapitan*, there is a large body of mounted men approaching Bethune from the other side. See, the smoke from the burning houses is blowing away and I can discern their uniforms. Why, they are all clad in white and are mounted on white horses. Who can they be?'

" 'I don't know,' I replied, 'they may be British Colonial mounted troops.'

" 'I know of no British Colonial mounted troops with white uniforms and white chargers,' he said, 'but anyway they will be blown to pieces now our heavy artillery are opening fire upon them.'

"We halted instinctively and stood watching those white uniform–clad cavalry advancing quietly through the smoke, their figures clearly outlined in the shining sun. We saw the shells breaking into death-dealing fragments and bursting amidst their ranks with shattering crashes which shook the ground, and this was soon followed by intensive machine-gun fire which raked them to and fro until it would seem impossible for anyone to survive.

"But the white cavalry came quietly forward at a slow trot and NOT A MAN OR A HORSE FELL!

"Resistless as the incoming tide they advanced and in front of them rode their leader—a fine figure of a man. By his side was a great sword—not a cavalry sword but similar to that used by the Crusaders; and his hands lay quietly holding the reins of his great white charger as it bore him proudly forward.

"Then a terror seized me and I found myself fleeing from that awe-inspiring body of white cavalry, frightened, terrified. All around me were masses of men, formerly an army, now a rabble broken and afraid; all fleeing from them also but more especially from that wonderful leader on his great white charger. . . .

· "The German Army is defeated. I don't say you will not have any more fighting, for this you are bound to experience; but I do say that we have lost the war and that it is due to the white cavalry."

He was right, for shortly afterwards the British and all Allied Forces came into action in full strength and pushed forward after the constantly retreating Germans. Fighting was often experienced but the main resistance of the enemy was definitely broken, and between April and November 1918, over 300,000 prisoners and 6,000 guns were captured; the Armistice being signed on the 11th of November, 1918.

During the years 1928 to 1939 I had evidence of this account from other sources, in one case from a man who said that he had captured many of the German prisoners at that time and that they could speak of nothing but the White Cavalry and their awe-inspiring leader from whom they had fled in such terror.

A lady who had been a nurse also told me that all the German wounded whom she had attended at that time spoke to her about the same incident, which had a similar effect upon all of them.

The same evening as she looked across the shell-battered country-side, she saw the sun shine on the white uniforms and white horses of a body of cavalry who were returning from the direction taken by the routed German Army. Then, as the sun set, they disappeared, leaving the countryside bare and shattered as it had been previously.

The White Cavalry had finished its work.

ETERNAL SOLDIER

Rene Boulay

I N MARCH 1945, THE WAR WAS WINDING DOWN IN EUROPE. MY OUT-
fit had just crossed the Rhine and we were at Division Headquarters near Heppenheim as part of a liaison team. Headquarters was a medieval castle which was mostly intact and had suffered
little war damage. From its ramparts, the castle afforded a commanding view of a major crossroad, which made it a stronghold today just
as it was in olden days. We were to stay here for a few days awaiting
our next assignment.

All enlisted men had to perform guard duty regardless of rank or
organization. So one night I found myself walking the parapet of the
castle. It extended for about 100 feet on the side facing the crossroad,
presumably the direction of any major threat.

It was just after midnight, since "Midnight Charlie" had just made
his run. Midnight Charlie was a lone German bomber. Every night at
midnight the plane dropped a few bombs on the intersection—
which did no harm—and then disappeared back to Germany.

Soon after its departure, I was at one end of the parapet and gazing
out onto the landscape below. The moon was nearly full and everything had an eerie appearance.

As I turned to walk to the other end of the parapet, I saw a figure
standing there. "It must be my relief," I thought. But it then occurred
to me that it was much too early for that. So I walked towards the fig-

ure to find out who it was; perhaps, I mused, it was someone with a cup of hot coffee.

As I came closer the figure became clearer. I could see that he wore a cape. Since it was winter and quite cold up there, it was not unusual for sentries to throw a blanket over their shoulders. As I approached to within 50 feet, however, I noticed that he wore a strange helmet, more conical than the GI issue and with something protruding from the top like horns or wings.

The figure held one stick upright. This stick looked like a spear or lance. He also wore a tunic which reached to his knees. But what intrigued me the most is that he wore a full beard. This was strange since beards were not permitted in the army—mustaches, yes, but not beards. The figure was not hazy or nebulous, but looked quite solid like an ordinary human being. My curiosity was so much aroused that as I walked toward him I completely forgot to challenge him.

As I came closer, the moon went behind a cloud and the ramparts were enveloped in darkness. Within a few minutes the area was again bathed in moonlight, but the stranger was gone! I searched everywhere, all over the parapet, but found no one.

At this time I began to have serious misgivings on being negligent of my duty in not challenging him. If someone were trying to play a trick on me, I could be in deep trouble.

But I dismissed these doubts out of hand. After all this was wartime and this was Division Headquarters; no nonsense was tolerated here. Besides it was a good way for a prankster to get shot, for we had orders to challenge and if not satisfied to shoot first and ask questions later.

I was not just an impressionable rookie at the time and had survived the D-Day landing and gone through several campaigns. I was certain that the soldier was like no one I had seen before.

We left the next day since our battalion was reassigned to a new sector. I never had the chance to discuss the apparition with other soldiers at the castle. It was not the kind of topic that you brought up casually.

Over the years I have become convinced that I may have seen the ghost of a medieval German soldier, destined for some unknown reason to eternally walk the parapet of this particular castle.

GHOST ARMY OF FONTAINEBLEAU

Warrington Dawson

F ONTAINEBLEAU PALACE IN FRANCE HAS NO REPUTATION FOR being haunted as does Versailles, and for this reason the experience of one of the palace guards, Pierre Andrieux, attracted particular attention recently.

Age 48, of normal health and living in the Sully Pavilion near the famous Parterre of which he had charge, Andrieux was not known to have reported abnormal occurrences of any kind in the past. But he claims that one night recently he witnessed from one of his windows an amazing spectacle.

He saw what he described as "an army of men 3,000 strong," passing bundles of straw from hand to hand and piling them up against the palace wall. Then they set the straw on fire with the evident intention of burning the building down.

To Andrieux the scene was so real and the danger so immediate that he ran for his pistol and fired into the ranks of the ghostly army.

The authorities had Andrieux placed in a hospital "for observation." Nothing more about the affair is known, evidently having been hushed up.

SEVENTEENTH-CENTURY BRITISH BATTLE REVISITED

Vincent H. Gaddis

O F ALL CIVILIZED COUNTRIES, IT IS GREAT BRITAIN THAT HAS experienced the most reenactments of marching warriors and battles. Is this due to the Anglo-Saxon values of tradition and ancestry, or is the veil more thin and tenuous there? Observers have sometimes noticed that the visions flow and ebb, clarify and fade.

Thus it was in Britain that the most incredible reenactment of a conflict took place with repeat performances.

The 1642 Battle of Edge Hill was the major conflict of the English Civil War. Although more than 4,000 men lost their lives, neither side won a victory. The carnage was so shocking that both sides refused to attack again the following day.

Religious fervor was involved—King Charles I was attempting to force Anglican ceremonies on the Scotch and Puritan clergy. So great were the emotions and psychic energies poured forth in the struggle that it is quite likely that no other similar vision in history has been so intense in detail and so vast in scope.

The battle was fought during the afternoon of October 23. Just two months later, on the night of December 24–25, between midnight and 1:00 A.M., the first reenactment startled bewildered witnesses. They heard the roll of drums approaching from a distance, then the sound was repeated close by.

Suddenly over the Warwickshire plain and on the slopes of hills, in the air above the heads of spectators, the battle scene appeared. They saw horses and men maneuvering, the clash of swords and the thrust of spears. They heard the fire of muskets and the discharge of cannons. They heard shouts and the groans of the wounded.

So vivid was the detail that survivors of the battle could see themselves fighting alongside comrades who perished. The scene continued for about three hours, then slowly faded away. At approximately the same time the following night the vision appeared again.

Never has a vision of this type been more persistent. The mammoth apparition appeared again at midnight of December 31–January 1, 1643. This time there were thousands of observers who had gathered on the plain from the surrounding villages. Some fell to their knees, praying to God for protection.

The next night it came again. The armies fought as ferociously as before, and terrified spectators watched. The battle continued for four hours. A week passed, then the scene returned on the nights of January 7 and 8 with the same violence and noise.

A report of the visions reached the king. He sent three of his top officers and three Oxford professors to conduct an on-the-spot investigation. All six men were witnesses the nights of January 14 and 15. So vivid was the spectacle that the officers recognized fellow officers whom they knew had been killed, including Sir Edmund Verney, the King's standard-bearer.

The visions appeared before thousands of witnesses a total of eight times. Obviously, we are not dealing here with spirits of the dead, since the human images included the surviving soldiers. This appearance was probably a recording comparable to a videotape that, when activated, re-created sight and sound to the consciousness of an observer. Nor would such phenomena be a display of the rare gift of clairvoyance, since all persons present could see and hear the battle.

THE MYSTERIOUS SAVIOR
OF HADLEY

Phillip M. Perry

O F ALL THE WARS FOUGHT BY AMERICANS, THE MOST COSTLY IN terms of percentage of casualties was King Philip's War of 1675, which is estimated to have killed one-twelfth of the adult male population of the Colony of Massachusetts. The conflict is named for Philip, son of Chief Massasoit and grand sachem of the Wampanoag Indians, who was credited with organizing the uprising against the white settlers who were violating their treaties by continuing to seize Indian lands.

Perhaps the turning point of the war was the decisive victory of the colonists at the village of Hadley on September 1, 1675. The curious omission of this battle from most textbooks surprises many researchers. But when one studies the still unexplained climax of that day's conflict the silence of historians becomes understandable.

Most of the town's population was attending a service at Hadley's Congregational church when the well-organized Indians began their attack. From the very first shot from a stolen musket the congregation was thrown into a panic, and no amount of pleading from minister John Russell could quiet the people and organize them for a counterattack.

At this moment, as if from thin air, appeared a tall man with gray hair and a beard. His sharp resonant voice cut through the noisy commotion and quieted the people. In 1764 Governor Thomas Hutchinson finally recorded the accounts told him by the family of his predecessor, Governor John Leverett, who supplied these details: "Suddenly a grave elderly person appeared in the midst of them. In his mien and dress he differed from the rest of the people. He not only encouraged them to defend themselves but put himself at their head, rallied, instructed, and led them on to encounter the enemy, who by this means were repulsed. As suddenly, the deliverer of Hadley disappeared. The people were left in consternation, utterly unable to account for this strange phenomenon."

Another eyewitness, the Reverend Phineas Cooke of Hadley, left this account: "All was alarm and trepidation. 'What shall we do? Who shall lead us?' was the cry from every quarter. In the confusion the stranger said, 'I will lead; follow me.' Immediately all obeyed their unknown general and prepared to march against the enemy. Though some were armed, their principal weapon of defense was an old iron cannon, sent there sometime before by the government; but no one of the inhabitants was sufficiently skilled in military tactics to manage it to much purpose. The marvelous stranger knew, and having loaded it, proceeded to the attack.

"Beholding this formidable array, the Indians retreated a short distance and took refuge in a deserted house on the Connecticut River. The cannon was so directed that, when discharged, the contents threw down the top of the stone chimney about the heads of the Indians, who took flight and fled with great terror and dismay. The commander ordered his company to pursue, take and destroy as many of the enemy as they could, and while they were in pursuit of the Indians he disappeared. When the pursuers returned he was gone, and nothing was heard of him afterward."

The stranger's inexplicable arrival and subsequent disappearance convinced the townspeople that the unknown commander "with silvery locks, venerable appearance and pale visage was a deliverer from another world." The apparition soon was dubbed "the Angel of Hadley" and eyewitnesses later commented that the stranger seemed to glow with an inner fire, that when he walked he seemed to make no noise and that his sword seemed to flash even inside the chapel.

In the face of this apparently supernatural event some historians tried to find a normal explanation. Ezra Stiles, the president of Yale College, in 1794 advanced the theory that the unknown commander was in fact Judge William Goffe, one of the jurists who years before had voted to condemn King Charles I of England to death when Oliver Cromwell had overthrown the monarchy. When the Restoration came in 1660 Goffe fled to New England and took refuge with John Russell in the Hadley church, according to Stiles.

This theory was discredited, however, by historian George Sheldon in 1905. He pointed out that Goffe's diary, willed to the Mather family, contained a complete record of his wanderings in Massachusetts and showed that Judge Goffe never had lived in Hadley.

Thus we are left with the mystery still unsolved. Who was the Angel of Hadley?

DEVIL RIDER OF
CHISHOLM HOLLOW

Harold Preece

W AR TALK MAY MEAN STOCK MARKET BOOMS IN NEW YORK
and huddles of statesmen in London or Paris. But to
psychic mountaineers of the Central Texas hill country,
the current military palaver means that the "Devil Rider" will soon
be galloping down Chisholm Hollow on his coal black horse.

It has been only ten years, on the eve of World War II, since he was
last seen travelling the gloomy chasm that the mountain people consider a direct gateway to inferno. But five times he has appeared during the 110 years since this section of Texas was settled by
Scotch-Irish hillmen from Kentucky and Tennessee. Living men
have seen him, and swear that every one of his manifestations has
been followed by the clash of arms in the world outside.

Moreover all witnesses agree on the description of the "Devil
Rider" and his steed. He measures more than six feet in his rusty
armor with its emblazoned insignia of a crown suspended over a
crouched lion. His face is completely hidden by a helmet suggestive
of a knight's headpiece. Long iron gauntlets encase his arms and the
hands with which he guides the huge, raven-colored horse that tow-
ers above the scrubby hill country mustangs.

Available evidence indicates that the "Devil Rider" set up residence in these last spurs of the Rockies long before the first mountain family ever drove down a homestead stake. When the earliest settlers came here in 1840, friendly Tonkawa Indians warned them of the strange apparition and urged them to avoid the forbidding hollow that was its abode.

The mountaineers, with the caution of the Celt about extrasensory phenomena, steered clear of the place. None would file homestead papers on the tract embracing the still-unnamed hollow. For six years stories circulated among both Indians and whites of sounds, like the clank of rifle barrels issuing from the gorge after nightfall.

Then in 1846 a rancher named McConnell, whose descendants still live in the hills, entered the hollow while tracking a wolf pack that had been preying on his calves. He was inspecting some tracks left by the wolves when he heard the creak of metal and the thud of hoofs. He looked up to see the armored warrior goading a phantom horse down the canyon's brink.

After he had jumped onto his own pony and ridden home in panic, he learned that General Zachary Taylor's forces had crossed the Rio Grande into Mexico. The Mexican War had begun.

McConnell's mountain neighbors knew nothing of ancient armory. But they did know their fundamentalist theology. They believed that the weird figure must be Lucifer, the Prince of Darkness, and that the hollow was one of his exits from the netherworld. So they began calling him the "Devil Rider" and his canyon haven, "Devil's Hollow."

Fifteen years passed before the apparition was seen again. His second appearance is substantiated to day and month by Emmett Ringstaff, the eyewitness who glimpsed him. I talked with Ringstaff, a realistic, practical man, before his death in Fort Worth, Texas, during the 1930s. His report corroborated the earlier description of the "Devil Rider" and added one detail.

The specter was dangling a pair of huge brass horse pistols, such as might have been used by early-eighteenth-century gentlemen-at-arms, when Emmett Ringstaff saw him on that unforgettable day of April 10, 1861. Ringstaff said that the pistols were swinging from a heavy gold-looking buckler bearing the inscription of the crown and the lion.

The old mountaineer recalled that the "Devil Rider" was moving at a slow trot, and that he "disappeared with his horse into thin air" at a bend of the hollow. A few days later word came that Fort Sumter had been fired upon by the Southern forces. America had entered the first stage of the Civil War.

Others had dismissed Ringstaff's account as the fantasy of an aging man. But a link in my own family tradition gives it a strong basis of truth.

During the early 1880s, my father and some other mountain youngsters disregarded strict parental orders and slipped off to the hollow. While playing hide-and-seek in a dense jungle of ferns, they found a moldering skull and a pair of odd-looking pistols uncommon for Texas where men carried revolvers of modern make.

The skull crumbled into dust when a boy touched it. But my father carried the pistols home. Emmett Ringstaff was one of the neighbors who came to examine the antique weapons. When he examined them his face paled. For the guns were identical with those that he'd seen in the buckler of the "Devil Rider."

Shortly afterward, the pistols mysteriously disappeared. "They were lying in plain sight on a wall rack one night," my father said. "They were gone when I woke up the next morning."

It so happened that Devil's Hollow lay directly on the Texas spur of the famous Chisholm Trail. Cowboys driving cattle herds up from the Rio Grande to Kansas often bedded their steers on its rim, and through the association of names, the chasm was eventually rechristened Chisholm Hollow. During that period several men picked up in the hollow other objects of supposedly Spanish origin. One of them was a ponderous silver spur that might have decked the boot heel of some grandee come to reap his fortune in the New World.

Still later, research by Southwestern historians revealed that a Spanish fort had been located in or near the hollow when Texas had been a province of New Spain. Their supposition was that the fort and garrison had been wiped out by the warlike Comanche Indians during the late seventeenth or early eighteenth century.

This cast the "Devil Rider" in a new light. Many of the mountain folk began believing he was the spirit of some Spanish soldier who had died during the Comanche attack. Certain events during the Spanish-American War would seem to confirm their belief about his nationality.

In the past, he had appeared to but one person at a time. But on the eve of the trouble with Spain he was seen on three different occasions by three different men—Arch Clawson, Ed Shannon, and Sam Bullock. Previously he'd paid no attention to the mortals who'd stood with gaping mouths, watching him ride by. But every one of the three claimed that they felt some eerie personal hatred flashing at them from beneath the heavy, creaking suit of mail.

"It was like having my limbs scorched by a look," Ed Shannon told me when I was visiting his cabin a few years ago. "And after the war started we might have been fighting Spain right here in our own hills."

The "Devil Rider" might have been a neutral omen of conflict during other wars fought by a nation that he'd seen emerge from the womb of history. But to this day, the mountain people blame his Spanish patriotism for the boundless trouble they experienced on the home front during that brief four-month fray between the young American republic and the decrepit Spanish monarchy.

The mountain men signed up *en masse* in Theodore Roosevelt's Rough Riders. All but one or two came down with malaria in Tampa, Florida, and never saw a day's service. The year of conflict, 1898,

was marked by much rain in Texas. Yet hill country springs and
creeks went unexplainably dry with cattle collapsing from thirst in
the sun-baked mud. Horses began dying of some baffling disease
that no veterinarian was ever able to diagnose. Corn withered in the
mountain patches, though there were bumper yields in areas outside
of the "Devil Rider's" domain.

After the defeat of Spain the hill people concluded that the spectral
horseman reluctantly accepted the capitulation of his countrymen by
vanishing from Texas. My uncle, a hard-headed man who scoffed at
"nonsense about ghosts," braved taboo by staking a homestead claim
on Chisholm Hollow. He invested all his savings in a new house that
he built at the canyon's edge. He'd scarcely nailed down the last shin-
gle when flames began shooting from every corner of the structure.
Today a charred, crumbling chimney remains as the only monument
to his attempt to tenant the place.

For almost the 20 years that followed, the "Devil Rider" remained
quiet. Only the bravest deer hunters entered the hollow which was
still shunned by the majority of the mountain folk. But roads and
telephones meanwhile had penetrated the hills, linking the somber
peaks with the larger world beyond. A younger generation grew up
to scoff at the hoary old tales of their fathers.

World War I broke out in Europe in July 1914. Two and a half
years went by with America remaining aloof from the holocaust. On
a late January day in 1917, a party of six scoffing young hillmen
descended into the hollow to look for deer signs.

"No deer here," one of them sighed in disappointment after sur-
veying the ground for tracks. "Maybe," he added laughingly, "the
'Devil Rider' scared 'em all off."

"Like all the war talk is scaring people," another commented. "But
the 'Devil Rider's' not scaring me—no more than Woodrow Wilson's
blowings. If he ever existed outside the old folks' yarns, let him show
himself. Let him ride out right here and now."

Suddenly the ground began trembling around the feet of the young skeptics. There was a clatter of hoofs and the flash of a gaunt, mailed figure riding by on a giant horse.

The youths scattered and ran for their lives. Within a few days—on February 3, 1917—the United States severed diplomatic relations with the German Empire. Two months afterward we were at war.

I knew all those six witnesses. All but one died on various battlefields of Germany and France. That man was Terrell Wallace who survived to tell me the story. But even more spectacular was the manner in which the "Devil Rider" announced World War II.

It was Sunday, December 7, 1941. The mountaineers had gathered in a country chapel to pray for peace. After services lasting well into the afternoon they dispersed down different roads toward their homes. One group loaded into a jalopy to follow a winding route leading past Chisholm Hollow.

At the hollow's head, the driver quickly jammed on the brakes when he heard the puffing snort of a horse in the nearby woods. Thinking that the animal was approaching the road, he waited a minute with the intention of giving it time to cross.

The bushes parted. Driver and passengers sat petrified as a coal black charger bearing a tall, armored figure strode into the middle of the road.

For a minute man and horse poised themselves squarely in the vehicle's path. Then they were gone even sooner than they had appeared. The frightened driver recalled that this was the first time that the "Devil Rider" had been seen out of the confines of the canyon proper.

He went home and turned on his radio. The first turn of the button brought him the news that the Japanese had bombed Pearl Harbor. And that, though he did not realize it then, was the prelude to the atomic bombing of Hiroshima.

THE CAPTAIN WHO CAME TO TEA

William H. Gilroy

HAVE YOU EVER ENTERTAINED A GHOST?

For those who scoff at such a possibility here is an unimpeachable account of a ghost who came to tea. The distinguished Briton, Admiral Sir William James, gave the following testimony to a group of 13 admirals and 500 reserve officers at a Trafalgar Day gathering in 1949.

"During the last war I lived for 18 months in Nelson's flagship, *Victory,* at Portsmouth.

"One day a friend asked if I would invite a retired sea captain to tea on the *Victory* and I made arrangements that he should come the following day at five o'clock.

"At half-past four another friend of mine arrived, and I asked him to help entertain the old captain who was disturbed by the recent bombing of Portsmouth.

"The captain arrived a few minutes past five o'clock. He was dressed in very old-fashioned clothes. He was quite familiar with the layout of the dockyard; however, some of his expressions seemed a bit quaint to us both. For instance, he referred to the Dover patrol as the Downs flotilla.

"Just as I was called away to the telephone I heard a bosun's pipe sound as a coastal force flotilla put out to sea.

"When I returned I found the old sea captain gone and, on inquiry, learned that he left soon after the bosun's pipe sounded.

"The phone call was from a London hospital. I was told that the old sea captain, whom we thought we were entertaining, had been injured in a bombing raid and could not keep his appointment with us for tea.

"I knew then that we must have been entertaining one of Lord Nelson's old sea captains. Which one it was, I do not know . . ."

Where Is Yesterday?

Harvey Day

MOST OF US ARE CONCERNED WITH WHAT HAPPENS IN THE future; the events of today are almost instantly relegated into the past. But sometimes past incidents are flashed back upon the screen of the mind so vividly that the eye can see them.

If the eye can see them, then there is some justification for assuming that the past is not obliterated.

Men and women have dreamt of crimes already committed; dreams that showed in detail the locality of the crimes, the faces and forms of the victims and those who killed them.

These were all conveyed to the dreamers' minds as if actually taking place, and with such accuracy that police have been led to the various spots by people who gave descriptions of such crimes.

What power or force is it that can snatch a picture out of the past and transplant it in a dreaming man's mind as if the incident were just taking place? If, as we think, the past no longer exists, then this should be impossible, for according to the school of Sartre the mere existence of something is proof that it is.

It follows, therefore, that if we can see an event out of the past, such as in the case of the remarkable Versailles story, then it must have an existence.

*   *   *

One of the most extraordinary of such cases occurred in a summer between the years 1746 and 1753, the nearest that Archibald Bell, a farmer of Inverary, could place the event when he recorded it many years later.

Bell wrote it down exactly as told him by his father and grandfather, a farmer of Glenary.

One morning Bell senior, wishing to transact business in Glenshiray, set out with his son. They crossed the hill into the town, finished their business and were on the return journey by midday.

No sooner did they approach Garron Bridge and turn towards Inverary upon the high road, than they beheld a vast concourse of men marching towards them.

The foremost ranks had then advanced only as far as Kilmalieu in regular order, packed close, and according to the writer, "they stretched from the point of the New Town near the Quay where Captain Gillies' house now stands, along the shore and the high road and across the River Arry near the Town, about the spot where the new bridge has since been built."

The army stretched so far into the distance that the rearguard could not be seen.

As it advanced, they walked slowly towards it, the old man noting that it had 15 or 16 pairs of colors and that the men marching nearest to them were walking six or seven abreast.

With them marched, as was the custom at the time, women and children, both above and below the road, carrying cans and other cooking utensils.

The men were clad in scarlet and the sun glinted on their muskets and bayonets, dazzling the two who watched this colorful array.

And somewhere in the middle distance was a large animal amid the ranks, the soldiers prodding it on with knives and bayonets.

*   *   *

Young Bell had never seen an army before, for large bodies of armed men did not often venture into the remote Highlands; but his father, who had served in the Rebellion of 1745, assumed that they had come from Ireland, landed at Cantyre, and were making their way south to England.

One peculiarity struck young Bell. "Why," he asked the old man, "are the rear ranks constantly running to catch up with those in front?"

His father explained that when on the march there was always some confusion in the middle of an army—for armies in those days proceeded like mobs—the rear ranks were constantly being delayed and consequently forced to hurry to keep their positions.

"If ever you get forced into the army," he advised, "always try to join the front ranks, which march at a leisurely pace and are never held up."

The army was now some 150 yards from them, and they observed a body of some 40–50 men led by an officer on foot, some little way in front.

A few paces behind rode an officer of Dragoons—or so they concluded from the trappings of his horse. He wore a gold-laced hat and a blue Hussar cloak with wide open sleeves lined with red, as well as boots and spurs.

Bell senior observed him so intently as to swear later that he would know him again instantly if they met.

At that period all able-bodied men went in fear of press gangs, for men were forced not only into the navy, but into the army as well, so young Bell felt it inadvisable to linger on the road, as he had little wish to spend years in some foreign land.

So both scaled a stone dyke behind some thorn bushes, and only when they felt safely hidden did young Bell look at the road to see the army march by.

The road, which a few moments ago had been thronged with humanity, was deserted!

He rubbed his eyes and asked his father to look, but never a sign of a uniform could they see!

Then it occurred to the old man that there had been no cloud of rising dust, which on those broken roads was always created by men, horses, and vehicles.

They clambered over the dyke again and onto the road as an old resident from Glenshiray, named Stewart, came towards them driving a horse. "What has become of all the soldiers?" they asked.

"I've seen none," said Stewart. All the information he volunteered was that as the heat had made his horse sag from fatigue, he had dismounted and was driving it.

To his dying day Farmer Bell believed that their vision was a peep into the future, but his son said that the uniforms and arms of the soldiers belonged to a past period.

They made guarded inquiries from people who must have seen an army if in reality an army had marched, but no one had. Nor, when they examined the road for footprints, could they find any.

Archibald Bell made careful notes of the story, which was recounted many times by both his father and grandfather, dour men not given to exaggeration. He could find no satisfactory explanation.

Was this a chapter of the past unfolding itself, and if so, to what purpose, and why to only two men? Or was it merely a mirage? There seems to be too much detail for this to be the answer.

PHANTOM RIDERS
ON SOUTER-FELL

Frank John Reid

ONE OF HISTORY'S MOST FAMOUS "PHANTOM ARMIES" appeared in the northwest part of England in the eighteenth century. The "army" was seen on a mountain called Souter-fell ("Cobblermount") and sometimes Souther-fell or Soutra Fell ("Southern Mountain").

Two accounts saw print in the 1700s. One of them served as the basis for several retellings in the nineteenth century, and later Charles Fort brought the story into our century. To the best of my knowledge the second account is given here for the first time since it appeared over 200 years ago.

The word "fell" implies a plateau- or mountain-pasture, but I doubt any part of Souter-fell actually was pastureland. The mountain is in Cumberland, about 17 miles south-southwest of Carlisle. The physical location was described in *The Gentleman's Magazine* for November 1747:

"At *Gisedale* the water turns both ways, so that in a sudden shower you may with your foot only, send the rainwater, either to *Carlisle* or

Cockermouth, by the channels of *Cauda* or *Lender-maken*.* This last springs under *Sadle-back*, a *Parnassan* eminence, with two prominent peaks; the most northerly is called *Blen-carter*, a surprisingly high precipice of the quarry kind.

"*Souter-fell* is a distinguish'd mountain of itself, encompass'd quite around with a *turbinated* trough, thro' which *Lender-maken* is convey'd. The West and North sides are barricaded with rocks, the East is more plain but withal steep, and seemingly 900 yards in height, but every where of difficult access."

It was on this steep eastern slope that the phantoms marched.

The more famous account, that published in James Clarke's *Survey of the Lakes* (1787), reports that the incident began with a sighting by Daniel Strickett, a servant, and his employer, John Wren. Wren's (probably quite small) estate, called Wilton Hill, was near the mountain.

After supper one summer evening in 1743, they saw a group of horses on the near slope of Souter-fell. The sight surprised them because the animals were galloping up a slope so steep that a horse could hardly be expected to traverse it at all. But the witnesses were even more surprised to see a man with a dog running after the horses but never catching up, yet going at such all-out speed that Strickett and Wren literally expected him to break his neck.

Horses, man, and dog all disappeared over the lowest part of the Fell. Wren and Strickett didn't investigate that night but the next morning they went up the mountain. It would be worth the trouble to pick up the horseshoes that surely must have been cast off in that furious gallop. And they fully expected to find the body of the man who had been running so recklessly.

---

*Today the River Cauda is called the Caldew; the other leads not to Cockermouth but to a lake called Thirlmere.

"Accordingly they went," Clarke wrote, "but to their great surprise found not a shoe, nor even a single vestige of any horse having been there, much less did they find the man lying dead, as they expected.

"This story they some time concealed—at length, however, they ventured to tell it, and were (as might be expected) heartily laughed at."

A year later, at 7:30 P.M. on Midsummer's Eve (June 23) 1744, Daniel Strickett saw the phantoms again. Although he was now working for William Lancaster (whose place adjoined John Wren's) he nonetheless observed them on the same slope of Souter-fell. Remembering the ridicule his story had earned him the previous year, he was at first reluctant to say anything to anyone. But there was no denying it—there *were* figures moving up there. After watching them for some time he went quietly to his employer.

Strickett told Lancaster that he had something curious to show him.

"I suppose some bonefire," Lancaster remarked. It was the custom for local shepherds to try to outdo each other with "bonefires" on St. John's Eve (which is also Midsummer's Eve). But no sooner had they come to the end of the house than Lancaster burst out, "Is that what thou has to shew me?"

"Yes, master," said Strickett, much relieved. "Do you think you see as I do?" Lancaster agreed and so did the rest of the family when they came out to look.

Men on horseback were moving, troop after troop of them, at "a regular swift walk" on the steep side of Souter-fell. Though not the gallop of the last year's mystery, the pace was still strangely quick for such treacherous ground.

The figures appeared at the lowest part of the mountain, a place called Knott. They moved along the side of the fell until they came opposite Lancaster's house, where they moved up over the mountain. They thus took a sort of curving course around the mountainside.

Blakehills, where Strickett and the Lancasters stood watching, was only a half mile from the phantoms' line of march. But the ghostly figures were seen by every person at every cottage within a mile. There were 26 witnesses in all, some nearer the horsemen than Blakehills.

"Frequently," Clarke remarked, "the last or last but one in a troop (always either one or the other) would leave his place, gallop to the front, and then take the same pace with the rest, a *regular swift walk;* these changes happened to every troop (for many troops appeared), and oftener than once or twice, yet not at all times alike. The spectators saw, *all alike,* the same changes, and at the same time, as they discovered by asking each other questions as any change took place."

This procession lasted at least two and a half hours, from 7:30 on, and perhaps longer—for it was still going on when it got too dark to see. Apparently, no one tried climbing up to confront the riders.

No one who saw the spectral horsemen could believe he was the victim of his imagination or of a mere illusion. Not at that short distance!

James Clarke, a land surveyor, went through the Lakes District of northwestern England about 40 years later. He wrote an account of the phantom riders, mostly from the testimony of William Lancaster (who seems to have been a son of the William Lancaster of the story, since Clarke describes Strickett as "his father's servant") and Daniel Strickett, who had since become a professional auctioneer. These two read Clarke's account and swore to a statement (July 21, 1785) affirming its accuracy and truth.

The other, even more contemporary account (already quoted) appeared in *The Gentleman's Magazine,* November 1747. It's part of a series of letters, for some reason published without the author's name, about interesting English geographical sites.

The first thing we learn from this article is that *the phantoms were also seen in 1735 and 1737.*

In the earlier sighting, in 1735, the only witness was "*Wm Lancaster's* servant," who was "discredited and laugh'd at" when he told his story (there apparently being no tradition of such phenomena on Souter-fell). Since the specters of 1743 aren't mentioned in this account, we can reasonably speculate that someone simply got his dates mixed up. On the other hand, the two stories are different enough to make us wonder if two different employees of Lancaster's were involved. Moreover, the accounts are supposed to be taken more or less verbatim from the witnesses' testimonies.

According to the *Gentleman's Magazine* writer, on Midsummer's Eve 1735 the unnamed servant saw the east side of Souter-fell "covered with a regular marching army for above an hour together; he said they consisted of distinct bodies of troops, which appeared to proceed from an eminence in the North End, and march'd over a nitch in the top."

Two years later, again on Midsummer's Eve, between the hours of eight and nine, William Lancaster saw what he took to be several hunters following their horses on foot (the sensible thing to do on a steep slope). About 10 minutes later he glanced toward the place again and saw that "they appeared to be mounted, and a vast army following, five in rank" exactly where the servant had seen phantoms two years before.

Lancaster summoned his family and together they "frequently observed that some one of the five would quit rank, and seem to stand in a fronting posture, as if he was observing and regulating the order of their march, or taking account of the numbers, and after some time appear'd to return full gallop to the station he had left, which they never fail'd to do as often as they quitted their lines, and the figure that did so, was generally one of the middlemost men in the rank." As time passed and it grew darker the figures abandoned their orderly march and behaved more like a crowd riding home from a market. But they continued in great numbers, visible as long as there was light to see them.

Because this is reminiscent of Clarke's account of the 1744 phenomenon, it's again possible that at least one of our sources has confused the stories. If so the likely source of the confusion is the younger Lancaster, who after 40 years may have run two separate events together. We are sure of the date of the 1744 sighting because Daniel Strickett backs it up. He may not have known of the sightings of the previous decade because he probably wasn't working for the Lancasters then. So the phantoms seem really to have acted much the same in their last two appearances.

The Gentleman's Magazine gives us some additional details about the 1744 incident. It tells us:

—that there were carriages interspersed with the columns of troops;

—that William Lancaster (senior, presumably) never thought the immense armies could be real "because of the impracticability of a march over the precipices, where they seemed to come on";

—that "horse and man upon strict looking at appear'd to be but one being, rather than two distinct ones";

—that they nonetheless were nothing like any clouds or vapors he had ever seen and that the weather was "extremely serene";

—that the visible length of the moving column was almost half a mile, which considering the long time they were seen marching means a positively incredible number of "horsemen."

This army seemed so real to some of the witnesses that the next day they climbed the slope in search of horseshoes, assuming some would have been left behind after the enormous procession of riders. But they found no trace of the presence of horses or men.

Our anonymous writer was attracted to the idea that the phenomenon was due to "an undulating lambent meteor" (a layer of mist) aided by "fancy" (imagination). But he rejected this explanation because there were too many reputable witnesses. And he couldn't figure how agitated mist could stop and start or "preserve so regular a system, as to appear still five in a line"—or (most important) why it should three times exhibit itself in this way only *on Midsummer's Eve*. (It seems likely to have been four times although we have no definite date for the 1743 sighting.)

James Clarke too was impressed with the number of witnesses and also with the phenomenon's habit of showing up on the same day of the year. The length of time during which people observed the figures further impressed him. Most apparitions, Clarke noted, were things seen momentarily by one or two persons.

"Is there any impiety," Clarke asked, "in supposing, as this (1744 phenomenon) happened immediately before that rebellion which was intended to subvert the liberty, the law and the religion of England, that though immediate prophecies have ceased, these visionary beings might be directed to warn mankind of approaching tumults? In short, it is difficult to say what it was, or what it is not."

The "tumult" which Clarke thought the phantom riders portended was the Jacobite Rebellion of 1745. This was the unsuccessful attempt to put a Stuart, Charles Edward ("Bonnie Prince Charlie"), on the throne.

Clarke's book went through several editions but today is very rare. Scientists of Clarke's time ignored the "ghost story," perhaps because Clarke's interpretation offended their sensibilities. "Divine portention" was thought to be superstition.

Eventually, however, Sir David Brewster presented Clarke's version in a chapter on mirages in his book *Letters on Natural Magic* (1836).

"The aerial troopers seen at Souter-fell were produced by the same process as the spectre (mirage) of Dover Castle, having been brought by unequal refraction from one side of the hill to the other," he wrote. "It is not our business to discover how a troop of soldiers came to be performing their evolutions on the other side of Souter-fell; but if there was then no road along which they could be marching, it is highly probable that they were troops exercising among the hills in secret previous to the breaking out of the rebellion in 1745."

To this Charles Fort responded sarcastically:

"With a talent for clear-seeing, for which we are notable, except when it comes to some of our own explanations, we almost immediately recognize that, to keep a secret from persons living upon one side of the mountain, it is a very sensible idea to go and maneuver upon the other side of the mountain; but then how to keep the secret, in a thickly populated country . . . from persons living upon that other side of the mountain—however, there never has been an explanation that did not itself have to be explained."

In any case the mountain is too rocky for troop maneuvers on horseback.

In *Medii Aevi Kalendarium* (1841) R. T. Hampson dismisses the whole phenomenon as mere imaginative "description of the shadows of smoke against the hillside, or of volumes of smoke itself." Nonetheless Hampson was astute enough to note that such phantom armies had been reported elsewhere although he hastened to assure readers this was all "absurd superstition." He pointed to the legend of the Wild Hunt, found in the traditional beliefs of all Scandinavian, Germanic, and Celtic peoples. The Wild Hunt in folklore was a terrifying apparition of a horde of armed riders. In the original story Odin led the hunt but in later, post-pagan times its leader was often identified as a local hero, the victim of a curse or the devil himself. Sometimes the Wild Huntsman rode accompanied only by spectral hounds. Most people believed the Hunt occurred *on specific days of the year*.

The Wild Hunt tradition may have grown out of real sightings of phantom horsemen like those on Souter-fell; there are many other similar cases. One is reported in the Anglo-Saxon Chronicle for the year 1126. Another (among the prodigies listed in the Puritan *Annus*

Mirabilis of the early 1660s) was seen for a half hour in Wales; then too the witnesses found no traces of hoofprints afterwards. Such phenomena have continued to occur through the centuries into our time.

The phantom riders on Souter-fell seem to have been neither "ordinary" haunting ghosts nor portents of war nor natural phenomena. But this observation explains only what they were not—not what they were.

THE GHOST OF
COLONEL WALLACE

Brigadier Humphry Bullock

O NE OF THE MANY ABANDONED MILITARY STATIONS SCATTERED across India and Pakistan is Sirur in the Deccan. This station housed a brigade of troops for over a century. The last soldiers marched away in 1907. For most of this period Sirur was the headquarters of a famous regiment of Indian cavalry, the Poona Horse, which always was quartered there when not engaged in one of its numerous campaigns. Now the barracks and bungalows are all fallen down. Nothing remains of the old cantonment except the burial ground—and the ghost of Colonel Wallace.

Wallace belonged to the 74th Foot, now the Second Battalion of the Highland Light Infantry. He led a brigade with great distinction in the war of 1803 against the Mahrattas, under command of a young major-general who was not yet known to fame as the Duke of Wellington. As a result of his exploits the people of the Deccan gave Wallace the name of *Sat Purush*, the Holy Man. He died at Sirur in 1808 at the age of 47, and the inscription on his tomb says that he was "a man respected and loved for his gallantry, devoted public zeal, ardent honorable rectitude, and noble character."

Before long his grave became the object of veneration. It became the shrine and focus of a cult and the local villagers worshiped there. At harvest time they brought their first fruits as offerings. The practice soon took a supernatural turn. It branched out along two lines and became rather confused. One branch led to a cult of a type familiar in folklore and ethnology. The other took shape as a ghost story.

The ghost was Colonel Wallace himself mounted on his familiar white charger. When the Deccan tableland around Sirur was to suffer from famine, pestilence, or other disaster the spectral nightrider on his luminous steed would warn his devotees by galloping around the cantonment. The ghost rode either on a night of full moon or on a night of no moon. It was then possible, his adherents believed, to avert the threatened calamity by making offerings at the tomb. These offerings became the perquisite of the tomb's custodian, the colonel's former syce (groom), who was specially pentioned off to take care of the tomb. In the course of years he was succeeded by his son.

The caretaker, of course, had an obvious motive for spreading the tale, which was calculated to appeal to the simple credulity of ignorant peasants, you may say. But before you dismiss the affair as just another racket, hear all of the evidence.

Ten years after Wallace's death the local General Officer Commanding proposed to stop the custodian's pension. Thereupon, we are told, the ghost "troubled the general" so much that he changed his mind and instead placed the sometime groom in charge of the whole graveyard—presumably with higher wages for this was an official post. Further details of this promotion regretably are lacking but, though it may have been consistent with a racket, the deception was plausible enough to delude a hard-boiled British general as well as the illiterate villagers.

The second incident occurred in the 1840s when the Reverend Oxro French, of the American Mission established at Sirur, felt impelled to stop the worship at the tomb. "The curse of the ghost rested on him who tried to interfere" it is related. In proof of this the visitor used to be shown the graves of three of the missionary's little children who all died at Sirur during the five years after 1842. It is curious that their ages at death were all much the same—from a year and three months to a year and five months. But of course in an old Indian cemetery such a row of small graves is no uncommon reminder of the frightful infant mortality in the days when unhygienic ignorance and lack of prophylactic measures failed to stem the attack of climate-bred disease.

The third incident was the Cat Plague of 1883. The riding spectre had gone his rounds more frequently than usual that spring, both in the cantonment and in the native village but the younger generation heeded neither the phantom's danger signal nor the monitions of their elders. No offerings were laid at the tomb. Then the cats began to die. Three hundred cats died in all—125 of them in the first three weeks of June. About the 18th of June the ancients of Sirur went in a body to the graveyard and took appropriate propitiatory action—and the Cat Plague ceased. What we should make of this is not clear. You never know with cats.

By 1888 a Bombay author wrote that since the advent of the American missionaries the Sirur ghost had disappeared. He could not have known of the last two incidents. In any case he spoke too soon. For before 1893 the Colonel's phantom appeared to completely trustworthy observers, one of whom gave an eyewitness account to a friend of mine in 1894. Here is the tale of the last verified appearance of the apparition. I will use initials only, though the full names are known to me.

C., a British officer of the Indian Army, was a big, heavy fellow who had seen active service in the ranks before he got his commission. By temperament he was notably stolid and matter-of-fact, "the last person one would think to fabricate or imagine a story" says my informant who knew him well. He belonged to a sepoy battalion and was marching with a detachment from it which halted for the night at

Sirur. The Poona Horse offered him their traditional hospitality and after changing into a mess jacket that evening he went over early for dinner at their Officers' Mess.

With time to spare C. and an officer of the Poona Horse, by name D., strolled over to the burial ground to have a look at Wallace's tomb, the local "must" for sightseers. As they approached it in the twilight they saw an oldish man in an old-fashioned white uniform rise out of the grave and advance towards them. Seized with unreasoning but understandable terror the two subalterns took to their heels, bolting to the Mess and safety.

C. could never find any natural explanation for the occurrence which satisfied him. The obvious one—that some Indian, perhaps a beggar or a vagrant, had been resting beside the monument and on hearing the approach of the sahibs had risen suddenly to his feet in the dusk—did not account for the overpowering but inexplicable terror which possessed C. His feeling of terror was the thing that made the strongest impression on him.

No later hauntings are on record, but the cult continued and probably survives today. Vows to avert barrenness are taken beneath the monument, illnesses are submitted for cure, pilgrimages are made, Thursday and Sunday being the days favored.

Few white men find their way to Sirur now. The days are gone when the guard of the Poona Horse on Piquet Hill turned out at midnight to pay the ceremonial compliments of his rank to a phantom on a galloping white charger.

THE GHOST ARMY OF CHIMNEY ROCK PASS

Edmond P. Gibson

IN A SPUR OF THE BLUE RIDGE MOUNTAINS LYING SOUTH AND WEST of Asheville, North Carolina, at a distance of about 20 miles on trunk line highway U.S. 74, the highway leading to Charlotte, is Chimney Rock Pass, at the east end of Hickory Nut Gap. Shaking Bald Mountain, famous for its bat caves and its subterranean rumblings, forms the north side of the valley. It is a mountain which shook almost continuously in a sort of chronic earthquake in 1874, and rather frequently ever since.

Chimney Rock Pass formed the stage upon which a ghost army rode and fought at a period which antedates by 50 years the Ghost Army of the Civil War, seen in Green Briar County, Virginia, in 1863. The vision of Chimney Rock Pass occurred in 1811, the year before the war between England and the United States began. Five eyewitnesses are known to have seen what seemed to them to be a spectral cavalry fight. Their testimony attracted a great deal of attention in Carolina journals of the time.

The tale attracted the attention of Wilber G. Ziegler and Ben S. Grosscup, who later noted it in their book of mountain travel entitled

"The Heart of the Alleghenies" published at Raleigh, North Carolina, in 1883. They state:

"The alleged witnesses of the spectacle were an old man and his wife, living in the gap before Chimney Rock Fall. So much interest was in Rutherfordton (which lies to the east of the Gap) by its recital, that a public meeting was held and a delegation, headed by Generals Miller and Walton, with a magistrate and clerk, visited the old couple and took their affidavits to this effect: For several evenings, while shadows filled the pass and sunlight still lingered on the mountain summits, they had seen, from their doorway, two bodies of cavalry advance toward each other across the sky. They heard the charge sounded, and saw them meet in conflict, with flashing swords, groans, shouts of victory, and then disappear. Three more settlers testified as witnesses of the same vision. They were all believed trustworthy, but evidently deluded by some material phenomenon. Giving credence to the tale, explanations were advanced, but none are satisfactory."

What is the true nature of these ghost armies? Mass hysteria is a common phenomenon, but mass hallucination is not. Were the witnesses gazing at fantastic cloud formations, or did they, by some extra-sensory means, look backward in time to a battle between Tarleton's horse, and the Continental cavalry? Did they look forward to the coming War of 1812? The vision occurred near the time of the battle of Tippecanoe, but Tippecanoe was scarcely a cavalry engagement.

Ghost armies do not fall into any of the usual categories of the paranormal, nor does there seem to be anything particularly purposive in these visions, as such. They do not appear to be cases of clairvoyance, or of vision of anything distantly removed in space. Ghost armies are "just one of those things."

THE UNEASY DEAD AT FORT MIMS

Sally Remaley

F LOYD BOONE, A YOUNG BRADENTON, FLORIDA, FAMILY MAN, graduate of the University of Alabama and employee of the state parole board, is probably one of the most logical and objective persons you could find. Yet a strange event, for which he can think of no logical or objective explanation, still bothers him after two years.

Boone is descended on his mother's side from Chief Red Eagle, the famous Creek Indian leader, and on his father's side from Daniel Boone, American pioneer. On March 27, 1966, he took a friend, a man employed as a county probation supervisor in Florida, and journeyed to his home in Baldwin County, Alabama, to visit relatives in the little settlement where his father and a few remaining Creeks still live.

Boone is collecting historical data about his ancestors. Hoping to add to his material and information he and his companion visited the site of the Massacre of Fort Mims. Because it was getting dark as they arrived they decided to camp overnight on the grounds and study further the place the next day. The night was calm and still, with no wind. The two men curled up in their sleeping bags about 10:30 P.M.

in the center of the barbed wire enclosure that now surrounds the site of old Fort Mims.

Back in 1813, news of the Massacre at Fort Mims spread across a shocked and saddened nation. A total of 516 men, women, and children were killed on August 30 that year by the Indians in one of the bloodiest slaughters ever recorded in American history. Today the event is almost forgotten. It even is unheard of by many persons living in this country today.

But Floyd Boone, who moved to Florida from his native Alabama in 1951, is a direct descendant of the famous Creek chief who at high noon on that day 155 years ago, led the attack on Fort Mims, Alabama, and he knows the story well. He has heard the tale since he was a little boy . . . from his father, his grandfather, and other members of his family.

The Massacre at Fort Mims, in Baldwin County, followed by a month the Battle of Burnt Corn, which was fought some 50 miles northeast of Tensaw in the same county. Both sites are approximately 35 miles north of Mobile, Alabama. The Burnt Corn battle was fought between the militia under the command of Colonel James Caller and the Creek Indians, then a powerful and proud nation. This battle, one in the historical conflict involving Spain, France, Great Britain, and the United States, ended in an embarrassing and disastrous defeat for the Americans. As a result the entire region of Alabama and surrounding area was fearful.

Terrified settlers began moving into nearby forts and stockades, preparing to defend themselves. One such was Fort Mims, which consisted of a stockade constructed around Samuel Mims's home, a large one-story frame structure with additional sheds, on land adjacent to Lake Tensaw.

Tension grew daily. Sentries kept a sharp lookout.

On August 29 two men, sent outside to herd cattle, rushed panic-stricken back to the safety of the fort crying, "Indians!" They reported seeing an unknown number of Indians wearing war paint.

The command at the fort immediately sent out a detachment of horsemen but these men found "no trace of Indians."

The next day, August 30, 1,000 Creek Indians, led by Chief Red Eagle whose American name was William (Billy) Weatherford, hid in a deep ravine just 400 yards east of the main gate at Fort Mims. As the signal of the dinner call sounded on a drum in the fort at high noon, the Creeks rushed across the open area surrounding the stockade, entered the east gate before those inside could close it, and in four hours slaughtered everyone inside the fort with the exception of a very few who escaped.

After the massacre, soldiers from other forts in the region came to bury the dead. Not much remained of what had been Fort Mims and the healing touch of nature and the surrounding forest soon softened, then covered, the hundreds of graves with a blanket of foliage.

General Andrew Jackson and his troops arrived at Fort Montgomery, not far from where Fort Mims had stood, and began the war to the finish with Chief Red Eagle and the Creeks. Skirmish after skirmish followed as more and more men joined the troops pledged to wipe out the Indians.

Only when the Creeks were almost all dead did the famous Indian chief, to save his nation from extinction, bow his proud head and surrender. History records the text of General William Weatherford's (Chief Red Eagle's) document of surrender, which he wrote beautifully by hand, since he was a well-educated man. He delivered this orally to General Andrew Jackson at Tohopeka, Alabama, on the Tallapoosa River when he surrendered on March 28, 1814, eight months after the Massacre at Fort Mims.

This surrender message read in part: "I am in your power; do with me as you please. I am a soldier. I have done the white people all the harm I could. I have fought them and fought them bravely. If I had an army I would yet fight . . . but . . . my people are all gone. I can do no more than to weep over the misfortunes of my nation.

"Once I could animate my warriors to battle but I cannot animate the dead. My warriors can no longer hear my voice. Their bones are at Talladega, Emunckfow and Tohopeka . . .

"On the miseries and misfortunes brought upon my country I look back with deepest sorrow and wish to avert still greater calamities . . .

"You are a brave man and I rely on your generosity. You will exact no terms of conquered people but such as they can accede to. . . .

"You have told us where we might go and be safe. This is a good talk and my nation ought to listen to it. They shall listen to it. I shall say no more."

Feeling was high against Red Eagle because of the massacre. To save the chief from mob violence General Jackson took him to the Hermitage, the Jackson family home, where he remained as his guest for several months.

Now, on March 27, 1966, Floyd Boone, camping out on the site of old Fort Mims with his friend, could not sleep.

"It was chilly and we built a fire to keep warm," Boone said. "Shortly after settling down, we began to hear unusual noises. They sounded like moans . . . soft . . . but like something human. I raised up but saw nothing. I had lain back down trying to tell myself I had imagined it when my buddy suddenly jumped up and looked around. He said he thought he heard footsteps close by us but there was no one there. By this time we were both wide-awake and decided the best thing to do was to stay awake and keep the fire going.

"Around 1:00 A.M., over the east gate of the fort, or where the east gate had been, we heard six loud drumbeats in succession. This was the entrance where Chief Red Eagle and his warriors entered the fort on the day of the massacre."

These drumbeats did not end the strange noises. In fact, the men said, they increased after that. Floyd's companion heard the sounds of horses' hooves, cries of human agony, muffled thuds, the sound of running feet, all the wild outcry of battle. And at 2:00 A.M. two loud drumbeats sounded over the west gate area.

But Floyd and his buddy stuck it out.

"I kept telling myself it *had* to be my imagination," Floyd said. "I never believed in ghosts."

Floyd's friend tried to tell himself the same thing even while he was actually hearing Indian war whoops, women screaming, men yelling, sounds so real it seemed to him the massacre was taking place all around him.

Still the two men could see nothing except the dark shadows of the lonely trees at the outer edge of the clearing and the moonlight shining across the field where the old fort once had stood. Not even a wild animal moved in the night although the wild woodsy area must have been full of game, the men said.

"At 4:00 A.M. we heard one drumbeat near where the blockhouse had stood," Floyd told me. "And that ended the strange incident. We heard no more unusual noises during the rest of the night but we sure were glad when morning came, believe me."

The two men think now that sleeping in the acre-square area where 516 bodies were buried in trenches by General Andrew Jackson and his troops isn't exactly the most inviting idea in the world.

"I don't know if I'd want to try it again or not," Boone confessed. "I wasn't really afraid. I was in familiar territory . . . I was born and raised in Alabama . . . but . . ."

Some persons who live in the area of the old fort and are familiar with its history suggest that perhaps the departed spirits of Chief Red Eagle, who led the attack on Fort Mims, and Major Daniel Beasley, who was commander of the fort at the time of the massacre, still are restless, still are wanting folks to know more about what happened and why on that long-ago day in August 1813.

History tells us that Major Daniel Beasley commanded the fort. General Claiborne, in command at Mount Vernon, came to Fort Mims August 7 to inspect this stockade and instructed Major Beasley "to strengthen the pickets and to build one or two additional blockhouses." Lieutenant William R. Chambliss stated after the attack, "And I further certify that Major Beasley received a letter, one or two days before the attack on Fort Mims, from General Claiborne (who was on his way to Fort Easley) advising him of the reported movements of the enemy."

Major Beasley ignored all warnings, calling them false, and sent two notes to General Claiborne assuring him of his "ability to maintain the fort against any number of Indians."

Weatherford (Red Eagle) later explained to General Jackson and Thomas Woodward why he chose to stay with the Creeks. He said he realized there was no chance for the Indians to defeat the whites but he felt it was his duty to stay with them, to try to keep the tribe from being utterly destroyed. He was drawn into the Fort Mims expedition but did everything possible to warn the garrison there of the intended attack and felt that he would have succeeded had the commander, Beasley, not been drunk. When he found he could not stop the Indians from their plans to attack he first sent a message to General Claiborne; later he sent messengers to the fort itself. The guards reported these warnings to the commander but were punished for "imagining" such a story and at least one Negro lookout was severely beaten for reporting the Indians' warning.

Red Eagle said he was surprised to find the fort in the condition it was but he was unable to restrain the Indians after the first shots were fired. During a lull of about one hour after the first attack he attempted to talk them into leaving the fort but they refused and even threatened his life if he interfered.

Jim Cornells had left Fort Mims on the morning of August 30 and ridden some miles upriver. Before noon he returned and halting at the fort gate shouted that the Indians were coming. In the argument that followed Major Beasley ordered Cornells arrested but the scout wheeled his horse and started for Fort Pierce. He yelled back once again that the Indians were coming, that if they would prepare to defend themselves he could take care of himself. But it seems that more of the garrison than Major Beasley were drunk on that day.

Later Cornells said, "Surely nowhere else in American history can an example be found where a fort was so poorly guarded, where a massacre was so needless."

T. H. Ball wrote in his book, *Fort Mims*, "This fearful massacre, one of the bloodiest in our land, has been placed as the beginning of the Creek War and its responsibility laid almost entirely upon Weatherford quite long enough. It is time that the real responsibility should be placed where it belongs."

And so perhaps those persons who believe the departed spirits of Chief Red Eagle and Major Daniel Beasley still are restless, still concerned with justifying their roles in the disaster, base their reasoning on solid history.

Boone told me, "Red Eagle did not want to lead the attack. History proves he was forced into it against his wishes. He knew most of the people in the fort. Beasley ignored the warnings of an impending attack. Those drumbeats over the east gate that we heard that night could have had something to do with the signals. Who can tell?"

Boone believes his illustrious ancestor would like the record set straight, that he, Chief Red Eagle, was not the villain, that he did not want to attack but was driven by pressures of the times.

Boone wonders, "Would the spirits of the massacred at Fort Mims, most of whom were friends of Red Eagle's and well known to him, be able to rest in peace if the truth were made known? Maybe they are trying to tell us the truth about what really happened at Fort Mims . . . and why."

THE GHOST OF GOLIAD

Author Unknown

IN 1936 TEXAS WAS PREPARING FOR ITS CENTENNIAL CELEBRATION and relics connected with Texas history were selling for high prices. A. W. Shaw of Goliad, who had earned a reputation for his ability to locate buried treasure, thought he might be able to find several buried cannon dating back to 1836. The weapons had been spiked and buried by men of the Texas army under Colonel James Fannin when advancing Mexican troops forced them to retreat from the mission of La Bahia at Goliad.

Shaw got permission to dig on the La Bahia mission grounds, provided he did so only at night. He used a metal locator during the daytime, then began digging with a crew of Mexican laborers after dark.

One night, frightened by the braying of a donkey, the Mexicans dropped their shovels and fled. Alone in the darkness, Shaw told Jimmy Walker, who reported the story in the *Houston Chronicle Rotogravure Magazine,* he heard the sound of marching feet. Although the sound seemed close at hand, Shaw saw nothing move.

Then, as he started after his Mexican workers, something that seemed to be a hand gripped his leather jacket and held him. Released a moment later, he swung his flashlight beam around but saw nothing.

The Mexican laborers refused to return to the mission. Shaw hired a new crew the next day and resumed work. As they were digging,

Shaw told Jimmy Walker, he suddenly saw beside him the misty figure of a Spaniard in buckskins. He says he knew, somehow, that the apparition's name was Manuel Caberra. Then, Shaw relates, the figure knocked him out with a blow on the head. He did not revive until his Mexican workers poured water on him.

Still dazed, Shaw was carried to the home of an old Mexican woman. When he told her of what had happened, she said her family had known Manuel Caberra, who had been a guard at the mission. She warned Shaw not to dig anymore because, she said, it was not yet time.

Continuing to dig, however, Shaw unearthed two cannon, a couple of skeletons, and numerous relics. Then he ran into legal difficulties over the ownership of the finds and this, added to his other troubles, made him give up his search. Although he says he knows the location of a dozen other cannon around La Bahia mission, he does not plan to interfere with Manuel Caberra's watch over them.

PHANTOM TROOPERS

Andre Nelson

IT WAS COLD AND FOGGY ON THE MORNING OF FEBRUARY 3, 1943, AS I drove an army jeep along the Burma-India border. The jeep lurched and slithered along the muddy track serving as a road between tea groves stretching to the horizon on both sides.

I had never liked that early-morning drive to the military airfield at Chabua, home of a fighter squadron and an air transport unit. As I made those trips it always seemed to me that I was utterly alone in a brooding, timeless land, although I knew there were hundreds of natives in white saris or loinclothes stirring in nearby villages and preparing for the day. On that cold, sodden morning I could distinguish the vinegary, sharp odor of the dried grass and dung fires over which the villagers prepared their morning meals. My nose also caught the strange earthy smell that came from dew forming on the mouldering thatches of their bamboo huts.

The clinging cold made my face ache. As the jeep shouldered through the eddying billows of mist, it seemed as if I had been driving for an eternity, that never had there been a time when I had not been jolting along that track.

Suddenly I heard the nonrhythmic clink of metal and the squeak of leather on leather. Glancing to my left, I saw that the source of the strange sounds was a troop of Indian cavalry riding in a column along the top of a broad earthen dike. The soldiers were mounted on bay horses and dressed in *alkhalaqus* (tunics) which looked green-black in the mist, gray trousers, long black boots, and scarlet Muslim turbans.

They were all seemingly unaware of me. As they slowly drove past, they would momentarily appear and disappear in the drifting banks of fog. The British officer heading the file of about 50 men was followed by a trooper carrying a yellow guidon inscribed with a black insignia that I could not see clearly. A second officer was riding in the middle of the column. The officers, burned by the sun until they were as brown as their men, were armed with sabers and pistols, while the troopers, to my surprise, carried long spears supported by a socket in the right stirrup. I did not notice if they carried other weapons.

No member of the column glanced at me as the troops rode by. Their faces were expressionless, each cavalryman sitting erect, staring straight ahead, each seemingly lost in his own thoughts. I saw the horses tossing their heads and mouthing their bits and I heard the subdued clink-clank of metal, the protesting squeak of leather.

In just a matter of minutes the column had drifted by me. It all happened so quickly and I had been so bemused by the sight that I had not thought of stopping to watch them.

Recovering from my surprise, I craned my head over my shoulder to catch another glimpse of them. All I saw were sliding banks of fog which twisted and writhed in the slight breeze, effectively concealing anything that may have passed. I listened intently, but by then the fog and damp ground of the dike absorbed even the sound of the horses' hoofs. All I heard was the sound of my jeep engine, which was greatly in need of maintenance. In retrospect I have often wished I had tried to turn around on that narrow track and catch up with the riders.

I was used to seeing tanks, landing craft, and cargo planes. They were a part of my wartime life. But colorful turbaned troops, horses, and spears were things one expected to see only in the days when the British Raj ruled India.

Continuing on my way, I stopped enroute at Tinsukia, a small village where a friend of mine, Captain John Burns, a red-faced, burly Scot, formerly head of the Shanghai Police, was now stationed in charge of troop transportation. I told him what I had seen.

He remarked, "We are moving troops down to Indo-China to counter a push by the Japanese up into this area. But I've not had any requests to move a cavalry unit there." He shook his head. "That's a long way to ride. . . ."

As the years passed, the war ended and I did not read of any engagement of cavalry against the enemy in that theater of war. Later as memories of that morning in India grew dim, doubt stirred in my mind. Had I really seen the troop? After all, at that time I was a young, credulous American soldier abruptly transported to an ancient land and culture. I had been attached to a British unit which still observed many of the unique traditions of the old British rule in India and I had been surrounded by remnants of the rich color and splendor of that epoch—all of which may have stimulated my imagination.

Possibly that morning as I drove through the banks of swirling fog, I had unknowingly been hypnotized and thought I had seen that troop rising out of the mist.

Whatever happened that morning in February 1943, it made an indelible impression on me. The recollection is still sharp and clear and one that every now and then I conjure up from the recesses of my memory. That vision serves to soften the clangor of the everyday world and brings me a fleeting movement of pleasure and of vicarious adventure.

THE PHANTOM ARMY OF THE CIVIL WAR

Frank Spaeth

I T'S THE MIDDLE OF THE NIGHT. THE AIR IS FILLED WITH THE sounds of battle—the roar of cannons and the screams of sol-diers. The shadows of phantoms in blue and gray lurk in every corner. War rages all around. It isn't just any war, but the Civil War, the most costly war in terms of lost lives—and lost innocence—in United States history.

Many Civil War battlefields are rife with stories and legends of ghostly soldiers and phantom armies, but there is one Civil War bat-tle that isn't relived on the battlefield. Instead, the horrors of war come to life in the New Orleans mansion of a famous Confederate general.

The Beauregard-Keyes house, located in the French Quarter of New Orleans, has a long, colorful history. Built in the 1820s, the mansion has been home to many famous people, including novelist Francis Parkinson Keyes. The ghostly rumors, however, surround another important figure.

General Pierre Gustave Toutant Beauregard moved into the man-sion shortly after the Civil War ended, although he may have resided there with his family during the war as well. Forced by illness to retire, Beauregard, a member of a prominent family in the New Orleans area, came home. He had graduated from West Point in 1838 and fought in the Mexican War. He was in command of the Confederate forces that fired on Fort Sumter in April 1861. A year later he led his troops at the Battle of Shiloh.

Shiloh was one of the most brutal battles of the Civil War. Over 23,000 men—10,000 Confederate and 13,000 Union—lost their lives in two days of intense fighting. Although the Union was the technical victor, the Battle of Shiloh was important to the Confederacy as well, for it stabilized their western position. In any case, the emotional scars of the battle were forever etched on every soldier who lived through—and died in—the Battle of Shiloh.

Nowhere may the eternal remembrance of Shiloh be more apparent than in the Beauregard-Keyes house. By day this beautifully restored Southern mansion, designated a National Historic Place, is a thriving inn. Guides in period costume entertain guests, showing them the house's intricacies. But late at night, those wandering around may be greeted by another, less pleasing spectacle.

Over the years, stories of a ghostly battle reenactment have circulated. Some nights at approximately 2:00 A.M., strange events take place in and around the mansion's ballroom. It takes on an otherworldly feel. The lavish furnishings seem to fade away, replaced by wide open spaces—battle grounds—and the hearty spirits of Beauregard's troops at the Battle of Shiloh. General Beauregard enters the battle from the ballroom's large double doors, riding his great white steed.

Legions of men under his command struggle against other spectral forces. Eventually the Confederate phantoms begin to show the wear of battle. The seemingly healthy ghosts change. Well-conditioned limbs become broken, mangled, and useless. Soldier's faces are wiped away, leaving fleshless skulls with hollow eye sockets. The stench of rotting death fills the hallway. Men groan in agony and cry for help. But even in death, the men can't escape their fates. Suddenly, daylight comes and silence falls over the area. The soldiers fade away. Their eternal battle will continue some other night.

Psychically sensitive people have been overwhelmed by feelings of anguish, confusion, and despair while visiting the hallway and ballroom of the Beauregard-Keyes house—emotions which most witnesses feel resonate from its spectral soldiers.

Psychic Luann Wolfe, who has visited the site of the actual Battle of Shiloh in Tennessee, says that these kinds of feelings are common in places where a tremendous loss of life has occurred. She felt the horror emanating from the Shiloh battlefield and has received similar readings at other battlefield sites as well.

Although many visitors claim to have witnessed this incredible ghostly battle, one woman questions the authenticity of the stories. Marion Chambon, director of the Beauregard-Keyes house, says that she does not know of anyone who has personally experienced the return of Beauregard's army. But, she adds, "This is a very old house and it can get a little creepy, not scary, at times. In the winter when it gets dark early, the house—or something—can sometimes 'spook' me, and for no reason I lock up very quickly and leave."

Chambon says, "If we do have ghosts or spirits here, then they are happy ones, and they leave us alone and we leave them alone."

Chambon is skeptical about the phantom army, but she has an open mind toward the possibility of other ghostly happenings around the house. She cites a book entitled *The Beauregard-Keyes House*, by Samuel Wilson Jr. This book shares another ghostly tale.

Apparently, General Beauregard and his wife had planned a grand ball in the house. Unfortunately, the general was called away on business and the ball never took place. It is said that every once in a while the ghosts of the Beauregards return to the ballroom to host the ball they planned but never gave.

Chambon relates a story that adds some credibility to the phantom ball tale. A young girl rented out the apartment below the ballroom one night. According to Chambon, the next morning, when the girl was asked how her night was, "She stated that she did not get much sleep that night because of the music and sounds of furniture being moved."

Was it the sound of long-deceased reveling debutantes coming to the ball that never took place? Or was it the sound of the hallway transforming into a battleground for ghostly soldiers? No one can say for sure, but many people have left the Beauregard-Keyes house feeling that there is more inside than the simple furnishings of a renovated Civil War mansion.

GHOST OF WAR

Cynthia Falconer

O N A HOT SUMMER DAY IN THE MIDDLE OF AUGUST, MY HUS-
band, some in-laws, and I were traveling the back roads
on the way home from a family wedding in Louisiana. We
had agreed to take our time on the return trip, to look for antiques
and nose through the towns that were no longer on the beaten path.

We meandered through aging schoolhouses and abandoned
church buildings, all of which had been converted into flea markets
and antique shops. Large window fans sucked warm, humid air into
the high-ceilinged rooms. We sipped ice-cold Nehis and RCs that we
had purchased from an old-fashioned grocery store.

In Washington, a small town about 10 miles north of Opelousas,
stands the Nicholson House of History. Locals told us that the house
had been used as a hospital during the Civil War, and that a fort was
maintained beneath it.

"And it's haunted, too," one of the men said. We asked for directions.

At the house, no one answered our knock. We were about to leave
when a woman drove into the driveway and came up the stairs. Her
name was Mildred, and it was her house. She was very friendly and
invited us in for a tour.

It was hot. Mildred asked for three dollars a person for the tour,
and while we were dropping the money into the jar, she went about
turning on the air conditioner units in the windows. We all felt faint.

Mildred directed us to a front room filled with early-1860s furnishings. She showed us a secret passage that led down to the fort. She told us interesting stories about the Civil War and about how the house, built on an Indian mound in 1812, held many memories. Mildred claimed to have seen the spirit of a Confederate soldier in full dress uniform coming down the stairs a few days before.

We were wiping sweat off our faces, wishing the air conditioning would kick in, when I felt the damp hairs on the back of my head rise. It startled me. I watched bumps form on my arms and felt them crawling slowly up the skin of my bare legs. I looked to the others, expecting to see a similar reaction.

Jane, my sister-in-law, looked like she'd been picking cotton in a hot Louisiana field. The others were also sweating. I folded my arms for warmth.

Mildred stopped in mid-sentence, her mouth formed around some unspoken thought.

"You!" she exclaimed. "Ooh, the Colonel must really like you." I just stood there, leaning on my husband, gathering my thoughts, and watching Mildred smile.

I felt the weary scent of the Colonel's dampened woolen coat, the pungency of tragedy collected in its gray threads. I sensed anguish, a never-ending sorrow.

Mildred assured us that the Colonel was a gentle ghost that would not bring harm to anyone.

"We may even be able to *see* him, if this keeps up," she said.

The attic was even hotter, at least it was for the others. Mildred said that wounded men were treated there during the war. Men who died were taken down and buried after dark.

During this time she kept smiling at me. I was still chilled while everyone else was sweating. My husband demanded to know exactly what the Colonel was doing with me.

"Well, he *likes* her," Mildred said.

My mind wandered during the remainder of the tour. I never felt frightened, but the presence of a ghost from the past was disturbing. I remembered the words to a song I'd once heard: "Memories can't ignore/The anguish of before/Rise, ghost of war . . ."

Standing out on the big front porch, getting ready to leave, I felt the cold crispness in the air all around me.

"Well, it's obvious how much he likes you, but I think he'll stay here," Mildred said. "He's lived here for so long."

I stepped off the porch. The walk to the car was warm. Settling into the back seat, I turned to look at the house as we pulled away from the curb. I couldn't see him, but I knew he was there—a tall, handsome Confederate soldier standing proudly on the porch in full dress uniform.

Soldier at the Door

Barbara Healy

FOR FOUR YEARS WHEN I WAS A CHILD MY FAMILY LIVED IN RURAL Kennesaw, Georgia, the site of a Civil War battle. The house had a long drive and a fenced yard. From the front door you could see the whole length of the drive. There were windows on each side of the door. We often heard a knocking at the door or the ringing of the doorbell, but when we answered it no one was there. One winter night in 1968, however, that changed.

My mother and I were home alone when the doorbell rang. We could see through the curtains that someone stood outside the door, but it was late and we were cautious. With the chain still on, we opened the door and saw a young man, blond and about 20 years old. He was wearing some sort of military uniform and a long gray overcoat. He looked disheveled and he was barefoot. He asked for Jimmy and said that he had served with him in the war and that Jimmy had told him to come by if he were ever in town. My father, James Lloyd Thomas, had served in World War II—but everyone called him "Tommy." My mother scolded the stranger, saying that he was too young to have served with my father, and she slammed the door.

As soon as she slammed the door, we looked out the windows and the young man was gone. He hadn't had time to make it down the drive. Although there was snow on the ground, there were no footprints anywhere. Was he a wandering soldier from the fateful battle of Kennesaw Mountain, which took place only six miles from our house?

GHOST WATCH AT WEST POINT

David Edwards

DESPITE ALLEGATIONS OF HOAX AND PERSISTENT OFFICIAL silence from army brass, the "West Point Ghost" remains an unsolved mystery. First published reports on the episode came in mid-November 1972 when the story was already a month old. And the subsequent "confession" by an Annapolis midshipman only further confused the already muddled picture.

The 168-year-old United States Military Academy, high on the west bluff of the Hudson River 60 miles north of New York City, dates back to the days of the Revolutionary War. In the past other ghosts have been reported to roam the superintendent's mansion and a house on Professor's Row, but there is nothing romantic about the locale of this latest disturbance—a sparsely furnished 16-by-12-foot room in 47th Division Barracks.

There are two quite separate and distinct accounts of what transpired. One was carried, with small variations, by the newspapers of the country, including the *New York Times*. The other was presented by the members of Company G-3, titled "A Modest Report," in *The Pointer*, which is published by the United States Military Academy itself.

According to the newspaper reports: On the night of October 21, 1972, Room 4714 was occupied by two unnamed plebes (freshmen). One of them, a 19-year-old plebe belonging to G Company,

Third Battalion, Fourth Regiment, awoke in the middle of the night and saw what he thought was a figure coming through the door of the room. He awakened his roommate but by then the apparition was gone.

The next night the strange man appeared again and this time both young men saw him. They said the apparition walked out of the bureau and stood approximately in the middle of the room. Cadet Captain Keith W. Bakken heard the plebes let out a yell and rushed to the room, which he later reported seemed unusually cold. The next night Bakken stayed overnight in Room 4714 with the two obviously shaken freshmen but saw nothing unusual.

The following night Captain Bakken brought a first classman from the battalion staff to sleep with the two plebes. About 2:00 A.M. all three saw "a figure partially extended out of the wall." The upperclassman placed his hand on the spot where the apparition had vanished and said it felt "icy cold."

The two plebes and the upperclassman agree the mysterious figure was of a calvaryman about five feet three inches tall, with a handlebar mustache, dressed in full nineteenth-century military garb and carrying a musket. Later they did some research in the West Point library and picked uniforms of the 1830s as being the most nearly like that worn by the apparition. They all agree, also, that the ghost wore boots and a plumed shako (hat).

Another upperclassman who slept in the room on the night of October 24 reported seeing "a face and shoulder" apparently come out of the wall locker. A few days later a first classman volunteered to spend the night alone in the room. "He was taking a shower prior to moving into the room," reports Lieutenant Colonel Patrick Dionne, the academy's information officer. "On leaving the shower (across the hall from Room 4714) he noticed that his bathrobe was swinging back and forth on the hook. The door was closed; the window was closed. So there was no breeze and there was no other person in the shower. He promptly put his bathrobe on and left the building."

Shortly after this incident Lieutenant Commander Michael Macdonald, tactical officer of the barracks, declared the haunted room "off limits" and transferred the plebes to other quarters. Even the furnishings were removed from Room 4714. The ghost had attained a private room and bath! But apparently he was not permitted much privacy. Curious cadets took turns sleeping in the room to see if the apparition would return. Various news reports stated that the ghostly visitor was seen as late as November 12.

From the very first report controversy has raged over the authenticity of the apparition. Skeptics point out that the apparition first appeared only five days after a lecture at the Academy by Ed and Lorraine Warren, self-styled "ghost hunters." However, the lecture was not open to plebes so the two young men who first saw the phantom had not heard the talk.

Officers who personally know the cadet witnesses vouch for their reliability. "I don't believe in ghosts myself but the lads saw something," information officer Dionne told the *New York Times*. Others were impressed by the similarities of reports from different witnesses. Opinion among the army cadets themselves seems evenly divided between belief and skepticism. West Point refused to tell the newspapers the names of cadets who had reported seeing the apparition but at least four different men, perhaps as many as a half dozen, had seen it on at least nine separate occasions. All reports agreed in general description and that the ghost was luminous and shimmering.

On Tuesday, November 21, 1972, Midshipman William Gravell of the United States Naval Academy at Annapolis, Maryland, claimed the West Point ghost really was a hoax he and another unnamed naval cadet had perpetrated. He claimed to have taken a photograph of a midshipman dressed in bits and pieces of old uniforms, overexposed it so it looked shadowed, and had a slide made of it. The two Annapolis men then had traveled up to West Point on Halloween—"an appropriate time to start"—equipped with the slide, a flashlight, some cheesecloth, and a fire extinguisher filled with carbon dioxide. He lowered himself by a rope from somewhere above Room 4714 and shined the flashlight through the slide to project an image onto the wall. The cheesecloth covered the flashlight to soften the beam, Gravell explained. The fire extinguisher was lowered through an "air shaft" and the sound of escaping gas awoke the sleeping plebes. The carbon dioxide was responsible for the cold place on the wall, he claimed.

Gravell's story is as incredible as it is ingenious. He fails to explain why he had to be suspended from above Room 4714, which is on the first floor and easily reached by ladder. The lower two-thirds of the room's windows are frosted and would not admit an image, leaving little leeway for Gravell's flashlight. Furthermore no air shaft or anything that resembles one exists adjacent to Room 4714. The most glaring discrepancy, however, is in the dates. Gravell was misled by a *New York Times* story by John Corry that incorrectly dates the first sighting of the apparition as October 31 rather than 21.

The exploding of Gravell's story, however, simply threw the situation back to where it had been before he dragged in his red herring. Still unexplained was: What did the cadets in fact see in Room 4714?

The confusion is further compounded by the quite different version of the haunting which appeared in the December 1972 issue of *The Pointer*. The article "A Modest Report" is attributed simply to "The Members of Company G-3." The story gives the names of the two plebes in Room 4714 as Jim O'Connor and Art Victor. But this version says the unexplained events started on Friday, October 20, with the swinging bathrobe incident—O'Connor rather than the anonymous first classman is the witness, however. Two days later, early on Sunday morning, O'Connor first sees the apparition, also in the bathroom rather than in the room across the hall. The report describes the figure as five feet six inches tall and "dressed in a worn full dress gray coat" with a Civil War musket in its hand. The glowing white eyes of the apparition terrified O'Connor.

The ghost's first visit to Room 4714 takes place the next night. Both Victor and O'Connor see "an unclear figure like the silhouette of a man's torso" floating about five feet above the floor. On Monday, October 30, the apparition returned and remained visible for 10 minutes. A pronounced cold accompanied both the swinging bathrobe and the apparition's appearances.

Except for the discrepancy about dates the second version now begins to parallel the earlier newspaper account. Bakken offers to sleep in the haunted room and is accompanied by one Terry Meehan, who is identified as "the platoon leader." Meehan sees "an image on the ceiling" at 1:45 A.M. and Bakken awakes too late to see anything but feels an abnormal cold. If we assume the "first classman from the battalion staff" is Meehan, this incident matches the newspaper version except that the earlier version would date the incident before October 24 and *The Pointer* would place it a day or so after October 30.

The next night, the later version continues, John Feeley, the "assistant brigade adjutant," shares the room with O'Connor and sees the ghost. His scream awakens O'Connor, who glimpses the apparition just before it disappears into the wall and reports that the spot on the wall is intensely cold. This seems to correspond to the events of October 24 in the newspaper account.

By far the most interesting additional details in *The Pointer* concern a later occasion, apparently about November 5. "The next night three cadets on the battalion staff stayed in the room with O'Connor. They had borrowed a thermocouple for measuring instantaneous temperature changes from the Department of Earth, Space, and

Graphic Sciences. The first remarkable reading was when the device measured –18 degrees Centigrade. It quickly returned to normal, 27 degrees Centigrade, and remained there until O'Connor returned to his room. As he walked in the device immediately dropped to a reading of 7 degrees Centigrade; the next time it dropped in O'Connor's presence it registered 14 degrees Centigrade. The cadets carried the thermocouple around the room and discovered that it was always coldest near O'Connor."

On Monday, November 6, cadets Joe Tallman and Gary Newsom slept in Room 4714 and experienced nothing unusual. But O'Connor, spending the night in an upstairs room, saw the "spirit on the wall." The details of the haunting as recorded in *The Pointer* strongly suggests that O'Connor is the unconscious center of the disturbance.

The Pointer also speculates on possible origins of the apparition. The dormitory building with the haunted room stands not far from the site of an officer's house that burned down in the last century. The officer perished in the fire. The old graveyard for Execution Hollow lies not far away and offers a second possible source of a restless spirit. But *The Pointer* also mentions a seance held during the visit of Ed and Lorraine Warren. The Warrens had conducted the session in the reputedly haunted superintendent's house, currently occupied by Lieutenant General William A. Knowlton, and *The Pointer* suggests that perhaps the seance drove the spirit out of the mansion into the barracks. A problem with this particular whimsy is that the mansion's reputed spectral inhabitant is "a 150-year-old milky iridescent maid named Molly, a tall, dark, domineering woman" whose best-known activity is rumpling the coverlet in one of the bedrooms. It seems unlikely that Molly would be mistaken for a Civil War soldier.

After comparing these two versions of the West Point affair one is left with the feeling that the discrepancies probably are due to the academy's reluctance to permit the original witnesses to be questioned. The newspaper reporters thus were forced to rely on hearsay accounts, many of them delivered some weeks after the unusual events and garbled in the retelling.

Neither account mentions anything unusual happening after the middle of November 1972. This West Point ghost seems to have vanished as mysteriously as he appeared and we are left with yet another psychic enigma.

GHOST ARMY OF JOHNSON'S ISLAND

Author Unknown

A STRANGE STORY IS TOLD IN CONNECTION WITH AN OLD CON-federate cemetery on Johnson's Island, a speck of land in Sandusky Bay, three miles from Sandusky, Ohio. During the Civil War Johnson's Island was used as a prison for some 12,000 Confederate soldiers.

At the turn of the century the major industry on Johnson's Island was stone quarrying. Most of the workers were Sicilians who lived in shacks near the cemetery. One March day a severe storm lashed the island and threatened to topple the stoneworkers' shacks. They fled outside where, whipped by freezing wind and spray, they sought shelter at the base of a bronze statue of a Confederate soldier, which had been erected as a memorial.

Suddenly, according to Grace Goulder, who related the incident in the *Cleveland Plain Dealer Pictorial Magazine,* the shivering Sicilians heard a bugle call. Their eyes widened in terror as they saw gray-clad soldiers, each shouldering a musket, rise from the nearby graves. In complete silence the soldiers marched off into the storm and disappeared from view.

A short time later the storm ended and the Sicilians returned to their shacks. The next day they rowed ashore and told of what they had seen. They were so convinced that their experience had been supernatural, that they refused to return to Johnson's Island.

THEY'VE BEEN WAITING

Robert C. Alsheimer

I LEFT DOWNTOWN LOS ANGELES, HEADING SOUTH TOWARD THE port city of Long Beach, a place seemingly as modern as one can get. But I was about to step back more than 100 years in time. I was going to visit the haunted Civil War museum.

What would an 1861 barracks look like now, restored and functioning as a museum in the midst of L.A.'s urban sprawl? I pictured a quaint wood building nestled within verdant park grounds. I was shocked when my directions took me to a densely populated residential street. In the middle of the block lay my destination. The Drum Barracks, named after Adjutant General Richard Coutler Drum, is so tightly flanked by modest homes that the only claim to prominence this historic site possesses is a double lot, which occupies the full width of the block, allowing the front entrance to be on one street and the rear entrance on another. Modest as it is, its presence dominates the area. Any trace of the twentieth century stops at its gates.

The building is a two-story, white clapboard structure. Window shutters are the only relief from the simplicity of its design. Single story wings extend from either side, forming a charming intimate courtyard, with a brilliant pink flowering tree gracing the center. A rooster cackles from a nearby backyard adding a final touch that helps the visitor shift centuries.

The barracks appears small from outside, so I was surprised by its vast interior. But this was only a perceptual illusion. Other surprises were not as easily explained.

Entering the courtyard, I thought about the ghosts said to reside here. I knew that *Unsolved Mysteries* felt confident enough about the authenticity of the hauntings to film a TV segment here. I wondered if I would only be reporting what other people told me, or if I would have experiences myself.

Marge O'Brien, the director/curator of Drum Barracks, greeted me at the door. Her effervescent personality sparkled throughout our two hours together, and her historical knowledge was disarming. Her ability to bring dry facts and dates brilliantly alive with anecdotes about life at the museum a century ago reminded me of a favorite history teacher.

As O'Brien explained, Californians had ambivalent feelings about the Civil War. The state had just become part of the Union and had far more immediate concerns regarding Mexico, not to mention the split affinities of its populace between North and South. O'Brien drew me into a world of very understandable concerns. As I glanced up at the 14-foot-high ceiling, she told me that this last remaining structure was once an imposing fort of 19 buildings centered on 60 acres of land, built to garrison troops of mostly European enlistees arriving from the Gold Country of northern California. I could almost hear horses outside in the courtyard.

As our tour began, O'Brien explained that when she arrived in 1986, her designated position was part-time caretaker. Back then the building was dilapidated and all of the rooms were bare. Most of the south wing that we walked through had been sealed off. With a worker's help, she tore out the wall and transformed the wing's abandoned rooms into comfortable institution offices.

We continued down the hall to the front of the museum. O'Brien opened the parlor door, announcing, "This is where most of the activity happens." I scanned the dim room. Shades on all of the 10-foot-tall windows were drawn. A deck of old-fashioned playing cards was arranged upon a beautiful inlaid wood table before two chairs, as if a couple were playing. When I entered the room a chill went down my spine. This had nothing to do with psychic premonition; the room was as cold as a refrigerator. "Feel the difference in temperature?" O'Brien asked, right on cue. "It's like this in here all the time." It was a cloudless California day, and the temperature was near 80 degrees. It was midday and the southwest room had been getting full sun all morning. Even with pulled shades, it should have been one of the warmest rooms in the house. Yet the chill persisted.

"They've moved the cards again," O'Brien said. "The deck was by the other chair this morning." Okay, I thought, there was no way to prove or disprove that. But the unaccountable cold was real and impossible to ignore.

I noticed a bricked-up fireplace and recalled the article I had read about Barbara Connor, the gifted psychic who had come here in 1991 and contacted many of the resident ghosts. Working with O'Brien's historical reference files, Connor and O'Brien were able to identify most of the spirits. I hadn't met Connor yet, but during a phone interview the following day, she filled me in on her experience in the parlor. She had seen the spirit of a Union officer sitting in one of the four parlor chairs closest to the fireplace. It was one of the most amazing experiences of her psychic career, she said, first because the Colonel's image was so distinct, with no haze or mist about it and without transparency. Additionally, he spoke to her; not through thought form—the way she usually experienced spirit communication—but with his actual voice. He asked that his chair be moved closer to the hearth. Even though the fireplace had been sealed in 1971, Connor could see it fully open. Only a weak fire was burning in her vision. The officer was trying to warm his extended left leg, which was too far away from the scant flames.

Connor's vision astonished O'Brien. The latest research had just disclosed that one of the commanding officers of Drum Barracks, Colonel James Curtis, had suffered severe frostbite during a winter Indian campaign in Washington. He would often sit here in the parlor, warming his aching leg by the fire. And it was his left leg, just as Connor had seen.

I noticed a portrait above the mantle. "I commissioned it to be painted from an old photograph of the Colonel that I found," O'Brien explained. "I wanted him to feel at home here."

"Colonel Curtis didn't die at Drum Barracks," Connor later informed me as we spoke on the phone. "He returned after death because he loved this place and spent many of the happiest years of his life here."

Connor also related her encounter with the woman on the stairs, "She, too, appeared quite clearly, wearing a long hoop-skirted dress. She communicated in thought form, identifying herself as Marie, an Earthbound spirit who was free to come and go as she chose, but who was very attached to the house. 'You would have to burn it to the ground before I would leave,' " she informed Connor. The spirit then clutched her side and began to moan. When Connor told O'Brien this, she realized the spirit had to be Colonel Curtis's wife, Marie, who had lived at the fort and had died years later of acute appendicitis.

Although O'Brien, a self-professed skeptic, had never seen a ghost herself, she could not discount the encounters she'd had there over the past nine years. Early one morning, while she was working in one of the offices, footsteps approached from the hall and stopped behind her. Assuming it was her assistant, she said, "You're early today, Todd." When there was no response, she turned around to discover that no one was there. But she still felt a presence in the room. O'Brien had also sensed the spirit on the staircase many times. The feeling of a woman, whose name began with the letter "M," was so pervasive that she started calling the invisible spirit Mary—years before Connor identified her as Marie.

O'Brien gave me the 14-page account of spirit activities recorded by Vincent Manchester, who was the volunteer caretaker of Drum Barracks from 1967 to 1975, during the time the building remained empty and neglected. "I saw a shadow move on the upper part of the stairs," reported Manchester. "I could see a triangle shape, like a girl in a long full skirt. She, or it, stood there long enough for me to realize there was actually something there. I turned my flashlight on the stairs . . . and it disappeared."

O'Brien added, "I may be the director here, but she is definitely the lady of the house." She also told me that as far back as 1927, neighbors had reported seeing strange shapes in the second floor windows. O'Brien herself had often witnessed window shades mysteriously rise before her eyes; not flapping up with a snap, but slowly rising, as if guided by an unseen hand. "They seem to enjoy basking in the sun—or at least having the rooms bright and cheery," O'Brien said.

Connor confirmed this. "I saw a number of unidentified soldiers in the parlor. A few of them were standing at the windows looking out. I didn't pick up any feelings of expectation from their behavior, just that the windows must have commanded a magnificent view back then, and that they found it very peaceful and relaxing to stand there, gazing out."

During her 1991 tour of Drum Barracks, Connor had also identified the source of some recurring ghostly thuds. Upstairs, she came upon the spirit of a young boy bouncing a leather ball in the hallway. He was shy. When Connor asked him to stop bouncing his ball, he did, and the thudding stopped. The request still works. Whenever the recurring noise becomes a distraction, O'Brien goes to the stairs and calls out to him to stop. "It always works," she said. Although O'Brien was unable to find any reference to a young boy at the fort, Connor had a strong impression that he was discovered by soldiers on maneuvers. The boy had been recently orphaned, she felt, and the soldiers brought him to the fort, where he stayed until he could be more properly placed. During that time the boy had bonded with a few of the soldiers who were like adopted fathers or big brothers to him. This boy's spirit, too, had returned because he had been very happy here while alive.

I hadn't heard any thuds that afternoon. But when O'Brien and I entered the upstairs artillery room, displaying every brand of rifle made during the Civil War as well as an authentic Gatling gun, we were surprised to discover the shades on all five windows in disarray. Most were raised at various lengths: One had been pulled well below the sill and another was missing completely from the 12-foot-high roller. "I checked in here this morning and all the shades were evenly pulled," O'Brien exclaimed. I wondered if this hadn't been pre-arranged, but I couldn't believe such a conscientious curator would actually rip down a shade just for my benefit. We searched the room. The missing shade was nowhere to be found. "Things like this have happened before," O'Brien said. "They always turn up in a few days."

A week later I asked O'Brien about the missing shade over the phone. Not only did it show up the following day, she told me, it was reattached to the roller and functioning perfectly. She said with a jolly laugh, "We've all become used to things like this around here by now."

In another room, I was shown a model of the fort as it stood in 1861. I was surprised that of the 19 original buildings, only this one remained. O'Brien told me the story of its preservation. After the Civil War, a number of barracks were lost to fire. Then the site became Wilson College. In the early 1900s it was turned into a high school. In 1910 the area became part of Los Angeles County, and Drum Barracks was purchased successively by two different families, who kept it from demolition, a fate that befell all the other fort buildings except for a now-dilapidated powder shed.

Ironically, when the Long Beach earthquake struck in 1932 many nearby buildings were damaged, but not even a window was broken in Drum Barracks. It stood empty and neglected, with only the old caretaker looking after it through the 1960s and 1970s until O'Brien arrived in 1986.

When my tour was complete, we continued speaking in O'Brien's office. I asked if we could return to the parlor to see if anything had been moved. O'Brien obliged me, stating, "Don't expect anything. They're reluctant to perform for visitors." She opened the parlor door. As we stepped in, we were accosted by a sudden, overwhelming noxious odor of musty mildew. Within minutes it was completely gone. Yet the open door led only to an inside hall where every other door and window was closed. Real mildew odor doesn't evaporate— it lingers and permeates.

That night at home, while reading psychic Barbara Connor's notes, I realized that she had encountered the same odor in another room, only she had identified it more accurately as the scent of unwashed uniforms.

Mysterious odors are not uncommon at Drum Barracks. Connor had also smelled melting wax in the parlor and lilacs in the bedroom. O'Brien has often encountered an inexplicable lilac scent, which, Connor explained to her, was Marie's favorite cologne, worn often while she was alive.

I wondered why these spirits were at Drum Barracks. Connor detected that they loved the place and that they were there to prove there was existence after death. I couldn't shake the feeling that their presence resulted from a more pressing need. I considered the notably short time period of a year and a half, the time between O'Brien's arrival as part-time caretaker in 1986 and the date in 1987 when she had acquired enough period furniture through donations to enable the once abandoned building to qualify as a museum. Her unrelenting dedication had resulted in gaining Drum Barracks certification as both a National Historical Site and a National Museum. Could these spirits have been waiting all this time for O'Brien's arrival? Each of them loved the place so much they remained for a century. Wouldn't their burning desire be to have the place restored to its former beauty?

Connor agreed. "They're helping Marge in every conceivable way, literally drawing the correct things and people to her." When I mentioned this to O'Brien over the phone, she gasped. "You're so right! Not that it isn't a lot of hard, tedious work, but things do seem to arrive here miraculously. Difficult doors to government and corporations always opened with ease and with remarkable success. I'm so glad you've seen this!"

A week later, I was back in the museum office meeting Barbara Connor for the first time. Connor hadn't been to the museum since 1991, and she graciously accepted my invitation for a final tour. The results were sublime. In the parlor Connor encountered the familiar presence of Colonel Curtis sitting near the fire. "He's content now that his chair is by the fireplace." She mentioned that a small group of soldiers was also there; some at the card table, others standing contentedly by the window. She focused her attention on the sofa. "There's someone asleep on it," she said. A moment later she gasped. "One of the soldiers just said to me, 'Don't worry about him. He's dead.' " We all laughed simultaneously. Living spirits commenting on the dead? Dead spirits? This opened a whole new level no one had considered before. Suddenly we all caught the scent of cinnamon. As we commented on this, it vanished.

At the end of the tour, Connor commented, "They're far more content now, especially Marie." She turned to O'Brien. "She trusts you now. She's very happy about the ongoing restoration in all of the rooms."

OUR CONFEDERATE GHOST

Christine S. Camp

O N THE FIRST DATE I HAD WITH MY FUTURE HUSBAND WE WENT
to his parents' home in Warner Robins, Georgia. The
house has a long hallway from the sitting room where Ashley and I were together. Night had begun to fall so the hall was dim. I
was on my way to the kitchen when, at the end of the hall, I saw a
large-boned man in a gray uniform, slant hat, and a belt with a large
brass buckle on it. My first thought was that we were not alone in
the home and of course I was right! But the third person there was
a spirit.

I asked Ashley if he had any kin in the Civil War and he answered
not that he knew of. But I felt sure someone in his family had been in
the Civil War fighting for the Confederate cause because thereafter
every time I went to his parents' home the gray-uniformed man
appeared; it was as if he were trying to tell me something.

Shortly after that day, seven years ago, Ashley and I were married. I
found out that Ashley has a very strong love for the Confederate
cause. He owns over 300 books on the Civil War and has collected
many relics. We decided to look into his family tree and to review
pictures in family almanacs to see if I could pick out his great-
grandfather, John Augustus Cox, who we were told had fought in
the Civil War.

After learning about his great-grandfather I could call my spirit by name. "Johnny" followed us whenever we moved, as if he were haunting us for some reason.

Ashley originally came from Americus, Georgia. The Coxes' old family home is in Plains, Georgia. We had come to a dead end after long hours searching the Georgia archives, and decided to call at Hugh Carter's antique shop in Plains to speak to his father, Alton Carter. When the Carter family first came to Plains, Mr. Carter had roomed with Johnny Cox and his wife Sarah Missouri. Mr. Carter told us of the days he spent with Johnny (he called him Gus) and Sarah Missouri, and told us that Miss Sarah "was the best cook in five counties." Then he told us how Gus would talk about the war . . . the Civil War! Mr. Carter told us Johnny was in the cavalry but he had no other information. We were very thankful for even that much.

One time Johnny appeared to two friends of ours who were visiting us after we moved here to Saint Simons Island. Both Janice and Laura said he had a very sad and puzzled look on his face. It seemed we had to try to give him peace at last. He stood at the top of the stairs and looked down at our guests on a number of occasions.

We went back to the archives and narrowed our search down to three John A. Coxes but we didn't know which one was Ashley's great-grandfather. That night I dreamed of a gravestone with the name John A. Cox on it and his battalion number. But the number wasn't clear enough to read. The stone was leaning against a garage in the country. I had never seen the place before. When I awoke I told Ashley my dream and described the house and garage and he told me it sounded like his Uncle Jack's home in Americus.

Uncle Jack was Johnny's grandson and knew all the family history but he had removed himself from all family ties; he was a loner. We tried to call him and ask for information but he wouldn't talk to us. He had had the gravestone for many years but wouldn't put it on Johnny's grave! Maybe that was what troubled our ghost.

We finally drove to Uncle Jack's home when we knew he wasn't there, and just as I had seen it in my dream, there was the gravestone, with all the information we had needed for so long. We couldn't have been happier.

We went home and ordered Johnny a gravestone just like the traditional one that goes on every Confederate soldier's grave. We awaited the truck that delivered the gravestone to us. And so did Johnny! He seemed to appear more in those few weeks than he had at any other time during the five long years. It finally arrived and we took pictures of Ashley in a Confederate uniform with the gravestone and as we were snapping the pictures I could see Johnny looking out the upstairs library window. He now had a smile on his face.

We put the gravestone in the car and drove to Johnny's resting place in the Plains of Lebanon Cemetery in Plains, Georgia, and dragged it to the grave site. In the blazing heat of May we dug a large hole in the red Georgia clay and placed the gravestone where it should have been for over 80 years. We also planted a Confederate flag at the foot of the grave.

Johnny finally is at peace: we have never seen him again. Sometimes I think I still feel his presence but I know that he has finally joined all the other proud Confederates and, most of all, his true love Sarah Missouri.

I am certain fate brought Ashley and me together and fate gave Ashley the Confederate family ties he so longed for. Ashley is now a member of the Sons of Confederate Veterans: he is a Brigade commander for the Army of Georgia, and best of all he is a Civil War writer, nationally published. He and Great-grandfather Johnny have finally found their places, but it took a Yankee woman to content the Confederates.

GHOST ARMY OF THE CIVIL WAR

John Phillip Bessor

A REMARKABLE PHENOMENON WAS WITNESSED A FEW MILES WEST of Lewisburg, Greenbriar County, Virginia, on the 1st of October, 1863, about 3:00 P.M., by Moses Dwyer, who happened to be seated on his porch at the time, as well as by others at or near the house.

The weather was quite hot and still; not a cloud could be seen; no wind even ruffled the foliage on the surrounding trees. All things being propitious, the grand panorama began to move. Just over and through the tops of the trees on the adjacent hills, to the south, immense numbers of rolls, resembling cotton or smoke, apparently of the size and shape of doors, seemed to be passing rapidly through the air, yet in beautiful order and regularity. The rolls seemed to be tinged on the edge with light green, so as to resemble a border of deep fringe. There were apparently thousands of them; they were perhaps an hour in getting by. After they had passed over and out of sight, the scene was changed from the air above to the earth beneath, and became more intensely interesting to the spectators who were witnessing the panorama from different standpoints.

In the deep valley beneath, thousands upon thousands of (apparently) human beings (men) came in view, traveling in the same direction as the rolls, marching in good order, some 30 or 40 in depth, moving rapidly—"double quick"—and commenced ascending the almost insurmountable hills opposite. They had the stoop peculiar to men ascending a steep mountain. There seemed to be a great variety in the size of the men; some were very large, while others were quite small. Their arms, legs, and heads could be distinctly seen in motion. They seemed to observe strict military discipline, and there were no stragglers. There was uniformity of dress, white blouses or shirts, with white pants; they were without guns, swords or anything that indicated "men of war." On they came through the valley and over the steep road, and finally passing out of sight in a direction due north from those who were looking on. Four others and a servant girl witnessed this strange phenomenon. On the 14th instant the same scene, almost identical, was seen by eight or 10 of the Confederate pickets at Runger's Mill, and by many citizens in that neighborhood: this is about four miles east of Percy's. It was about an hour passing.

THE RETURN OF PRIVATE DUPOY

Raymond J. Ross

PRIVATE JEROME DUPOY WAS ONE OF THE MOST POPULAR MEN IN the ranks of Company D, Seventh Regiment. Soon as word reached New York that good old Abe Lincoln called for men, Dupoy had lost no time in enlisting his services. And he was the jolly type, the kind of soldier that helps his buddies keep happy. When he fell dead at the battle of Olustee, Florida, with a bullet in the back of his head, a cloud of sorrow settled over Company D Camp.

The report of his death in the official war records might have read "killed in action" except that Sergeant Frank Broes had the strange conviction that Private Jerome Dupoy had been shot by someone in his own outfit.

Sergeant Broes voiced his suspicion and the camp buzzed with the question "Who did it?" Each man looked at his buddy and wondered.

A week later on a calm moonlit night Private John Rawley, a substitute for a New York drafted man, came off guard duty looking very unwell. Beads of sweat zigzagged down his sunburned cheeks. His gray eyes stared in terror.

Sergeant Broes noticed Rawley's hands trembling. "Are you ill, John?" he asked. "No-no," Rawley chattered, "I'm-I'm fine." With shaking hands he spread out his blanket and lay down.

Sergeant Broes removed his own boots and lay down too—still puzzling over Rawley's nervousness.

It later seemed to Broes that he was asleep only a few minutes when the dead Jerome Dupoy stood before him. He was pale, bloody, his lips moved several times but Broes couldn't make out his words. The sergeant sat up, shook his head, and was awake. His dream seemed very real. It was over an hour before Broes could go back to sleep.

During the next day Broes was haunted by the dream. It seemed that whenever he looked at Private John Rawley the dream and the vision of Dupoy returned to him with renewed impact.

That night a full moon rode the sky along an avenue of clouds. Sergeant Broes leaned against a shell-torn tree watching some of his men clean their rifles. His eyes fell on John Rawley who sat against a water keg. Broes saw a slow mist rise up behind Rawley. He watched it, fascinated as it formed a human figure—even the features became plain. It was Private Dupoy!

Chills ran up and down the sergeant's spine as he saw the figure point to Rawley. Then it was gone. Broes now felt he knew the meaning of his dream. He walked over to Rawley.

"Private Rawley," Broes' voice rang like steel, "I just seen Dupoy!"

Rawley leaped up. His face was drawn; his eyes started from their sockets; his mouth opened but no sound came. Then he bolted past Broes. But the sergeant grabbed his arm and spun him around.

"Rawley, listen, you can't run away from the dead! Speak man, speak what's on your mind! What happened to Dupoy?"

"Please, please Broes," Rawley begged, "keep Dupoy away. I'll confess. I'll tell you everything. He's—he's been appearing. That other night on guard I seen Dupoy, his face pale, bloody. Oh God, Sergeant Broes, please, I'll confess!"

A few minutes later in a candle-lit tent Sergeant Broes, with several picked soldiers, listened as Rawley told what happened at Olustee.

"Dupoy and I," Rawley's words were slow, "had a quarrel in the barracks in St. Helena. He stabbed me. I swore that if I ever got a chance I would kill him. Then at the battle of Olustee he was beside me. I fell back a few feet and raised my rifle. I got him in back of the head."

Broes saw hate building up in the eyes of the listening men. Outside the company troops were waiting.

"That isn't the only man I killed!" Rawley continued. "I killed a sailor on a gunboat coming down here. I killed a man in New York too, one who fixed it so I had to leave my family and go as a substitute for a drafted man last fall. But Dupoy is the only one that has ever troubled me. Since I killed him, I dread the nights, for I see him—see him plain as I see you. I see him standing in front of me, his face and head covered with blood. In my dreams he comes, he stands—I can't bear it any longer."

Before Broes could stop him, one of the men slipped out of the tent. Broes knew he would spread the news of Rawley's confession.

"Hang the rascal!" were the words that raced through the camp.

Broes opened the tent flap and stepped into the circle of men. "As long as I'm in command here and until an officer arrives to take over, there will be no killing. Rawley will stand a just trial."

Broes never finished. From inside the tent came the sound of a shot. He ran toward the tent.

Inside Rawley lay with a bullet in his chest. His guard had been knocked out by a blow on the head.

"Sergeant," Rawley gasped, "look! Look! Dupoy! Keep him away . . . Broes." Rawley tried to rise, then fell back.

Thus Rawley died—to escape from the ghost of the man he had killed—Private Jerome Dupoy.

KINDRED SPIRITS

John J. Lamb

I NEVER BELIEVED IN GHOSTS . . . UNTIL I VISITED GETTYSBURG," said the grizzled Union soldier, his voice subdued but full of conviction.

We sat before a flickering campfire watching sparks spiral lazily skyward into the darkness. Around us, 25,000 mock Civil War troops were bedding down, preparing for sleep. It was July 1998, the 135th anniversary of the Battle of Gettysburg, and we had assembled less than two miles from that famous battlefield to re-create the three days of savage combat. As a ghost researcher and Civil War reenactor, I found this a remarkable opportunity both to participate in the grand event and to collect dozens of fresh accounts of spectral sightings from one of America's most haunted towns.

The reenactor continued his story: "Last year I came to Gettysburg to walk the battlefield in uniform. It was always my dream to do that. So I left my family in the motel and set out before dawn because I wanted to avoid the crowds. By the time I got to MacPherson's Ridge, the sky was getting lighter, but I was alone. I was walking along near the railroad cut when I saw him."

I knew the place described by the witness. It was about a mile west of Gettysburg along U.S. Route 30. This was where the battle began, as Yankee cavalry and infantry attempted to stop the advance of a much larger Confederate force. By the time three days had passed, the ferocious fighting had claimed 53,000 dead, wounded, and missing, and Gettysburg had become a vast charnel house.

There was a long silence, but I was patient. As I had discovered, many reenactors were initially reluctant to speak of their unearthly experiences, so it did no good to try to hurry a story. I lit my clay pipe and waited.

His eyes peering into the fire, the reenactor finally murmured, "I don't know where he came from. He was just there . . . a Union soldier. I'd guess he was about 25 years old, a skinny guy wearing a forage cap. He didn't have a rifle and he just stood there looking at me. He looked so damn real, I thought he was another reenactor, so I raised my hand to say hello. No sooner did I do that than he disappeared."

The bewhiskered reenactor fixed me with a defiant gaze as if to dare me to deny the reality of the episode. He spoke again: "He didn't run away or drop to the ground. He simply vanished. At first I was surprised, then I got scared because I wondered what else I might see out there. I ended up going back to the motel."

Is Gettysburg the most haunted place in America? The town and battlefield have a long history of ghost sightings and poltergeist phenomena. Indeed there are so many reports it is only natural to suspect rampant witness suggestibility and outright fraud. But it is possible there is another reason Gettysburg produces such a prodigious number of paranormal events.

Richard Senate and other noted ghost researchers theorize that the living can play a pivotal role in energizing a haunted site. Senate christened this process "restimulation" and suggested that when historical episodes are re-created on or near a spectral landmark, they sometimes provide a venue for paranormal activity. In particular, Senate believes that Civil War reenactors may prime the spectral pump of a battlefield.

Members of that martial hobby invest large amounts of time and money to re-create the lives of the soldiers from the 1860s. Reenactors wear woolen uniforms, carry authentic rifles, and live in crude canvas "dog-tents." They eat salt pork and hardtack, sing sentimental tunes from the era, and stage dramatic mock fights, sometimes involving thousands of combatants. A visit to a Civil War reenactment is like stepping backward in time. Therefore, if there is even a kernel of fact to Senate's intriguing hypothesis, it isn't surprising that reenactors so often encounter the restless phantoms of Gettysburg.

An excellent example of this theory is provided by the experiences of Stanley and Ruth Bukowski of northern Illinois. Although born in "Yankeedom," Stanley is a proud member of a local Confederate regiment, and Ruth portrays a civilian. In 1992, the couple and several thousand other reenactors assembled on the battlefield to appear in Ronald Maxwell's splendid film *Gettysburg*. During preparations for filming the climactic scene, Pickett's Charge, Stanley Bukowski and others had a mysterious auditory encounter with an invisible army.

Stanley recalled the episode: "It was about 8:30 in the morning and there were thousands of us in line, waiting to advance across the field. We were all pretty excited because we were standing on the precise spot where the Confederates advanced toward the Union lines. Then the assistant director asked us to give a rebel yell, which we did. But a few seconds later, I heard another collective rebel yell from the woods behind us. I turned around and saw that there was no one in the woods, but the sounds continued."

Perhaps there was a natural explanation, I suggested. Could the chorus of voices merely have been an echo?

"Not likely," countered Stan. "We were facing Cemetery Ridge when we shouted, and the cheer we later heard came from behind us. An echo doesn't behave that way. Besides, this was a huge open field with nothing for our voices to bounce off."

Is it possible that the gathering of several thousand reenactors on the battlefield activated a place memory of the famous Pickett's Charge? On July 3, 1863, 15,000 soldiers marched across that field and into history in a spectacular and unsuccessful attack on the Union lines. Or could it be that the spirits of those brave troops who died in the battle shouted to signify their approval of the efforts of the hobbyists?

Ruth Bukowski, too, had a ghostly encounter in Gettysburg. During the filming the reenactors lived in an authentic camp, in an area likely occupied by a Confederate field hospital during the battle. Sleeping in a tent isn't always the most comfortable of experiences, but Ruth is a seasoned campaigner and ordinarily slumbers peacefully. Yet one night, at about 2:00 A.M., she was inexplicably awakened.

"Something caused me to wake up," she said. "I sat up and saw the distinct shadows of soldiers by lantern light as they passed my tent. You could even see the silhouette of their hats and muskets on the tent canvas. But what was really strange was that they were marching with fixed bayonets!"

Could it have been reenactors performing nighttime picket duty, I asked?

"That's what I thought at first, but I later learned the reenactors weren't posting guards at night," she replied. "When I looked out the tent flap, they suddenly were gone and it was completely dark."

The following morning Ruth casually mentioned the episode to another woman who confirmed that she too had seen the spectral figures passing her tent. After two more nocturnal visits from the spectral squad, Ruth became convinced that the silhouettes were the spirits of Confederate soldiers watching over the women in the camp.

"Like true Southern gentlemen, they were protecting the ladies," said Ruth with a chuckle.

* * *

Ghosts abound at Gettysburg, but research seems to indicate one region in particular is infested with revenant spirits. This is in a southern part of the battlefield near Devil's Den, the Wheatfield, and Little Round Top. During the second day of fighting, this area became hell on Earth as the Yankees and Rebels fought each other with inhuman fury. Echoes of that fighting seem to persist to this day.

John Rushoe is a Union reenactor and resident of central Pennsylvania. Early one evening in October 1996, Rushoe and a party of family and friends visited Gettysburg and decided to go on a playful expedition in search of ghosts. They didn't expect to encounter any specters, but in this the amateur ghost hunters were mistaken.

The group's destination was the grotesque playground of boulders known as Devil's Den. While walking eastward near a stream called Plum Run, Rushoe and others in the party heard the distinctive sound of drums and fifes approaching through the dark woods. The tune was somewhat familiar and certainly from the Civil War era, but neither Rushoe nor his friends could remember its name. At first, Rushoe thought that someone was playing a practical joke or perhaps a reenactment musical group was practicing in the gloom. But this seemed improbable, for he had seen no one in his journey from the nearly empty parking lot.

"I tell you, a chill went down my spine as that music continued to move toward us," recalled Rushoe. "But there was nobody there. The music seemed to be coming right out of the air. Then, when the drums and fifes got to about Plum Run, the music stopped abruptly."

Rushoe later wondered if he and his friends hadn't experienced an auditory echo of the fighting. On the second day of battle, Confederate troops had swept eastward across the Emmitsburg Road and through the boulder-strewn Devil's Den. The fighting had been so savage and casualties so heavy that Plum Run turned red with human gore and became known among the combatants as Bloody Run.

Stunned by the spectral music, Rushoe and the group nonetheless decided to continue their expedition to the nearby hill called Little Round Top. However, as Rushoe walked along the pathway leading along the slope of the promontory, he was in for yet another shock. In the darkness, Rushoe saw a gray luminescent mist possessing a vaguely human form. The vaporous figure was gliding among the trees toward the hill's stony summit. Rushoe gasped and pointed to the apparition, but no one else in the party could see it.

"It wasn't ground fog, I can tell you that," Rushoe declared. "The shape was over five feet tall and about a foot wide and had sort of a human shape. I'd never seen a ghost before, but I knew I was looking at one now. I watched it for about a minute or so and then it vanished."

Rushoe believes the apparition might have been the revenant spirit of a Union soldier from the 20th Maine, a regiment that courageously defended the hill. But considering the phantom's movement toward the hill, the spirit was just as likely of Confederate origin, perhaps a former member of one of the regiments from Alabama that attacked Little Round Top. Regardless, John Rushoe is firmly convinced that specters abide on the Gettysburg battlefield.

If an individual reenactor could restimulate a haunted site, I wondered what effect 25,000 uniformed hobbyists would have on the ethereal environment. The answer wasn't long in coming. On the third day of the event, stories began to circulate that several reenactors had been awakened the night before by the marching tread of many troops. I spoke with one of the witnesses whom I shall refer to as Mike since he requested anonymity.

* * *

"I was asleep in my tent when I suddenly woke up to the sound of a lot of troops marching past. It's a real distinctive sound: footsteps and tin cups clanking," said Mike, who is a member of a Federal infantry company from the Midwest. "It was real late, about 2:00 A.M. I'd guess, and I wondered who would be stupid enough to march troops around in the dark. So I got up to take a look."

The puzzled hobbyist searched for the origin of the sound, but no troop formations were visible. Indeed, the camp was dark and all appeared normal. Yet Mike had no doubt that he had heard a spectral regiment pass in the darkness. Later, the reenactor learned that others, too, had heard the mysterious noise.

It is difficult to identify the specific source of the invisible marchers, but it is known that a portion of General James Longstreet's Confederate force was encamped near the modern reenactment site. Therefore, it is possible the hobbyists were fortunate enough to experience a 135-year-old auditory echo of troops marching to or from their camps.

Mike doesn't consider himself so fortunate. Said he: "It was spooky as hell hearing those guys march past and I'll be happy if it never happens again."

On the final day of the battle reenactment, the spectacular Pickett's Charge was staged. In excess of 12,000 rebel troops emerged from the woods in perfect parade order, their rifle barrels glittering in the sun. Into the maelstrom of cannon and rifle fire the formation marched, and before 15 minutes passed, their course was littered with countless mock corpses. The scene was surreal, and I struggled to appreciate how so many men could have died in such a brutally short time.

It was then that I realized the valiant spirits of the dead, both Union and Confederate, are far closer than we can ever imagine.

Some of the ghosts might be unaware of their violent passing, and a few may be trapped in their own private hells, but I'd like to believe the majority of specters remain as a phantasmagoric honor guard for this sacred place. Whatever the reason for their spectral occupation of Gettysburg, I can only salute the restless warriors and pray they finally rest in peace.

The Ghosts of Tunnel Hill

Connie Scott

S TRANGE SCREAMS COMING FROM THE WOODS LATE AT NIGHT, dark figures and headless phantoms lurking around an abandoned tunnel, mysterious ghost campfires, marching dead Confederate ghost soldiers, and smells of rotted human flesh—these are all things one might expect to read about in the pages of a Stephen King novel. According to some residents of Tunnel Hill, Georgia, the same images also apply to their little town. Especially when it comes to the long-deserted train tunnel and the fields where some of the bloodiest battles of American history were fought.

Ken Sumner of Woodstock, Georgia, claims to have experienced numerous encounters with ghosts in Tunnel Hill. Widely known in the area as a Civil War preservationist and reenactor, Sumner became interested in the Western Atlantic Tunnel, more commonly referred to as the Tunnel Hill Tunnel, seven years ago.

Desolate and bordering on decay, the tunnel was in danger of destruction when Sumner and others decided to save it. Rumors of a ghostly presence in the abandoned tunnel circulated for years. During preservation efforts, Sumner experienced a bizarre occurrence firsthand. While taking a group of people to see the tunnel, Sumner was surprised to see a shape take form out of the fog.

"As we drew closer," Sumner said, "it became obvious that the shape was a distinct outline of a human male standing just inside the tunnel mouth."

Intrigued, the group began walking toward it, only to see it dissolve.

Not far from the tunnel lies property owned by Kenneth Holcomb, on which reenactment of Civil War battles periodically takes place.

Civil War General Patrick Cleburne and his soldiers camped there from 1863 to 1864 during the coldest winter on record for the area. Conditions were harsh, and the soldiers suffered. There were very few blankets and not much to eat. Clad in ragged clothes, some of the soldiers didn't even have shoes left on their feet. In addition to the winter cold and the lack of adequate supplies, there was always the threat of Yankee invasion and possible death hanging over their heads. Five to seven battles took place there, with 277 Yankees killed in one battle alone.

"There continues to be no truth to the rumors that this field is haunted," Sumner, captain of the 35th Tennessee Infantry Regiment on the reenactment battlefield, used to tell newcomers to the site. He doesn't say that anymore.

"The joke was on me, because the field definitely is haunted," he now claims. "Peculiar experiences began happening to me in 1993 and have continued since that time with varying degrees of intensity."

Sumner and a group of reenactors set out to clear an area for the reenactment campsites. While walking through a heavily wooded area, Sumner was overwhelmed by a sickening odor.

"It's like a death stench, the smell of rotted human flesh. On the first occasion I was affronted with it, only I smelled it. None of the other men did, even though they were only a few feet away from me," Sumner relates. Since that time, many others have smelled it, sometimes as many as five or six at a time.

Strangely, each time the death smell presents itself, some people experience it while others do not.

In the heat of the battles fought in Tunnel Hill, countless soldiers were slaughtered. The smell that has come to be known as the death smell is a constant reminder of the tragedies that took place there.

Several reenactors have seen ghost campfires over the years. On one occasion, campfires appeared along the side of a hill. Sumner and another man went to check it out.

"When we got about 75 feet away, we saw legs in gray uniform pants behind the fire. A set of hands reached out to the warmth of the fire. Then we saw another set of legs. As we approached the fire, the legs disappeared without a trace. Then when we retreated to the top of the hill, the fire reappeared," Sumner said.

That night the fire lasted two and a half hours, but the soldiers materialized for only a few minutes.

"It was a cold December night. Most of the sightings I've experienced in Tunnel Hill happen in the coldest part of winter," Sumner relates.

On that same night, Sumner saw a Confederate soldier walk the length of the picket fence behind his tent.

"It was a particularly windy night. Every so often the wind would just stop without warning. It would get dead still. That's when I heard the footsteps. It got a little scary that night," he relates.

Sumner believes the ghost he heard and saw that night was that of a camp guard, because it was performing the duties of a guard.

"I've seen soldier ghosts walk around the perimeter of the camp in spring, around a big fog that rises up that time of the year on the battlefield. It's a circular type of fog that surrounds the camp. They just walk around the edge of the fog like camp guards securing their posts. I've also seen some of them trying to get in, and that gets scary, but they haven't ever really bothered us," Sumner says.

*   *   *

The ghosts have gotten so active in one particular area that some of the reenactors won't go back there. Some of the things the ghosts do to scare their human visitors include banging pans together, banging logs against trees, and generally just walking around. Once a group of people witnessed a ghost lantern floating across the field, and campers have reported hearing strange screams coming from the woods at night.

The ghosts are most commonly described as dark figures in human form. Their faces are hard to distinguish, according to Sumner.

The reenactors wear Confederate uniforms that look authentic. When they camp out, it sometimes feels as if they have been transformed back in time. It's not always easy to distinguish reality from supernatural.

For example, one night a Confederate soldier walked out of the fog beside a reenactor sitting on a gun position. The reenactor thought it was a buddy until the soldier disappeared before his eyes.

On another occasion, a group saw a Yankee soldier lying beside the road at the campsite. He had his head lying on the pack and had apparently fallen asleep. The group carefully passed him, in an effort not to wake him, only to look back and see no one.

"Last year at the seventh annual reenactment, a Whitfield County historian informed me that where I built the artillery fort is where the actual fort was located during the war," Sumner says.

Sumner named the fort after a captain he admired, a man by the name of Keys. It became Keys Battery Fort. Sumner could have been knocked over with a feather when he learned that the name of the fort had actually been Keys Battery Fort.

"This is something I just learned last year. Prior to that, I had no knowledge," Sumner insists. Strange parallels continue to amaze as area history is researched.

The artillery fort is where most of the hauntings occur.

"Out here your imagination can get away with you," Sumner says.

"But when groups of people see the same things, it's pretty clear something is going on.

"Ghosts have to remind everybody, 'Hey, we suffered here.' If you're sincere, they pretty much leave you alone. If not, they try to run you off. If you don't hold reverence, they aren't always pleasant. I've seen people run out of the woods screaming," Sumner says.

He believes the ghosts just want visitors to the fields to remember the suffering they endured. He believes they want the war participants to be remembered, whether Northern or Southern. But most of all, he believes they want us to learn from them and never repeat what happened to them long ago.

Sumner will continue to camp the battlefields of Tunnel Hill. He expects to see ghosts. Especially if it's cold and windy.

CIVIL WAR GHOST

Marion Bradner

AT TWILIGHT ON OCTOBER 6, 1962, I WAS DRIVING SLOWLY along a road strange to me, Route 5-20. About two miles west of Waterloo, New York, I suddenly spotted a man wearing what appeared to be a faded blue Civil War uniform walking directly ahead of me on the wrong side of the road. Tooting warningly, I braked to a stop. But when I glanced back nobody was in sight.

Nearby I noticed a lighted farmhouse. Deciding he must have fled in that direction I drove there, reasoning that he probably was costumed to participate in some local township's centennial celebration.

Having heard my car brakes squealing, the farmer, a man named Lohr, walked to the road's edge to meet me. When I inquired about the uniformed man he said, "You must've seen James Johnson's ghost. Folks here says he keeps trying to come home. His Scythe Tree down the road a piece draws him."

By daylight I journeyed back to examine the Scythe Tree. There I learned that on October 29, 1861, 26-year-old James Johnson, having joined Company G, 85th New York Volunteers, stuck his scythe into a then-young sapling in the family farmyard, requesting that his parents leave it there until he returned.

On May 22, 1864, at the Confederate Hospital at Raleigh, James died of a thigh wound he'd suffered on April 24, 1864, at Plymouth, near Albemarle Sound. He was buried in an unmarked grave. Until the day of her own death in 1883, his mother awaited his return, refusing to believe he'd been killed. Though the farmhouse passed to another family after Mrs. Johnson's death, folks still fly an American flag near the Scythe Tree, from sunrise to sunset each day, in James Johnson's memory.

THE MOST HAUNTED
BATTLEFIELD OF THE CIVIL WAR

Vincent H. Gaddis

ONE OF THE PLACES WHERE GHOSTLY BATTLE REENACTMENTS have occurred is the most haunted battlefield of the American Civil War. The Battle of Cedar Creek in Virginia was a bitter one, especially for the South.

On the morning of October 19, 1864, General Philip H. Sheridan's Army of the Shenandoah was camped on hills beside the creek. Sheridan himself was at Winchester on his way back from a conference in Washington. He had no idea that a Confederate force led by General Jubal Early had been marching day and night, existing on short rations, to deal the Union army a stunning blow.

Early's surprise attack came out of a chilly autumn fog. After one round of musketry, the camp was filled with shouting rebels. The Union soldiers not taken prisoner fled while their own artillery, now in Confederate hands, fired at them from behind. The starved Southerners, who had not eaten well for months, ignored their officers and fell upon the abundant food supplies in the storage tents.

But their victory was short-lived. Sheridan woke to the ominous rumble of cannons. He quickly dressed, leaped into the saddle, and raced toward the battle. Thirty minutes later he met his leaderless, disorganized troops moving north in defeat. He successfully rallied his men, turned them around, and straightened his lines. As the Union forces advanced, the charging cavalry and infantry broke through the prolonged Confederate line in a dozen places. The rebels were broken up, scattered, and flung back up the valley, and the Shenandoah campaign ended in a triumph won from the shadow of defeat.

Here, where the Union exulted in victory and the Confederacy suffered the anguish of disaster, men knew the agony of pain and the shock of sudden death. The effects of violence and strong emotions linger at this place. From time to time sensitive souls can hear the clash of conflict, the call of bugles, the shouts of men, the whine of shots, and the distant booming of spectral cannons. In a nearby church that was used as a hospital, one can occasionally hear the cries and moans of the wounded. Especially disturbing are the screams of patients whose limbs were amputated without anesthetics. Very few survived this crude surgery.

Sometimes after the sounds of suffering fade away, the music of a martial band plays. Perhaps it is a requiem for the shades of long-dead comrades.

A Mysterious Guide and Phantom Troops

Mary Crawford

I N 1989, STEVE CRAWFORD WAS STATIONED AT SEYMORE AIR BASE IN North Carolina. He was 21 years old and newly married. He found a small apartment in Goldsboro, and he and his wife Karen settled in. They enjoyed taking short sightseeing tours whenever Steve was not on duty.

During one of their excursions, they decided to visit the Bentonville Museum and Battlefield 10 miles away. It was springtime and the weather was fine. Upon arrival, they were disappointed to find posters stating the site was closed for the season. They browsed through the visitor center and small self-service museum, then decided to walk around back to get a closer view of the museum building. This building was a colonial-style two-story house—what one would expect of an old Southern mansion, complete with slave quarters and such. As they drew closer to the house, a woman came down the walk to meet them. The lady's dress and mannerism certainly looked authentic to the Civil War era. She introduced herself (later, Steve could not remember her name) and asked whether she could be of any assistance. They said they had hoped to have a tour of the museum, but had seen the signs indicating that it was closed for the season. It was officially closed, she said, but she had some spare time and would be happy to serve as their guide.

Steve and Karen agreed that this lady was the most knowledgeable guide they had ever encountered. As she directed them through the old mansion, she told stories about each room—important people who had been guests there in better times and so on. As they approached the landing of the second floor, she turned into a huge room with a fireplace. "This room served as a hospital ward during the war." She described the men brought with mangled limbs and bodies. Some had amputations under the crudest conditions, only to waste away and die in that very room.

The tour lasted approximately two hours. Steve and Karen thanked the woman and left with a promise to return when the museum officially opened. Something about this tour stayed fresh in their minds. They learned that a reenactment of the Bentonville battle was scheduled to take place in a couple of months. They were anxious to return for that event.

On the day of the reenactment, they arose early and left at 6:30 A.M. Neither wanted to miss any of the action. The drive seemed to take forever, but the weather was lovely and they enjoyed looking at the landscape. Suddenly, they were shocked to see a cotton field that still had scrap cotton clinging to half-rotten burrs and stalks. This was highly unusual for the time of year. Ideally a farmer would have had the land turned and replanted by this season. As they discussed this, they were in for another surprise. A whole regiment of troops was making its way across the cotton field. This would not have seemed strange, with the reenactment about to take place, had it not been for the sorry condition of this group. The men were a sad-looking bunch, weatherbeaten and clad in tatters and rags. The horses looked even worse. Steve remarked that such appearance would make the reenactment seem more real. But he wondered where they came up with such pitiful horses. He pulled to the roadside to get a closer view. The troops looked straight ahead, determined to keep pressing on. Two women walked along with the troops carrying something—neither Steve nor Karen were sure what.

After the scrappy regiment passed, Steve and Karen drove on for another five miles before arriving at the site of the museum and battlefield. To their surprise, the actors all wore new uniforms, and the horses all looked sleek and well fed! They enjoyed the reenactment, then moved on to the museum for another tour. When the guide arrived, it was a lady, but not the one who had given them their first tour. Steve and Karen agreed that this lady was not nearly as well informed as the first had been. As they walked through the house, they noted that all the doorways had red ropes and chains across their openings. When they asked about this, their guide explained that no one was allowed into any of the rooms. When they stated that an earlier guide had allowed them inside all the rooms, the guide said, "You must be mistaken. Since we opened this site, we have never allowed visitors into any room."

Intrigued by the unexplainable events that transpired at the Bentonville site, Steve visited the local library to do some research on the battle. He learned that the actual battle had not taken place at the site of the museum—it had been fought in a cotton field about five miles away. He also learned that the reenactment had been scheduled on the anniversary of the actual battle. Since he could not remember the name of his mystery guide, he was not able to determine where she fit into the scheme of things. Could she have been one of those ladies who accompanied the troops as they trudged into battle? Unfortunately, there is no way to know. But the memory of their visits to Bentonville is still vivid in the minds of Steve and Karen.

CUSTER'S LAST STAND?

Author Unknown

A T FORT RILEY, KANSAS, THE PHANTOM OF GENERAL GEORGE Armstrong Custer—who died with his men in the massacre at Little Big Horn—is reported to be haunting the house he occupied with his wife after the Civil War. On dark, moonless nights, when the wind blows south across the parade ground, it is said that the clank of a saber and loud footsteps are heard in the gallery and the high-ceilinged library.

This is confirmed by occupants of the house, Major and Mrs. William A. Gribbons. "My husband has seen Custer standing beside the fireplace in the living room with his arm resting on the mantel," Mrs. Gribbons told a reporter. Strangely enough, the paint is worn thin near the edge of the mantel where an elbow would rest. And below, on the tile hearth, is a chipped place which spurs might have made.

Major and Mrs. Gribbons have made friends with the ghost. The family that preceded them in the house asked to be moved because they "couldn't stand the noises at night, especially on the stairs."

Custer was a large man, six feet tall, and according to the couple the "ghost" does make a lot of noise on the stairs. Sometimes he is observed looking at a picture at the foot of the stairs hanging just inside the front door. It is the picture of "Custer's Last Stand."

Ghost of the
Cibecue Creek Massacre

Connie Cutac

I NOTICED A STRANGENESS ABOUT THE WINDSWEPT ARIZONA MESA the very first time I set foot on it in the summer of 1965. I had driven a short distance out of the Indian village of Cibecue because I wanted my dog Corky to have room to exercise without my having to worry that she would get hit by a car.

I parked my pickup off the road. Corky and I walked around the base of a small knoll. She quickly picked up a scent and raced off, disappearing among some juniper trees at the crest of the knoll.

Having nothing better to do, I took a leisurely stroll and picked up the flint that lay scattered along the hillside. When I reached the knoll's top, Corky was nowhere to be seen.

As I started to walk across the top of the knoll, I was overcome by a sense of foreboding, as if I were in sudden danger. For no reason at all I was scared silly.

I've roamed the desert for years and am used to its stillness and isolation. I often took solitary hikes, so being alone in a deserted area was nothing out of the ordinary for me.

But the feeling I had on that knoll was definitely out of the ordinary. I was absolutely terrified. Goose bumps rose on my arms and the hairs on the back of my head stood up.

My instincts were to run but I forced myself to walk slowly and calmly. When I whistled, Corky came racing back, wagging her stubby tail. Whatever had scared me hadn't bothered her at all. It was reassuring but puzzling.

With Corky scurrying ahead of me, we went into a tight clump of cedar. There I caught sight of a weathered wooden fence. It was so old that it had fallen down in places, the wood gray and splintered with age. As I walked closer, I found what I had been certain I would: an old grave, the inscription on the marker erased by the elements.

The panic I experienced on the knoll didn't leave me until I was in the pickup and driving down the road. After a mile or so I breathed a sigh and began to feel a little ashamed of myself. I had convinced myself that if there had been anything up there to be afraid of, Corky would have sensed it—be it animal or supernatural—hence I had been foolish to react as I did.

Still, the mystery of the knoll and my strange feelings nagged at the back of my mind. For several days I crossed the Cibecue Creek, drove on up the mountains and hunted fossils. It was a peaceful time but my mind still drifted back to that knoll.

I couldn't shun the knoll altogether because the main road between Cibecue and the nearest highway leads along the flat at the base of the knoll.

One night after dark I drove along the main road, near the wash at the base of the knoll. Suddenly Corky growled a warning and sat bolt upright on the seat beside me.

Her attention was fixed on the bottom of the wash and I glanced quickly in the same direction. Drifting along the bottom of the wash was a pillar of white mist. It was just that, a standing, elongated wisp of mist. It held its shape for a while and suddenly it disappeared. It didn't break up; it just vanished. It hadn't blown or drifted away. One second it was there, the next it wasn't.

I was terribly shaken but my curiosity was fully aroused. What was the secret of that knoll? Up to then I had been reluctant to tell anyone about the sudden fear I had experienced atop the hill because I knew full well I might be laughed at. But I didn't care anymore. I just had to find out if anyone else had seen anything unusual.

It didn't take me long to find out that I wasn't the only one who felt the place was haunted. Some people even made a point of avoiding the knoll and the surrounding area after twilight—because on many nights they claimed the ghost comes and dances on the edge of the hill.

My mother Elsie Lucas tells this story:

"My husband Wesley and I saw the ghost at Cibecue while he was supervising the building of a road there—for the Bureau of Indian Affairs—about 20 years ago. We lived at Cibecue on the Apache Indian reservation and had been to Show Low, Arizona, to get groceries.

"It was dark when we started for home. We were a few miles from Cibecue, driving slowly because it was a rough road. It was a clear, cloudless night. There was no fog or mist. Halfway down a hill we saw the ghost come up from a ravine to the left. This white, human-size thing floated across in front of our car and our headlights shone full on it. The lights did not shine through it as they would have if it were merely smoke or mist. Both my husband and I were aware that this was something strange, something supernatural.

"The ghost continued to float to the right, on up the hill. My husband said, 'Now I understand why the Indians refuse to work near here, after the sun sets. They want to get past this hill while it's still light out.' Later one of the Indians mentioned that it was common knowledge that a ghost can be seen, on or near that particular hill, after dark."

Later, as I was doing research for an article on the fossils in the Cibecue area, I learned of a battle between the U.S. Cavalry and the Indians. The newspapers of the period called it the Cibecue Creek Massacre.

On August 30, 1881, a detachment of 85 cavalrymen was sent from Fort Apache to arrest a medicine man named Nokay Delklinne. This Indian shaman had been holding a series of Ghost Dance rituals, prophesying he would raise some of the mighty dead Apache warriors and they would chase the whites off the Indian land.

Colonel Eugene Asa Carr, along with Captain Edmund G. Hentig and five other officers and 23 Indian scouts, followed the military trail that led west from Fort Apache to the old Indian village of Cibecue. When they reached the vicinity of Cibecue, they found more than 300 Indians nearly hysterical as they watched their holy man arrested.

While the soldiers were making camp, their own Indian scouts turned against them and fired on them. Captain Hentig was killed instantly and before the battle was over 10 soldiers were dead; about 20 Apaches were killed, including some of the scouts.

Although the medicine man had surrendered peacefully, he was shot down in cold blood by one of the troopers. Forty-seven Indians were taken prisoner. Three of the turncoat scouts were hanged and two others were sent to prison in Alcatraz. The massacre site was about two miles from the village of Cibecue, although there was a running battle as the troops retreated.

I still don't know whose restless ghost roams near Cibecue but I suspect it has to do with the slaughter that occurred there. It may have been a cavalry soldier, who died thousands of miles from his family and home, or an Apache who was killed in his own stomping grounds. All I can say for sure is that an apparition appears around the battle area. I've seen it.

SILENT SENTRY IN VIETNAM

James E. Gentry
as told to C. T. Bowden

I JOINED THE MARINES IN APRIL 1963 IN MY HOMETOWN OF DE-
troit, Michigan. In October 1965 I was sent to Vietnam and
served with the Second Battalion, Fifth Marines, First Marine
Division at Chu-Lai. In September and October 1966, just a few
weeks before I was due to return home, my outfit got hit hard in
"Operation Allegheny." After suffering heavy casualties we were billeted temporarily in an abandoned French fort deep in the jungle to
await new orders and, hopefully, replacements.

The old French fort was called just that on military maps. It was
built up against a bluff with the inner compound and front protected
by stone and mud-brick walls. Lacking aircraft the Viet Cong could
attack the fort only by a frontal assault and naturally we felt more
secure there than in the more usual chopped-out jungle clearing.
Night sentries were stationed at the gate and along both the inner
compound and outer walls.

Our first night at the fort one of the sentries was killed by a stab
wound at the base of his throat. Apparently he was attacked from
behind. This threw us all into dismay. It seemed impossible for an
enemy soldier to be within the boundaries of a sentry post and not be

seen. To sneak up and kill a sentry from behind within a walled enclosure seemed incredible. Naturally the mysterious death of the sentry was foremost in my mind when I was placed on guard duty the following night.

My post was to patrol both walls and the corner of the inner compound where they met. Through an overcast sky the moon shed enough light so I could see the limits of my post clearly. The warm night was so quiet that at times I could hear the night cries from the jungle beyond the outer walls. My first three hours of duty and the routine visit from the sergeant of the guard passed uneventfully.

As the final hour moved more slowly I began to feel uneasy. I could see nothing unusual but had the feeling I was being watched. Several times I slung my rifle to wipe perspiration from my hands, yet my body was cool as if I had a chill. I reasoned I might have a touch of malaria, the common affliction of American troops in Vietnam. I stopped walking and backed into the corner of the walls to get control of myself.

Then I spotted the figure of a man up against the wall where I was certain nothing existed a moment before. The stranger was not wearing Viet Cong attire but did have on boots and a bush hat. He seemed to be looking down, with his chin on his chest, but at the same time I could see his face, white in the moonlight. As he pointed, arm outstretched, to the wall behind me I noted a diamond insignia on his shirtsleeve. I raised my rifle to challenge the unknown visitor, at the same time trying to watch the wall toward which his hand pointed. At the base of the wall a stone was slowly sliding forward. As the stone was pushed beyond the wall the figure with the bush hat vanished. And through the opening in the wall crawled a Viet Cong, knife in hand. I shot him, then knelt and fired the remainder of my ammunition into the tunnel.

The unknown man who had warned me never was seen again.

Our men were not required to wear their steel helmets inside the fort and no one in the company owned a bush hat. At the time I attributed the apparent hallucination to a touch of malaria or combat fatigue. I hesitated to mention the strange visitor in my report for fear of being sent to the hospital for observation just when I was due to return to the States.

When we explored it the next day the tunnel turned out to be a very old one extending several hundred yards to an entrance in the jungle beyond sight from the fort. When I told my story to the officer of the day, Lieutenant Phinney, and later to the commanding officer, Major J. Kiley, I felt a twinge of guilt at being given credit for discovering the tunnel. If the unidentified figure in the bush hat had not pointed to the wall there is no doubt I would have wound up with my throat cut like the sentry on the previous night.

By early November 1966 I was on my way home. A commercial airliner flew a planeload of us veterans to Okinawa and then nonstop to California. During the 15-hour flight I sat next to Staff Sergeant C. T. Bowden, who had served as a helicopter pilot in many of the same battles where I had fought on the ground. We swapped tales of our experiences and soon were conversing like old friends. Bowden had flown several times over the old French fort and I told him about being stationed there. Eventually I found myself explaining about the tunnel used by the Viet Cong assassins and mentioned the strange figure in the bush hat, although I still thought the hallucination was due to malaria.

After our in-flight dinner Sergeant Bowden directed the discussion to famous military units, uniforms and battles and in particular the French Foreign Legion. I confessed that my only knowledge of the Foreign Legion was from the film version of *Beau Geste*. Nor did Dienbienphu mean much to me other than that it was the site of a famous battle in Indochina before the United States was involved.

A number of years later I heard again from Bowden, who was

doing research for a book on Vietnam. He explained that the French Foreign Legion had served many years in Indochina. The first attachment arrived in Tonkin in 1885 and legionnaires served there continuously until the last group were flown in as reinforcements during the siege of Dienbienphu in 1954. Over the years there had been considerable change in their uniform, he said. The sparkling white I recalled from *Beau Geste* had been replaced by modern khaki and for jungle duty in Vietnam the military cap was replaced by a bush hat. Most significant of Bowden's discoveries was that the insignia of the legionnaires sent to Dienbienphu was a white diamond shoulder patch.

Was the figure I had seen that night at the old French fort a deceased legionnaire? Was he perhaps one who had himself been assassinated by a Vietnamese who sneaked into the fort by that hidden tunnel?

I still am inclined to attribute the apparition to malaria or combat fatigue but there is no question that the strange figure in the bush hat, wearing the legionnaire's insignia on his pointing arm, saved my life that night in October 1966.

•

I Wrestled a Ghost

Charles H. Clark, D.D., Ph.D.

DURING THE WAR WITH SPAIN I RETURNED ON A CONVALESCENT furlough and was sent to Washington Barracks for treatment of a disease of the left leg resulting from typhoid fever. In the ward where I was being treated were two men who play a part in this story. One was Kengla, convalescent from yellow fever; the other was Smith, an undesirable character who was rather unfriendly toward me.

I got up and got some water for Kengla at his request. He drank about half of the contents of the glass and I placed the rest at the head of Smith's bed and went back to my own. At about 4:00 A.M. on the morning of December 31, Kengla woke me and asked if Smith was dead. I looked, and it seemed to me that he had died in an effort to get the water that had been left in the glass. He had to be buried early the next day for the stench that was coming from his body was unbearable.

I was returned to duty the following day—New Year's—and was assigned to a tent outside the barracks. It was cold and I was assigned to be tent-watch and delegated to go to the barracks cellar for coal—a distance of about 200 feet.

I had never been a religious man but as I was about halfway from the tent to the cellar entrance I was stricken with livid terror. The thought was so real that I cried out, "My God, I'll be in Hell before morning."

Shaken as I was I filled the bucket with coal, returned to the tent and put the coal on the fire. Then I sat down to read. As I settled myself, the tent flap opened and the materialized spirit of Smith entered. He moved toward me saying, "I've come after you."

I replied, "You'll have a hell of a time getting me." I made a rush at him, but though I am a strong man physically he threw me to the floor.

The other occupants of the tent came in shortly and saw me struggling on the floor. They could see nothing of "Smith" and picked me up and put me on the bunk. I swear to this day that I was not delirious and was not under the influence of drink.

THE UNKNOWN SOLDIER

A. B. C. Dario

WE LIVED ABOUT THREE MILES FROM YAUCO, ON THE WAY TO Guanica, Puerto Rico. Guanica is the place where the American troops landed on July 25, 1898, to take possession of the island from the Spanish at the end of the Spanish-American War.

About two miles from Yauco there is a hill where the Spanish soldiers waited for the signal to attack. However, at the moment the Spanish lookout tried to sound his bugle a bullet went right through it, killing him instantly. Because of this the American troops took over without further bloodshed. But in the confusion following the surrender, for two days the body of the dead Spanish lookout remained on the spot where he had fallen. Then charitable people from the vicinity buried him right there, piling stones on his grave and marking it with a wooden cross bearing the inscription "The Unknown Soldier." About 15 or 20 years later a monument was raised on the site, and tourists now stop there to take pictures.

At a time when I was already out of school and working as a store clerk in Yauco I traveled by bike every day to and from my job. Many times I passed by the monument late at night and never saw or heard anything until one Sunday night when I was returning from the movies.

That night, as I came uphill toward the monument and when I was about 300 yards away, something very heavy jumped on the back of my bike. I tried to stop, but the brakes would not work. The lights went out and would not go back on. And, although I was going uphill, my speed seemed to increase. Exactly when I was in front of the tomb and ready to start downhill something like a heavy bundle fell off the back of my bicycle. Immediately the lights came back on again, by themselves.

I got home safely but very shaken. The next day I could not go to work; I was running a high fever. But everybody laughed at me when I told of the incident.

THE EARTHBOUND SOLDIER

Bill Wharton

HERMANUS VAN RENSBURG WAS LATE FOR WORK ON THE WARM evening of December 21, 1947, as he hurried across the desolate sun-parched veldt from his railroad cottage to the small whistle-stop, Dalmanutha, in the Eastern Transvaal, on the track between the towns of Belfast and Machadodorp.

The tall, blond-haired station employee skirted the 47-year-old war cemetery on its little rocky hill overlooking the long sloping valley, and cut across from the rough-hewn track to the railroad through dried-up mimosa trees to save time.

The stolid Afrikaner was about halfway through a little hollow below the cemetery and passing the ruins of an old farmhouse when he saw, quite clearly on the side of the hill, a man walking towards him. The railroad employee hurried on. A train was due to pass through the whistle-stop in about 15 minutes and he had to be there to pick up any mail and parcels for the local people.

He was about 100 yards farther on and less than a quarter of a mile from the railroad track when it occurred to him that the stranger he had seen was not a local man. He was tall, over six feet, and there was no one in the district taller than Van Rensburg, who stood only five feet 11 inches in his bare feet.

He stopped and looked back. The man was standing looking down at the ruins. In the late sun's glow there was no mistaking the figure. The man seemed to be dressed in some kind of uniform. Van Rensburg glanced at his watch and decided he still had a few minutes to spare; maybe the man was looking for someone.

He turned and walked rapidly over the veldt towards the man and as he came nearer he saw that it was a soldier, an officer, but the uniform he wore was not a modern one. It was scarlet and khaki—the kind of uniform British soldiers wore during the Anglo-Boer War of 1899–1902.

Van Rensburg, a man nearly 40 years old, with over 20 years' railroad service, and a trusted employee of the South African Railways, was within hailing distance of the stranger when he stopped, puzzled. There was something eerie about the man, something Van Rensburg could not fathom.

"Hey!" he called out. "Hey, there! You looking for someone?"

Van Rensburg, whose home language is Afrikaans, knew that his English was poor but even so the man should have understood. He approached within a dozen feet of the man before saying in a normal voice, "Hullo there, can I help you? You are a *vreemdeling*—stranger, aren't you?"

Then the officer turned and looked at Van Rensburg. The officer, who wore the uniform of the Eighth Hussars, had a sad expression on his face and looked pale in the fading light of the day. He looked steadily at Van Rensburg for a minute or more and then began walking up the low hill towards the mimosa trees encircling the cemetery.

Van Rensburg remained standing there another few minutes, then, hearing the distant whistle of the approaching train, ran to the station.

As soon as the train had gone, Van Rensburg picked up the mailbag and three packages and walked down to the small village where he delivered the bag to the postmaster.

"Who is the stranger in the old uniform?" he asked. "I was on the way to the station when I saw this man come over the hill—"

Meneer Pieter Calitz dropped the bag and said, "Was the stranger wearing a scarlet tunic and khaki trousers?"

Van Rensburg nodded. "Ja, he was. He looked like the *Rooibaadjies* who fought against us Afrikaners in the Boer War."

"The man you saw was the Sad Soldier," Calitz said. "He comes in October and sometimes in December. You have only been here six weeks; you will find out all about him. Go and ask old Meneer Schoemann, he knows the whole story."

"Are you telling me I have seen a spirit, a ghost?" Van Rensburg asked. "I don't believe in those things. I have walked through cemeteries at night; I don't believe in rubbish."

Calitz said soberly, "There are 200 people living in this area. Nearly all of them have seen the Sad Soldier. The spiritualists have come down from Johannesburg to speak to the Sad Soldier and a man came up from Durban, a psychic man. The Sad Soldier spoke to no one."

In that year of 1947 when Van Rensburg saw the Sad Soldier, only one man still lived who knew what was believed to be the true story of this officer of the British Eighth Hussars, an old farmer named Cornelius Schoemann who fought against the British in the Anglo-Boer War and who was actually engaged in the Battle of Geluk close to the Dalmanutha railroad stop.

Although Mr. Schoemann, now over 80, does not claim that the Sad Soldier is the man involved in one of the most poignant stories to emerge from that bloody guerilla war between Boer and Britisher, all the facts fit into place like the parts of a jigsaw puzzle and leave one with the conclusion that the Sad Soldier was Major Vernon, the man who fell in love with an enemy girl.

"Caroline Potgieter," Mr. Schoemann related, "was about 20 years old in 1900 when the Boers were driven back by the British towards the Portuguese East Africa border. The Boers dug themselves in about 12 miles from here and the British occupied the Geluk-

Dalmanutha area. In the Potgieter family was only Mrs. Potgieter, a woman of 40 or so, and her daughter, Caroline. They lived on a small farm about a quarter of a mile from Dalmanutha station."

The British forces commandeered whatever accommodation was available and Major Vernon and three other officers were quartered with the Potgieter family.

"I remember Caroline Potgieter quite well. She was a tall, beautiful girl with startling dark, almost black, eyes and dark chestnut brown hair. It could have come as a surprise to no one that Major Vernon fell in love with her. Her father was with the Boer forces and her mother was totally opposed to the British," Schoemann related.

After three weeks, during which the British forces built up reserves and rested, fighting only spasmodically with the entrenched Boers, the order came for the Britishers to attack, and on the night when they were due to leave Vernon asked Caroline to marry him when the war was over.

No one knows what took place between the Boer girl and British officer but the story has it she told Vernon she would marry him if he laid down his arms and no longer fought against her people.

Vernon, Mr. Schoemann related, was unable to do this, of course, as it would have meant a field court-martial and a probable death sentence for desertion in the front line. But his love for the Boer girl was stronger than the call of duty and when the British forces moved on Vernon was missing.

He was reported as a deserter but during the bitter engagement fought about 30 miles from the farm, where he was hidden in an attic by the girl, no effort was made to find him simply because no soldiers could be spared to hunt for him.

"Caroline's mother bitterly opposed her daughter's love for the Red Coat, as the Boers called the Britishers, but Caroline was determined to marry Vernon and the two planned to leave for the Portuguese border, only about 50 miles away, and to live there where British law could not touch Vernon," Schoemann said.

On the night before they planned to go, at a time when the girl had gotten six fresh horses and a buggy for the journey, the British returned. The Boers were gaining the upper hand and the Red Coats were falling back to await reinforcements. An old native servant of the Potgieters came running to warn Caroline and Vernon that the soldiers were coming, and Vernon fled up the hill to hide among the rocks while Caroline got the buggy and horses harnessed.

"The girl was on the point of leaving when the first of the officers arrived," Mr. Schoemann related, "and as Caroline boarded the buggy she saw her mother speaking to one of the officers."

Fearful that her mother might be betraying Vernon, the girl whipped up the horses just as an officer screamed at her to stop: She whipped the horses around the hill and shouted to Vernon to come. He ran down the hill and leaped aboard the buggy, but the soldiers and officers were already in pursuit on their own mounts, and after several shots had been fired at the fleeing couple, with bullets striking the buckboard, Vernon pulled the reins and stopped, fearful that Caroline would be hit.

A field court-martial was held outside the Potgieter's home on the *werf* the next day and Vernon was found guilty of desertion in the face of the enemy and sentenced to death. The papers were sent immediately by dispatch rider to army headquarters 15 miles away and before the day was out the confirmation of the court's finding and sentence were back.

Caroline hurried to army headquarters-in-the-field to plead for Vernon's life, but British army law is inflexible, and the next morning Vernon's arms were bound behind his back, he was stripped of the insignia of his rank, led up the hill, placed against a mimosa tree and shot. Caroline watched the execution from a distance and after the British soldiers had buried Vernon she placed a wreath on the grave.

That same night a mysterious fire razed the Potgieter home and when the flames died down the charred remains of a woman were found. Caroline had been about five feet seven. inches, but her mother was a short woman of about five feet four inches, and, according to a medical doctor, the remains were those of a shortish woman.

Of Caroline there was no trace.

"She simply vanished," Mr. Schoemann related, "and she has never, to my knowledge, been seen again. Some say that she walked alone into the mountains, died there, and still lies somewhere there under the bushes; others said she went to Cape Town to forget her dead lover. The truth of what happened to her no one knows."

The ruined farmhouse was never rebuilt. Through the years the ruins became mossy and overgrown with weeds and the story of the soldier who died for the love of an enemy girl became one of the Eastern Transvaal's legends—until about 10 years after the end of the war.

Some frightened Africans reported to the local magistrate that they had seen a British soldier walk down from the hill and stand looking at the ruins. There were no British soldiers in the area and the magistrate discredited the story at once.

The following year, on the night of October 13, several men reported to the magistrate that they had seen the mysterious red-coated soldier and a watch was kept, but in vain. It required two dauntless Afrikaners named Van Blerk and Coetzee to keep watch the following October 13. Soon after sunset when it was still quite light the two men, keeping watch from a distance of about 50 yards from the ruins of the old Potgieter farmhouse, saw the soldier coming down the hill.

They told the magistrate later that they were close enough to see a black bullet hole in his uniform over his heart and stains around the bullet hole.

Natives in the area now live in superstitious fear of the wandering soldier and each year in October and just before Christmas they lock their homes up more securely than usual. They believe that anyone who sees the Sad Soldier will come to harm.

No spiritualists took an interest in the matter until after World War II when two men and a woman traveled down from Johannesburg, spent an evening near the ruins and then reported that they saw nothing. But the night they spent there was October 22. The following night only one of the men went there. He saw the Sad Soldier and, according to his statement, endeavored unsuccessfully to speak to him.

"This apparition appears usually every year on the evening of October 13, but it has been known to vary its appearance from October 13 to October 24 and also to appear around December 20 to December 22," Mr. Schoemann related. "I have tried to trace back a possible reason for its appearance in October and December but I haven't succeeded.

"There is no proof whatever that the apparition is Vernon who was shot for desertion," the Boer War veteran said, "but from the known and proven facts one must come to the conclusion that it is he. He was the only British officer shot in this area for desertion, although others were killed in action. I have lived in these parts all my life and know of no other case comparable to that of Caroline Potgieter and this man Vernon. If it is not Vernon, why does the apparition come straight down to the old farmhouse? I don't believe in ghosts myself but I have seen, not once but many times, this man from another world come from the mimosa and old cypress trees, walk down to the ruins of the farmhouse, stand there for a time and walk back up the hill to the small cemetery."

Last year another Johannesburg spiritualist questioned the apparition but received no reply. In answer to her, "Who are you? Who do you seek?" the soldier from another world merely looked at the ruins, then turned away sadly and walked back up the hill.

CAPTAIN CROCKETT'S MESSAGE

Belle C. Ewing

C APTAIN CAREY I. CROCKETT OF THE PHILIPPINE CONSTABULARY was a professional soldier and had taken part in many battles. His body was covered with knife and bullet scars. He was tough, matter-of-fact. There was nothing visionary about Carey Crockett.

The United States had been having trouble with the Visayans, one of the unruly tribes in the Philippines in the early days of the century. Captain Crockett garrisoned the town of San Ramon, on the east coast of the island of Samar, while Lieutenant Stanley Hayt, of the Philippine Scouts, garrisoned the town of Dolores in the interior of the island.

In December 1904, Lieutenant Hayt was attacked by a large force of Visayans and his entire force, with the exception of a sergeant, was massacred. Lieutenant Hayt had a small fox terrier that was his constant companion. The little dog was by his master's side during the fight but disappeared after the lieutenant's death.

Three months later, in February 1905, Captain Crockett was returning to the stockade at San Ramon after a scouting trip in the interior of the island.

The captain and his company of 60 men were camped for the night. The exhausted officer was asleep, when he was awakened by his sergeant who reported that something white had been running back and forth before the sentries for the past half hour.

Captain Crockett arose, strapped on his revolver, and stepped out into the black night. As the captain approached the White Something, incredulity swept over him. It was Lieutenant Hayt's fox terrior! That a dog used to the protection of civilization could have survived in the wild jungle for three months was amazing.

Commiseration for the little animal filled the captain's heart. He stopped to pet it. As his hand touched the terrier's head, from some-place, somewhere—he was never able to explain it, even to himself—this message was flashed to him:

"Go back to the stockade . . . It is going to be attacked . . . *Go back to the stockade!*"

The stockade at San Ramon was a day's march away, down a twisting mountain trail. It was 9:00 P.M., and a heavy tropical rain was falling. The company had been marching all day and the men were exhausted. Yet Captain Crockett was so deeply impressed with the message that he broke camp immediately. He and his men faced a night of wind and rain. Black clouds overhung the jungle and the crashes of thunder rolled over the tops of the trees.

The weary soldiers stumbled on through the night, reaching San Ramon at five o'clock in the morning. At 5:15 the stockade was attacked. Sixty-five Visayans were shot off the top of the 14-foot wall; 100 were killed altogether. Had not Captain Crockett returned when he did with his 60 men to assist the 65 he had left at the stockade, the garrison at San Ramon would have been wiped out.

Captain Crockett cared for the little fox terrior as long as he lived. But he never again gave any supernatural messages. Was Lieutenant Hayt able to part the Veil and send his little dog to warn his friend of impending disaster? Captain Crockett thought so.

PHANTOM FLIERS

Dwight Whalen

O N SEPTEMBER 1, 1914, ONLY DAYS AFTER CANADA DECLARED war on Germany, residents of Niagara Falls, Ontario, heard alarming news. A militiaman guarding the Park Street military prison reported hearing an airplane flying over the city before dawn. Word spread quickly. People feared the plane carried a bomb.

"The fact that none saw the supposed aeroplane and that the whirr of its motor only was reported leads to the belief that it is but a case of nerves," said the *St. Catherines Standard*. "However, the militiamen have orders to fire at sight of an airship of any description. The Canadian government has sent a request to Washington to forbid the flying of Americans over the dominion during the war. . . .

"This may have been the same airship which a local merchant dreamed he saw going over St. Catherines that same night. He says he saw it go over the east end of the city and drop out of sight towards Merritton."

If fears of aerial German emissaries bombing Niagara were mere dreams and war nerves, what explains the following?

"Captain Scobell, adjutant, 19th Regiment, on guard at the Welland canal, reported to the *Standard* this morning that during the past four nights the soldiers on the canal have seen airships flying over the city," the *Standard* reported on September 12. (The word "airship" is evidently used to mean airplane, not dirigible.) "They carried red lights. One of them dropped a rocket large enough to wreck a house had it hit it. The soldiers found the rocket in the morning.

"Friday night an airship flew so low over the city that the soldiers at Lock seven could plainly discern the framework. . . .

"A well-known citizen told the *Standard* this morning that while motoring home from Hamilton the other night, he saw two clouds in the sky, which looked for all the world like biplanes. Others with him noticed the same thing and remarked on it."

The *Standard* never mentioned the rocket-bombing incident again. Perhaps the report proved unfounded or perhaps further news of it was censored. Whatever the case, the *Standard* (along with other area newspapers) continued to report mysterious sightings of unidentified aircraft over the Niagara district until early 1916.

The primitive state of aviation technology in this region prior to that time makes these reports of advanced aircraft extremely difficult to explain. Their nature, purpose, point of origin, and destination are as unfathomable today as they were when their startling appearance sent chills through soldiers and citizens of wartime Niagara.

The next sightings of a "phantom flyer" occurred over Niagara Falls, Ontario, according to the *Niagara Falls* [N.Y.] *Gazette* of October 13, 1914:

"Reports have been circulated that an airship has been seen flying over the city during the last few nights, which has caused anxiety in some circles. The military guard are keeping a sharp lookout at night.

"The [Canadian] government has issued a proclamation prohibiting any aeroplanes of a private or public nature being used in Canada during the war crisis. Many residents have been attracted by the noise of the machine at night and have seen a light traveling across the skies which they believe is carried by a flying machine."

Under the headline "Saw an Aeroplane!" the *Gazette* reported another Niagara Falls, Ontario, sighting December 12:

"Mr. James Healey, the well-known automobile liveryman, on Bridge Street, reports that he saw an airship on Thursday night passing over this locality about 8:00 P.M. It could be plainly seen in the heavens, he stated."

The winter of 1915 saw a flurry of unidentified aircraft sightings over Niagara. On January 30 the *Niagara Falls* [Ontario] *Evening Review* noted:

"We are told by a trustworthy informant that three nights in succession—Wednesday, Thursday and Friday—between 12:00 midnight and 1:00 A.M., an aeroplane, carrying a green and red light, and flying low, has hovered over this district and along the river coastline."

On the night of February 3, according to the *Review,* a sentry at the local armories "heard what sounded like the hum of a motor and on looking up perceived a gray shadow creeping across the sky."

The *Standard* described another sighting, probably of the same mysterious plane:

"Niagara Falls, Ontario, February 4—Superintendent Alex Collins of the city waterworks department reported this morning that he saw an aeroplane pass over the city about 10:30 P.M. The aircraft was a considerable distance away, but Collins claims the outline of it against the sky could be seen distinctly. The aeroplane carried no lights. It seemed to be passing over Victoria Park when Collins saw it."

A few nights earlier guards at the Toronto Power Plant on the Niagara River saw an airplane. "It carried a red and green light," according to the *Standard,* "and the men said they could hear the noise caused by the exhaust of the engine. While the military authorities were at first inclined to take the aeroplane stories as a joke, they are now making a secret investigation to find the owner of the aeroplane. It is understood they have enlisted the aid of the police of the surrounding places on both sides of the river to help find the mysterious airman."

They had no luck. Niagara's nocturnal "Flying Dutchman" was back on February 19—this time for a daylight flight over Buffalo. According to the *Review,* thousands clearly saw a plane flying at an altitude of 2,500 to 3,000 feet shortly before 8:00 A.M. "The outline of the aircraft could be plainly discerned, and at times the machine seemed to head directly for the Canadian shore and then quickly swerve back again. . . . It was going at a terrific pace and caused considerable excitement."

The skeptical reception these reports received in many quarters is understandable. Historical records show that except for a few rickety seaplanes no airplanes were operating in the Niagara vicinity before May 1915, when American aviation pioneer Glenn Curtiss established an airplane factory and flight school at Buffalo to meet a huge British wartime order for "Jennies," the Curtiss JN-3 aircraft. At the same time Curtiss set up an aircraft-manufacturing plant at Toronto and a nearby pilot-training school at Long Branch. But for almost a year afterwards unknown craft continued to buzz Niagara Falls and St. Catherines. Might some of these have come from Buffalo or Toronto?

Wilfred Stead of Niagara Falls, Ontario, was a Canadian member of the Royal Flying Corps. When I interviewed the 90-year-old man shortly before his death in January 1983, he told me that when he took his flight training in Toronto in 1917, flights to the Niagara area were not part of the school's instruction program.

Furthermore, R. E. Norman of Islington, Ontario, secretary of a veterans' group called World War I Flyers, says, "I asked one of our members who trained [at Toronto] if they did any night flying or were likely to fly as far as Niagara. His answer was no. They were very short of machines. On the day that he went solo, there was only one machine serviceable."

A. J. Shortt, assistant director of the National Aeronautical Collection at Rockcliffe Airport, Ottawa, remarks, "I very much doubt that any of the [Toronto] school aircraft would have flown as far as St. Catherines as the students' skills even on graduation were rather basic and the performance of the Curtiss F boats and Curtiss JN-3 aircraft they flew was marginal."

What about Buffalo? The British-ordered Curtiss aircraft built there were shipped disassembled to Canadian destinations by rail, not delivered "on the fly." Yet, although Canadian war regulations declared that American aviators could not fly into Canada without official clearance, pilots from the Curtiss flight school at Buffalo are known to have flown over the American and Horseshoe Falls and into Canadian airspace as early as August 1916.

Months earlier, however, in October and December 1915 and in January and February 1916, the Niagara region was visited again by more untraceable aircraft: "Their lights were seen and the whirr of their motors distinctly heard. . . . An aeroplane passing over the peninsula was distinctly seen last night. . . . The craft was high up and carried lights. . . . A number of residents of Grantham Township claim they saw two aeroplanes fly over last night about 8:00 P.M. headed south and coming from the direction of the lake."

All but one of these unexplained sightings from September 1914 to February 1916 occurred at night. This is an amazing statistic, since in those days it was hazardous to land a plane at night. A. J. Shortt doubts that "any night flying was done in the [Niagara] area during 1915–16." And Wilfred Stead says night flying was not part of his training at Toronto.

Just as strange is the curious fact that more than half of Niagara's phantom flyers appeared in winter months. "There was little or no winter flying done at this time as skis had not been developed," says Shortt. "RFC Canada operations at Beamsville did not begin until April 1917, although Camp Borden, Leaside and other stations began in February 1917. The first winter operation was during the winter of 1917–18," when student pilots were sent to Texas for flight training. (In France, however, flying continued in winter.)

And what explains the mention of lights on so many of these aircraft? The Jennies and other conventional planes of this period were not equipped with night lights of any kind. "We did not have wingtip lights in France at the time of the Armistice," says R. E. Norman. Certainly no known aircraft, Canadian or American, flying at Niagara in the winter of 1916 matches the description of this strange illuminated vehicle:

"A large monoplane was seen over Stamford on Thursday evening with many lights on. It was seen by a number of residents on Portage road and through glasses appeared to be of a great size. Mr. A. T. Smith, Wilbur and Mrs. Fitch, and R. F. Jolley, wife and daughter, all saw the aeroplane through glasses. They could distinctly see red and white lights at each side, and counted in all 27 lights. There was a headlight of great power. It travelled in the direction of the Welland canal, then circled and took a westerly course." (*Evening Review,* January 15.)

Could some of these reports have resulted from misidentifications of fire balloons or illuminated kites? Perhaps—but this explanation does not account for those reports in which witnesses not only saw a clearly defined aircraft but heard its motor as well.

War hysteria? F. Robert van der Linden, an aeronautics research assistant at the National Air and Space Museum of the Smithsonian Institution, Washington, D.C., says, "The sightings were either a general 'war hysteria' or perhaps atmospheric phenomena [*sic*]."

It is difficult to imagine what "atmospheric phenomena" would convince people they had clearly seen and heard airplanes. Hysteria is another matter. The *Niagara Falls Gazette* never reported any "phantom flyers" on the American side of the Niagara River during this period. The United States was not yet in the war. Its citizens did not share the Canadians' fear of enemy aircraft; America was officially a neutral country then.

War hysteria is not an unreasonable explanation but it does have some drawbacks. The phantom flyers were almost always seen at night and usually during winter nights—a time when most people, including hysterics, are indoors. No sightings at all were reported in spring months and almost none in summer. Are people so much more susceptible to hysteria in cold weather?

On the other hand, to believe that somebody was flying around Niagara before March 1916 is to credit an unknown flyer or flyers with the night vision of a cat, the hardiness of a polar bear, uncanny lighting inventiveness and a vanishing act to beat Houdini.

Perhaps one day some long-lost documentation will surface to clear up this mystery. For now the sky keeps her secrets.

THE FLYING COFFIN

Harold Helfer

ONE OF THE GHOSTLIEST OF ALL AIRPLANE STORIES CENTERS around a real-life incident of World War I.

On April 28, 1916, officers and mechanics at a small airdrome in France, behind the front lines, were engaged in their daily routines when suddenly one of them uttered an exclamation and pointed into the sky. A single-seat Neuport fighter had come out of the clouds and was circling about crazily.

Every man on the field stared in grim fascination as the plane came nearer. It was identified as the plane of Lieutenant Peretti of the *Cignone* (Stork) *Escadrille*. The craft had been riddled by enemy bullets.

As it descended toward the field, the pilot did not cut the throttle. The plane droned along at the same steady speed. Everyone held their breath, expecting disaster. Then smiles broke out as the plane managed to make a perfect three-point landing.

But the sighs of relief were short-lived for the plane did not stop. It went into a ground loop and crashed.

Field attachés rushed to the plane and pulled Lieutenant Peretti out—but he was dead. The strange part of it was that he had not been killed in the crash. It was discovered that he had been shot cleanly through the head.

Death, almost certainly, would have been instantaneous.

How, then, with a dead man at the controls, had the plane managed to get back so unerringly from the front to its home base? It remains one of aviation's strangest mysteries.

THE HAUNTED SUBMARINE

Peter King

AMONG THE MANY MYSTERIES OF THE SEA, NONE IS STRANGER than the story of the German U-boat UB-65. That submarine was more than jinxed; it was haunted.

At the height of World War I great armies were locked in combat in France and Belgium. A new weapon, the British aeroplane, was in the skies—but the Allied Forces faced a worse threat. Beneath the oceans the deadly U-boats were sinking millions of tons of shipping. If their successes continued France and England would be effectively blockaded, literally starved for food and war materiel.

In July 1916 Germany began construction of 24 new undersea vessels with which they planned to win the war. The Naval Staff applied to these new UB-type submarines the lessons they had learned from the U-class craft. The new ones were lighter, having a displacement of only 650 tons. With a complement of three officers and 31 men, each submarine carried 10 torpedoes and a 105 mm gun and had a range of 4,000 miles—truly an awesome threat.

However, one of these boats, the UB-65, seems to have been jinxed practically from its beginning. A week after its keel was laid a steel girder slipped from its sling and crashed into the hull, killing one workman outright and injuring another who died within a few hours. Only four weeks later, while the engines were being tested, the engine room filled with chlorine gas and three men were suffocated.

In the shadow of these misfortunes the UB-65 put to sea for a trial run. One day out a tremendous gale sprang up and a crewman was washed overboard and lost. During the first test dive a leak developed in a submersion tank and the UB-65 lay on the bottom for 12 hours before the crew could bring her to the surface. On the way up another leak developed and water reached the batteries, filling the ship with poisonous fumes. Officers and men were half-asphyxiated by the time they surfaced and were able to force open the hatches.

The UB-65 returned to port after her disastrous trial voyage in April 1917, a time when the attacks on Allied shipping were intensifying. She was ordered to take on a full load of fuel and armaments and put to sea immediately. But as the torpedoes were being winched aboard one of the warheads exploded. Four crewmen and the second officer, one F. Richter, were killed instantly, a dozen men were badly injured and the UB-65 had to be towed to the dockyard for extensive repairs.

A few weeks later, the damage having been almost repaired, a new date was set for the UB-65 to leave port. One day, as the time approached, a panic-stricken seaman rushed up to the captain, Friedrich Hönig, who was in the wardroom.

"Sir, the dead officer is on board!" he shouted.

Captain Hönig at first accused the man of being drunk but soon determined he was completely sober. Nevertheless, he told an unbelievable story. He claimed that while standing on the foredeck he had seen Second Officer Richter climbing the gangplank toward him. The seaman insisted he was not mistaken and held stubbornly to his story even while admitting he knew the second officer was dead.

The man was so insistent that the captain agreed to go with him to the foredeck where the second officer had been seen. They climbed the ladder and made their way past the conning tower. There, to the captain's astonishment, another crewman, Seaman Petersen, crouched—gibbering and pale with fear.

His stammered answers to the captain's questions made no sense at first. Then when it was clear that he was not to be reprimanded, Petersen said he had just seen the second officer whom he knew was dead. Richter, he said, had walked along the main deck, had passed the conning tower and had gone on to stand on the foredeck looking out to sea. Petersen said he was so terrified he had hidden behind the conning tower. He admitted, however, that now as he looked over the ship the officer was nowhere to be seen.

The independent evidence of the two men convinced Captain Hönig that something extraordinary had happened and he recorded the incident in the ship's log. But he wanted to let the matter drop rather than risk having the whole crew affected. It was too late, however. The story raced around the ship and morale sank. The day before the UB-65 was due to put to sea on its first war cruise, Petersen deserted, telling his shipmates they were doomed.

On January 1, 1918, the UB-65 left Heligoland bound for the English Channel. There, for three weeks, she searched for Allied ships. Her log shows that on January 21 she was cruising on the surface 15 miles off the English coast in extremely rough weather. The starboard lookout strained his eyes watching for telltale lights or the dim shapes of enemy vessels. Glancing down he was amazed to see a figure on the plunging deck. It seemed impossible for a man to survive the great waves sweeping over the ship. It was equally impossible for anyone to be there. In such a raging sea all hatches except the conning tower were battened down. Just as the lookout started to yell a warning the figure turned. In the twilight his features were clear. It was dead Second Officer Richter.

The terrified lookout staggered from the bridge only to collide with Captain Hönig, who cursed him for leaving his post. When he heard the man's almost incoherent explanation the captain pushed him aside and went forward to stare down at the deck below. With his own eyes he saw the second officer. He shouted for a man to come to the bridge immediately. Three seamen obeyed—and they all saw the ghost of the dead man.

Then the submarine hit a particularly heavy sea and the foredeck dipped out of sight. Icy water sprayed over the ship and when she once again reared out of the waves the mysterious figure was gone.

The captain relieved the lookout, who quickly spread the story. In minutes a terrible fear gripped the crew. The captain knew he must dispel their terror in some way or the whole working of the ship would be affected. Yet what could he say? He himself had seen the specter.

Despite these problems the rest of the voyage was relatively uneventful. Two steamers were torpedoed and sunk, two others raked with gunfire. Under different circumstances the UB-65 would have closed in and finished them off but the captain, like his crew, feared that the appearances of the ghostly visitor presaged his ship's doom. On the excuse that hidden guns on the crippled steamers might sink his vessel the captain broke off both engagements and put the submarine into Bruges on the Belgian coast.

In March 1918 while the UB-65 was being outfitted for her next voyage British bombers raided Bruges' submarine shelters. Captain Hönig was on his way back to the ship from leave when a bomb splinter took off his head. His headless body was taken aboard the UB-65. That night one of the crewmen awakened everyone aboard by racing through the ship yelling like a madman. When he was finally subdued he said he had seen the ghost of the second officer coming out of the cabin where the body of the dead captain lay.

The stories of the ghost aboard the UB-65 soon spread through the fleet and inevitably reached the high command. In April 1918 Commodore Michelsen visited the ill-fated submarine and person-ally interviewed every member of the crew. He was skeptical at first, saying that a rational explanation must exist. But the longer he stayed on the UB-65 the more convinced he became that the men were seeing *something*. So much corroborative data and the unshakable testimony of so many sailors persuaded him that the men were certain the ghost of the second officer roamed the UB-65. Examining the full record of every man in the crew the commodore learned that all had excellent records in the submarine service and all were considered reliable by their superiors.

Finally every man in the crew requested a transfer to another vessel. Although these requests were officially refused, on one pretext or another all but three men were transferred. An almost totally new crew took over the haunted submarine.

Just before the UB-65 was to sail on her next mission a Lutheran pastor came aboard to conduct an exorcism ceremony. The immediate effect of this well-intentioned move was to unnerve the new crew. The men began asking questions of the dockworkers and the crews of other vessels and soon the stories of the UB-65's unwholesome career came to light. The new captain heard them too but was determined they should not affect his crewmen. He threatened severe disciplinary action against any man who mentioned the phantom officer or spread tales likely to cause unrest.

The next two voyages were uneventful. Several enemy vessels were sunk but nothing out of the ordinary happened aboard the UB-65. The submarine returned to port and her captain was relieved. The new captain was Lieutenant Commander Heinrich Schelle.

In May 1918 the UB-65 set out to patrol the coast of Spain. After two days out, Hans Eberhard, one of the torpedo gunners, seemed to go mad. He screamed that a ghost in the uniform of a second officer was following him around the torpedo room. Eberhard was one of the new crew members and he did not recognize the officer. The captain dosed him with morphine to quiet him but after a brief quiet spell Eberhard suddenly became violent again and jumped over-board. Despite a long and intensive search he was not rescued.

Off the coast of the French island of Ushant the submarine encountered bad weather. The chief engineer was washed off his feet and his right leg fractured. The leader of the gun crew, Richard Meyer, was blown overboard and never seen again.

Then on the run back to Bruges the UB-65 encountered a flotilla of destroyers and dived just in time. Depth charges exploded all around for more than an hour and many of the crew were injured. However, the submarine managed to limp into port, but before the ship docked Coxswain Heinz Lohmann died from his injuries.

One petty officer reported he had seen the ghost of the second officer three times during this cruise. On numerous occasions it was seen by several seamen at the same time. Yet other sailors in the same group had not seen the phantom even when it was pointed out to them. Nevertheless, in the debriefings after the cruises it came out that most of the men on the haunted submarine had seen the ghost.

After repairs and refitting the UB-65 again sailed from Bruges on July 2, 1918, into the North Sea, around the northern tip of Scotland and south into the Bristol Channel. On July 4 she radioed that she had sighted a British submarine and was going to attack. She gave her position as 51° 7' north and 9° 42' west—just off the south coast of Ireland. This was her last message. The submarine was never heard from again.

What happened to the UB-65? In his book *U-Boat Intelligence, 1914–1918,* a factual account of the tracking and sinking of U-boats, Robert Grant of the University of Chicago refers to the disappearance of the UB-65 as "the most baffling mystery of the U-boat war."

British naval records show that despite the UB-65's report on July 4 no British submarine was in the area that day. However, an

American submarine, the AL-2, and the German UB-108 were near the area.

The theory has been advanced that a stray torpedo from the UB-108 may have hit the UB-65. The UB-108 had sighted the AL-2 and had fired its torpedos but every one missed. Another guess is that the UB-65 fired at the AL-2, having mistakenly identified it as British in its radio message, and that her own torpedos exploded in their tubes due to some malfunction. The AL-2's log showed instrument contact with another submarine but reported that no engagement took place.

No wreckage was ever found which could be linked with the UB-65. Her fate remains unexplained to this day.

The German Naval High Command requested Professor Hecht, a renowned psychologist, to investigate the remarkable story of the haunted submarine. The members of its first crew were scattered, transferred to many different ships, but Professor Hecht interviewed all of those he could locate. He examined all the logs—except the last—and when the war was over Professor Hecht published his findings, concluding: "The phenomena do not lend themselves to explanation on any rational grounds. . . . The case of the UB-65 is undoubtedly the best-documented ghost story of the sea."

GHOSTLY SOLDIER SAVES FRIEND

Boczor Iosif

DURING WORLD WAR I, ON THE NIGHT OF AUGUST 3, 1916, THE
guns were silent near Brusilew, Russia. It was the lull before
the storm. The staff of the Austro-Hungarian army knew
that the next day the Russian army would begin a brutal assault.

Alpari Imre, a Hungarian sergeant, lay on a straw mattress in a
trench. Alpari was a doctor in civilian life, but he had been pressed
into service to fight for his country.

That night an apparition of Imre's best friend appeared in
the trench. Alpari had not seen his friend since the war began. His
friend looked pale, and he wore a full-dress uniform with all his
decorations.

His friend spoke to Alpari: "I want to help you because there is
danger ahead. If you listen to my advice you will be saved. Tomorrow
a bayonet will wound you. Then a grenade explosion will cause you
to lose consciousness. When you regain consciousness, you must
run toward the Russian front, where you will find a wounded Aus-
trian officer. You will help him, but then you will be captured. After
16 months you will be released." Alpari's spectral friend took out a
golden amulet and gave it to Alpari. Then the vision vanished into
thin air. That night Alpari wrote a letter to his parents describing his
strange encounter.

Early the next morning the Russian offensive began. Alpari was injured by a bayonet and knocked unconscious by the shock of a grenade blast. Regaining consciousness, he headed toward the Russian front, where he found a wounded comrade lying on the ground, unconscious. Alpari picked the man up and carried him to a Russian first aid station. He was taken prisoner, and remained in a prisoner of war camp for 16 months.

During his captivity, Alpari never parted with the amulet he had received from his ghostly friend. When he reached Hungarian soil after his 16-month prison stay, he held the amulet in his hand and prayed. Then he stuck the amulet in his pocket. He never saw it again. It simply vanished, like his friend had that night in the trench.

Alpari later learned that his friend had died in a battle in Russia in 1914—nearly two years before Alpari had been visited by him!

The Phantom of the Cruise

Raymond Lamont Brown

FOR A NUMBER OF YEARS MRS. CYRUS P. MACHRAK HAD WANTED TO make a long cruise "to see some of the places I have never visited before," she said. So a month after the death of her husband, the New York society lady, who was visiting her sister-in-law in Gloucester, England, booked a four-week voyage around Africa for the summer of 1938. Mrs. Machrak was to pick up her ship, the *Llanstephan Castle,* at Tilbury, some 20 miles east of London on the north bank of the river Thames.

The advent of the Munich crisis—Adolf Hitler's threat to Czechoslovakia—made it problematical for a while as to whether or not the cruise would in fact take place. As she waited for the crisis to clear, Mrs. Machrak did some shopping in London. Also, being of an inquiring mind, she took time off to look up some data on her cruise ship, the *Llanstephan Castle.*

The 11,346-ton ship was built in 1914 at Govan, Scotland, for Great Britain's famous Union-Castle Line. Designed to carry 229 first-class passengers and 202 tourist-class passengers, the liner had served as a troopship during World War I. During the years 1919 to 1939, however, the liner was on the London–East Africa run.

The international crisis was settled, at least temporarily, and *Llanstephan Castle* prepared to depart. Mrs. Machrak joined the ship at Tilbury on a damp and dismal day in September 1938. Three days out of Tilbury the *Llanstephan Castle* encountered bad weather and was badly battered by heavy seas. A considerable amount of damage was done to her fittings; three members of the crew—Wilson, Smith, and Harper—were badly injured. At Gibraltar the weather continued so rough that it was quite impossible for passengers to go ashore. A Royal Navy hospital tender came alongside and removed the injured seamen.

By the time the ship steamed away from Gibraltar, gregarious Mrs. Machrak had made friends with the cabin staff. One evening as she was served an after-dinner coffee by her stewardess Mary Richards, Mrs. Machrak asked the young woman about the morale of the ship. The girl admitted that "strange things were continually happening aboard." It appeared that accidents happened which "should not have happened," things were mysteriously missing, and more than one passenger reported to the ship's doctor with strange feelings of depression and a desire to commit suicide—one passenger on the previous trip had actually done so.

At the time Mrs. Machrak dismissed the report as superstitious gossip and enjoyed the cruise ports of Tangier, Genoa, and Port Said and the trip through the Suez Canal to Beira. She noted, however, that as the ship steamed down the East African coast her fellow passengers seemed to become depressed. During the past few days Mrs. Machrak had been a guest at the chief officer's table, together with six other passengers. "But," she later reported, "we never seemed able to really get together . . . an air of mental subversion surrounded us all."

On the way south to Durban, in perfectly calm seas, the *Llanstephan Castle* suddenly developed an alarming and unaccountable list. As they entered Durban, Mrs. Machrak discovered that one of the ship's cooks, Pete Archer, had vanished, no one knew where. No lifeboats were missing and it was too far to swim ashore.

Then Mrs. Machrak began to have "strange encounters." Her account of what happened was set down on papers found with her will in 1947 when she died at her home in Chicago. Of these happenings she said, "We were just leaving Durban and I went out on deck around ten o'clock for a breath of air before going to bed.

"Nobody else was in sight and all I could see was the dim light burning over the main entrance to the saloon. I stopped walking and looked up at the sky; it was a lovely night. And then something indistinct approached me; it moved slowly and with what seemed to be a cold purpose. And as it came nearer I saw that it was the spectral figure of a man in uniform and that the clothing was dripping with some strange greenish slime. I knew then, why I cannot say, that it intended taking hold of me and pushing me over the ship's rail. I was so terrified, I was unable to move or to call for help."

Very afraid, Mrs. Machrak prayed hard, then:

"I found I was able to move and I ran as fast as I could towards the bow of the ship and finally reached my cabin in a roundabout manner. There was a window, not just a round porthole, over my bed and it was open about six inches. I flung myself at it and tried to close it but something on deck outside prevented my doing so. How long I stood there I cannot say but in time I reopened my cabin door and ran across to the nearby bathroom; somehow I thought I would be safer locked in there. And as I locked the door I knew that this thing in tattered uniform was with me. I managed to unlock the door and fled back to my cabin. The window was still open and I watched the fingers of a hand take hold of the upper sash. I ran from the cabin again and managed to reach the cabin of a woman friend [Amy Rogers] and there I spent the rest of the terrifying night."

Not long afterwards a woman—dressed in a negligeé—was restrained from jumping over the rail into the sea. She later told the ship's doctor that she had been pursued by "a phantom sailor all dripping with slime"; the specter had tried to push her into the sea. The doctor entered a diagnosis of hysteria in his medical log.

Discreetly Mrs. Machrak told one or two of her fellow passengers of her encounter and one of them admitted to a similar meeting with the "phantom sailor." In the end Mrs. Machrak informed the captain of what she had seen and he promised to notify the owners.

No note made by the captain on the subject ever came to light. But in 1956 ghost hunter Warren Armstrong interviewed an Irish lady, Hester O'Mara, who had been aboard the *Llanstephan Castle* on the cruise with Mrs. Machrak and who had seen the same thing. She too had informed the captain. In all, four people are known to have seen the ghost during the 1938 trip, but no official record was logged by the Union-Castle executives.

Whatever the "ghost" was, its haunting ground is no more. The *Llanstephan Castle* was refitted in Belfast during World War II and went back into the African service. She was sold for breaking in March 1952.

Psychic researchers who have studied the case have put the occurrences down to "the death of a naval officer, probably during World War I, causing a psychic atmosphere disturbance aboard the ship."

All of which explains nothing!

BROTHER AGAINST BROTHER

Lonnie E. Legge

JIM DANIEL, OF LOGAN COUNTY, WEST VIRGINIA, JOINED THE ARMY early in 1917, and was among the first of the A.E.F. to arrive in France. His letters at first came regularly to his girlfriend, Darlene Mastin, then they stopped entirely.

Darlene continued to write for some time, not knowing that Will Daniel, Jim's older brother, was intercepting their mail. Will also was in love with Darlene. He finally faked a telegram, stating Jim had been killed in action. Showing Darlene this telegram, he played so cleverly on her anguish that she agreed to marry him.

Will and Darlene were married in October and all went well until Christmas Eve 1917. Darlene, who was preparing supper, heard the front door open and recognized Jim Daniel's voice saying to her husband, Will, who was sitting in the living room: "I know what you have done to Darlene and me and I have come to kill you as you deserve."

Darlene knew that mountain people weren't in the habit of speaking without meaning what they said. She realized that Will either had made a mistake or deliberately had lied to her about Jim's death, as Jim was back home and seemed very much alive.

There was a blast from a gun and Darlene ran into the front room just in time to see a man in uniform go out the door. Will lay dead on the living-room floor, a hole in his forehead and a look of disbelief in his dulling eyes.

How long Darlene stood rooted to the spot, staring down at her dead husband, she never knew. A brisk rapping on the front door brought her back to reality. Opening the door she saw a boy with a telegram. It was from the War Department and read: "To William Daniel: . . . Regret to inform you that on December 21, 1917, your brother, James Daniel, was killed in action in Germany. . . ."

The murderer of Will Daniel never was apprehended. There was no trace of anyone, other than the Western Union boy, ever having been there that night. No gun ever was found and it was proven that Will Daniel never had owned a gun. Darlene insisted that the ghost of the wronged brother had returned after death and done the killing. Of course, the law took a dim view of this explanation.

TALE OF TWO GHOSTS

David Barron

I'M A SKEPTIC WHEN IT COMES TO GHOST STORIES, BUT THAT HARD-nosed attitude was jarred a few years ago when a friend gave me an old copy of a book entitled *Spooks Deluxe*. He called my attention to a chapter that mentioned the summer resort of Groton Long Point, Connecticut, where I had lived as a teenager. Although the book has vanished from my library since that time, my recollection of the story remains vivid. The ghost story told of a mystery that has stayed in my mind for 40 years.

Attempting to find the names and dates relating to the original story, I alerted friends and relatives to my need for the book. Then I set about interviewing several elderly residents who might recall the strange event. As luck would have it, I wound up with conflicting names and identities of the persons involved. At last I located relatives of a former owner of the cottage where a ghostly appearance supposedly took place. What I learned from them helped me to understand my own experience.

In 1944, I was a high school student earning spending money by delivering newspapers. This involved walking several miles around the resort and dropping off papers at the homes of the two dozen "winter" families. One cold December evening, nearing the end of my paper route, I trudged through the snow and approached the cottage of my last customer, Miss Elsie Raymond.

Glancing toward the end of the deserted road, I was startled to see the figure of a young man standing under the pale yellow beam of the wartime-hooded streetlight. The black, icy waters of Long Island Sound beyond the seawall, coupled with the gently falling snow, made an eerie contrast, giving me the impression that I was looking down an endless tunnel.

To my amazement I recognized the man as a sailor, dressed in summertime "whites," wearing no coat or jacket against the cold. I bounded up the steps of Miss Raymond's side porch, tossed the paper behind the snow-matted screen door and hurried back to the street, eager to see the stranger again. I was surprised to find him gone. He had vanished without a trace.

The fresh snow cover showed where he had stood for some time. His footprints had packed down the spot beneath the streetlight. Something was terribly wrong: There were no footprints coming to or leaving the site.

I knew I hadn't imagined the sailor. The footprints proved that he had been standing where I had seen him. I remembered the way his hat was cocked on his head, his restless-looking posture as he stood there, and his lack of winter clothing. He appeared to have been waiting for someone or something.

As I hurried home, bewildered by the whole incident, I could hardly wait to ask my father, Seth Barron, a retired Coast Guard commander, if it wasn't unusual for a sailor to be dressed in whites instead of the regulation winter uniform blues.

"The only explanation I could give," he told me, "is that the sailor might have just recently been transferred here from a tropical zone where whites are mandatory."

Choosing not to bring up the matter of the sailor's unusual vanishing act, I let the subject drop, even though I would remember it for years thereafter. World War II ended and I went off to college. Then I came upon *Spooks Deluxe* and the story of Miss Raymond's ghostly encounter.

According to the book, Miss Raymond had been at home one dark, snowy evening, about to empty some dishwater out of her door when she was startled by the sight of a strange man on her porch. Her rented summer cottage had its windows and front door sealed up to conserve heat and the only entrance was from the side of the house facing Middlefield Street.

The stranger entered her house, brushed past her, leaving a trail of wet snow prints on her newly waxed linoleum floor, and proceeded into the living room. She closed the door against the wintry blast of air and hurried after him.

By the time she got to the living room, he was gone. Only his footprints, ending halfway across the room, remained. Gun in hand, she searched the rooms and closets to no avail.

A strong, self-reliant woman, Miss Raymond kept the incident to herself until the following spring when she mentioned it to her neighbor Marie and her mother when they returned from a Florida vacation. Marie owned the small inn next door.

Her elderly mother took special interest in Miss Raymond's story. Danton Walker, the well-known New York journalist who owned the cottage, stopped by for a visit several weeks later and asked how Miss Raymond had fared during the winter. She reported the strange encounter with a man with "piercing black eyes" and a "lumber jacket . . . and a felt hat that had been trimmed around the edges in scallops."

Then she added that the intruder's appearance tallied precisely with that of Marie's mother's deceased son, the inn owner Marie's brother. Clothes identical to those she had described were stored in the attic of the next-door inn, the old lady informed Miss Raymond. The son, who suffered from war-related lung problems, had spent a lot of time in the cottage and loved the place. When he left Groton

Long Point, he was taken to the veterans' hospital and died there. Walker included this story in *Spooks Deluxe*.

There were two inns at Groton Long Point in those days. Both were operated by women who had lost sons in war. The owner of the Farm House Inn, Mrs. Palmer, lost her son Bruce when his ship went down in the South Pacific about the time of Miss Raymond's experience. I learned that Bruce Palmer had been a frequent visitor to the cottage and was good friends with the old lady's son.

During a lengthy telephone conversation with George McKay* I learned that the cottage's history included the suicide of a former owner who hanged himself in the house. Several years later, so the story goes, another tenant was found murdered in nearby Haley's Woods. Subsequent tenants, although unfamiliar with its strange history, have complained about "peeping toms" staring through the windows.

When I finished reading Walker's remarkable story, I wondered about its connection with my own experience. Had the spirit of the young sailor come back to the house where his best friend lived, expecting to be welcomed—as the interviews had suggested? Or, as Walker's story implied, had the spirit of the World War I veteran returned? Or was it the suicide victim's ghost or that of the murder victim attempting to return home?

---

*Pseudonym. Real name on file at FATE's editorial office.

VISION OF WORLD WAR I

James Leigh

NOT ALL THE TRUE GHOST STORIES OF THE GREAT WAR WERE enacted on land. The late Lord Halifax vouched for the following case, which was, at the time, "general knowledge among the senior submarine officers."

Among the commanders of submarines operating from the southeast coast of England was an officer whom we will call Ryan—a man of striking appearance and charming personality.

These submarines had a special "beat." They would do a patrol of from two to three weeks off the Dutch shoals and the entrance to Jade Bay. Working on the surface at night they were driven undersea during most of the daylight by the numerous German aircraft.

Ryan left on one of these patrols. His ship never returned and in due course it was written off as lost.

About two months later another submarine was operating on the same beat. She had just broken the surface with her periscope to have a brief look around. The day was fine and sunny and the officer who was searching the seas through his periscope suddenly exclaimed, "By jove, there's jolly old Ryan waving to us like mad from the water."

The tanks were immediately blown to bring the vessel to the surface. Men crowded into the conning tower and went out on deck with lifelines. But now no sign of Ryan was to be seen. The officer, still positive that it really was Ryan he had seen, was not the type of man who would suffer from illusions nor could anyone be in doubt about Submariner Ryan's characteristic appearance.

Suddenly there was seen in the sea "right ahead and on the course the submarine had been steering, two mines which would undoubtedly have blown them skyhigh had Ryan's ghost not put in its most opportune appearance!"

Did the spirit of the dead submarine commander return to rescue his friends from the kind of death he had himself experienced? That, I think, would be the accepted answer of the former British War Minister, Mr. Hore Belisha, who admitted his belief in spirit return.

"The dead are always with us," he said, "to gird and to sustain us on our march, to lift us up when we fall with exhaustion."

GHOST SOLDIER IN OUR ATTIC

Etna Elliott

MY HUSBAND AND I, WITH OUR THREE CHILDREN, LEFT PORTland, Oregon, in the hot summer of 1928, to join my parents in the high mountains of California, five miles from Georgetown, where they had purchased a gold mine and were working it together with my uncle Charlie. There were no buildings at the mine and they rented an old farm which was badly in need of repairs. It had been unlived in for several years and my folks spent some time making it livable, so that it was comfortable by the time we reached there with our family.

During the day, while the men were busy at the mine, Mother and I went to work in the attic, which we reached by a very narrow, steep stairway. We piled old trunks, boxes, a very tiny old-fashioned organ, an old music box, and other discarded articles of the departed family, all in one end of the attic.

As we were working, I suddenly felt as if someone had walked up behind me, but turning I saw nothing but the cobwebs which hung from the peak-roofed ceiling. I told Mother that I had the odd feeling of being watched, but she only looked at me queerly, then talked of other things.

Later on I ran downstairs to get something for Mother. As I came back up the steps someone brushed by me, almost knocking me back down the stairway. Still, I could not see a thing, although I had felt the contact distinctly.

We worked up in the attic for several days before we had it ready for use. During all that time, I felt an unseen presence near me. After what had happened on the stairway, I wouldn't let my mother out of my sight and followed at her heels the whole time. We had put two beds side by side in the narrow room, leaving only a two-foot space between them. Then we hung thin lace curtains in the doorway to hide all the things piled in the other end of the attic. And still, air from the two windows at each end could circulate through the area where we were to sleep.

My husband did not like the idea of going up into that hot attic to sleep, so he put his bed under an old apple tree near the front porch. Therefore, our small daughter and I slept in one bed and our two boys in the other. That first night I was terribly nervous, so my mother turned the kerosene lamp down low and said to just let it burn if it would make me feel better. But even with the light burning I still could feel that unseen presence, and I don't think I slept over five minutes that whole night. I was terribly tired the next day, but still I could hardly bring myself to go to bed that next night.

Finally the children could not be kept up any longer, and I slowly climbed those steep stairs, with cold chills running up into my hair. I got the children into bed and climbed in beside my little daughter. I forced myself to close my eyes and finally fell asleep, only to be awakened much later by an icy wind blowing over my body.

With my eyes wide open, in the dim light of the kerosene lamp, I saw him!

Standing just outside the lace curtains was a young soldier in uniform. He was tall and straight and looking intently at me as if he were about to speak. The curtains blew out toward me and he started moving in my direction. I screamed and then was unable to move until my parents came dashing up the stairs. I sobbed out what I had seen, and I thought there was a look of horror on their faces. My mother slept up in the attic with us the rest of the night, but she wouldn't talk much about it the next day.

The following night I forced my feet up the stairs. I did not want the children to know how frightened I was. Mother stayed up there with us until the children were asleep and I had become quite calm. I tried to make myself believe that I had imagined the whole thing, and when morning came and there had been no frightening experiences during the night I almost believed this.

A week passed, and I was feeling quite safe as we went to bed and almost at once I fell into a sound sleep, only to be awakened about two o'clock in the morning. I felt as if some one had shaken me. I sat right up in bed, wide awake and trembling. My body was as cold as ice.

There sitting on the edge of the other bed, right against my small son, was the same young soldier. He was looking into my face, smiling, and he had his elbow on his knee. He held a hat in his hand, which he was swinging back and forth. I recognized the hat as a soldier's hat of World War I. It had a wide brim with a heavy, bright cord around the crown. It, or a hat like it, had been hanging in the hall when my parents moved into the house, and I had been wearing it as a sun hat since coming to the mines.

Now this ghostly soldier had the same hat in his hand as he smiled at me with his face not over a foot from my own. He leaned toward me, closer and closer!

I have never remembered making a sound, but I must have for my parents were soon there. This time I could still see the soldier long after they were in the room.

I was weak and trembly for several days after that, and my dad put up a cot at the other end of the attic, just outside the lace curtains, and slept there himself every night. So things settled down, and I was beginning to think and hope I would not see the soldier again.

When I quietly slipped into bed beside my little daughter on this particular night I felt quite safe with my dad so near. Turning on my side with my face to the wall, I was soon fast asleep. But sometime in the early morning hours I was suddenly wide awake and again as cold as ice. A large, heavy hand was pressing down on my shoulder. I tried to rise but I was held tight by this pressure. Turning my face up I found myself looking right into the eyes of the soldier. His face was only inches from mine, and I still felt his hand as plainly as I have ever felt the hand of my husband. I felt as if I were dying.

I still think I would have died, and the soldier would have taken me with him, except that at that very instant my small daughter sat up in bed screaming the most unearthly screams I have ever heard. Still, it seemed her screams receded farther and farther from me.

To this day, that child, now a woman grown, thinks a soldier was taking me away.

Her screams, of course, brought Dad and Mother, and my mother had her arms around me before that soldier took his hand from my shoulder.

They finally got me downstairs, and in my hysterical condition I managed to make them understand that I wanted the children brought down at once. My dad and husband hurried to do this, and my mother held my little daughter until she cried herself to sleep. We all sat in the kitchen the rest of that awful night.

My husband was very doubtful of what I had seen. He said that he wanted to sleep upstairs the next night and see for himself what was going on. I begged him not to but he was determined. He went off to bed and the next morning said he had slept fine. This continued for almost a week. Then one night about midnight he came bounding down the stairs, blankets and all. We never could get him to say what he had seen or what had happened. He was very pale and said only that he would never sleep up there again, that this house should be burned and the ashes buried.

Then in the bright light of day my parents told us what the old lady had said to them when they rented the house. She had looked at them for a long time and then said, "You are welcome to live in the place if you can stand it!"

Pointing to great piles of rocks all over the place, she continued, "See those rocks? Well, I have piled them just to have something to do, to keep me out of the house. For my husband still lives there, although he has been dead many years." Then she added, "Yes, and the boys come back too, so I have left the house to them most of the time."

She explained that her husband had died in a drunken stupor in that house; one of her sons had dropped dead on the back porch; her youngest son had died in the kitchen while having a fistfight with his brother; and her oldest son, a soldier in World War I, had come home after being wounded and died in his sleep in his bed in the attic.

"This house is bad!" she had gone on to say. "But if you can stand to live among them, you are welcome."

Now at last my parents believed her. The men went to work at once and built a large cabin at the mine. My husband and I stayed there only long enough to help my parents move out of that house with its ghostly inhabitants before returning gratefully to our home in Portland.

THE PHANTOM BARRAGE

Edward D. Fuller

I WAS ASSIGNED, DURING THE FIRST WORLD WAR, TO THE THIRD Battalion of the 137th Infantry Regiment as one of the signalmen. Our battalion was holding a portion of the front line trenches near Verdun known as the Manhuelles Sector. It was comparatively quiet and at places our trenches were separated from those of the enemy by a valley over a mile across, leaving a wide "no man's land."

Our battalion headquarters was situated in an excavated area atop a high hill that presented a rocky perpendicular front to the enemy and was only about 100 yards in the rear of our own front line trenches. We had several observation posts located on this perpendicular area, which commanded an unobstructed view for several miles both up and down the valley.

On the night of August 15, 1918, I was on duty in the signal lookout station and had the 2:00 A.M. to 4:00 A.M. watch. All was quiet along the entire front. The signalmen on watch with me had just returned from the kitchen with coffee and sandwiches for our lunch. It was perhaps 2:15 when we heard the swish of artillery shells passing overhead. At first there were five or six a minute, then they increased until the noise was continuous. We phoned artillery headquarters to verify our observations and were told that no guns in that sector were in action. We asked if there were shells bursting in the back area but were told there were not.

We couldn't hear any shell bursts on either side, nor could we hear any gun explosions and assumed it must be long-range cannon firing from our extreme back area. We entered our observations in our reports and also called and alerted all 137th regiment officers. This bombardment continued for over an hour and then ceased as suddenly as it had begun.

There was much comment the next day as to who fired the shells and what had been their target. Two nights later some German prisoners were taken. They told our officers that two nights previously they had been moving supplies and artillery up from Metz under cover of darkness and were preparing for a drive on our sector when suddenly and with extreme accuracy our artillery had sent over a barrage which completely demolished every piece of equipment they had. Our officers attempted to ascertain which artillery unit had fired this barrage but in every case all artillery in the entire area reported no action that night.

The old French soldiers wisely nodded their heads, took another sip of Vin Rouge and said, *"Il na passe pas"*—"those who died before Verdun have seen to that."

Steve Came Home

Robert A. Bahr

THIS TRUE STORY HAPPENED TO MY GRANDMOTHER, MRS. MARY Whitley, in 1918, when she was 31 years old. The First World War was drawing to a close.

One sunny Wednesday afternoon she was sitting in a chair in front of the huge bay window, a broom in one hand and a dust cloth in the other, resting. Cool spring air swept into the room, bringing with it the fragrance of new flowers. Mrs. Dunn passed with a number of bundles in her arms.

"Hello there," called Mary. "Lovely day. Hope it stays this way till Steve comes home."

Mrs. Dunn smiled and waved, then went on her way. She had lived next door to the Whitley's for years. Her brother, Steve, was fighting overseas, but was expected home in a few weeks.

Mary glanced up the street. It was empty, except for a few playful sparrows and a soldier. As he drew nearer she thought she recognized him as Steve. But he wasn't due home for weeks yet.

He was almost at the front of her house now and Mary was certain he was Steve. Somehow he seemed to be surrounded by a thin mist. She called to him, and he turned toward her and smiled. His voice seemed far away as he said, "Tell my mother that I'm all right."

Mary did not understand what he meant. His face and the tone of his voice frightened her. He turned away and walked up the street, still in the small cloud. Then she could see him no more.

She was shaking now. She didn't want to believe what she had seen. Yet she found it impossible to pass it off as a figment of her imagination. Either I am going crazy, she thought, or Steve has actually approached me for some reason.

Convinced of the reality of the incident, Mary went next door to Mrs. Dunn. She hesitated before knocking. Mrs. Dunn had a very weak heart. The shock might hurt her. But since it was important that Mrs. Dunn be given Steve's message, Mary knocked.

Mrs. Dunn was shocked when Mary told her. She wept and finally she whispered, "He's dead." Mary said softly that there was no cause for her to think that, but the woman only sobbed, "He's dead. I know he is. God will take care of him."

Ten minutes later a letter came from the War Department stating that Mrs. Dunn's brother Steve had died of influenza, a common sickness at that time, while in camp. If that letter had come a few minutes earlier, Mrs. Dunn probably would have died of a heart attack. Her life was saved, because Steve came home.

The Phantom Soldier

Eileen Hart Prentiss

I N NOVEMBER 1918, ONE OF MY TWO BROTHERS WAS IN FRANCE with the army and the other, in the marines, was expected home soon on a short leave before going overseas. My mother, my sister and I were alone in our Lorain, Ohio, home.

One cold night after we had prepared for bed and turned off the lights, my sister and I sat at our bedroom window and watched the snow falling. Soon the lawn was covered and the street light made the snow sparkle. Mother's room at the top of the stairs was still lighted. Our old-fashioned house had no upper hall. The stairs went directly up to Mother's room.

Our fox terrier, asleep on a chair by the front window downstairs, suddenly growled as she did when a stranger came around. We saw nobody and so we called down through the floor register to quiet her.

The door at the foot of the stairs squeaked open and there was the sound of someone starting up the stairs. Mother called out, "Who is there?" As she went to the top of the stairs the footsteps stopped.

Mother saw no one on the stairs but she opened her bedroom window and called out to the man next door, who was visible through a window as he sat in his dining room. He came running when he heard Mother's urgent call. Another neighbor, about to enter his house across the street, also came running.

The dog continued to growl until the two neighbors came. We

went down to unlock the door for them. Both front and back doors were bolted on the inside. We all had heard the dog, the footsteps and the squeaking of the door, yet the neighbors found nobody in the house and said theirs were the only footprints in the snow-covered lawn outside.

The neighbor from across the street said he had noticed a young soldier walk up to the house and enter it. He had thought that one of my brothers had come home. Neither neighbor, however, had seen anyone leave when Mother called out the window.

Three weeks later, just before the Armistice, we were told that a boy who had lived in the house before we bought it had been killed while fighting in France. He had been killed the day before we had the visit from the phantom soldier.

THE SMIRKING AIRMAN

Herb Kugel

I N 1975, THE 78-YEAR-OLD RETIRED AIR MARSHAL SIR VICTOR Goddard published the story of a photograph that he had kept for many years. It was a group photograph of his squadron. It was taken in early 1919 at the end of World War I and portrayed some 200 men and women who survived the fighting. It was an official RAF photograph. Nobody could have tampered with either the photograph or its negative at any time. When the photo was developed, it was placed on the squadron bulletin board so that those who wanted copies could sign up for them. There was one thing wrong, though. There was an extra face in the photograph, a face belonging to the late Airman Freddy Jackson. Jackson was a mechanic, who died by heedlessly walking into a spinning propeller two days before the squadron, which was to be disbanded, posed for the photo. In fact, his funeral took place on the day the squadron gathered for the photo. In the photo, everyone is wearing a hat but Jackson. Everyone is looking grim except Jackson, who is smiling enigmatically. The others had reason to look grim—they had just returned from Jackson's funeral.

Is the face in the photo really that of Jackson's spirit? Goddard and others of the squadron were convinced that it was. Goddard, in his book *Flight Towards Reality*, suggests that Jackson's expression seemed to say: "My goodness me—I nearly failed to make it—They didn't wait or leave a place for me, the blighters!"

THE OFFICER WHO RETURNED

P. C. Cumine Russell

While working during the war and afterwards as Honorable Organiz-
ing Secretary and then as Chairman of the Polish Children Rescue
Fund, I came across many Poles. Those who served on the committee
with me I naturally got to know well, as I worked for the fund for seven
years.

Otton Laskowski, well known in Poland as a historian whose books
have been translated into English, was on our committee. When
talking one day on psychic subjects he told me the following story. I
have recounted it to various people, who have all begged me to pub-
lish it.

I then approached Laskowski to give me a written and signed state-
ment of the account he gave me, which I reproduce at the end of this
narrative.—P.C.C.R.

O TTON LASKOWSKI'S COUSIN W— MADE AN UNHAPPY MARRIAGE.
Her father, at the time of the marriage, which she insisted
on making, settled on her a small property with a country
house, which was fully furnished and staffed. When the daughter
separated from her husband she decided to take up residence on her
estate, which had been prepared for her by her father in case such an
eventuality occurred.

She asked Otton Laskowski and his uncle Otton Myssuna to
accompany her to this property.

They arrived in the afternoon at the house, where the land agent met them, and they were settling down to a meal when the front doorbell rang.

The butler went to the door, and returned with a visiting card on a salver, which he presented to W—. On it was engraved the name Captain von der Wert, and he said that this gentleman was at the door and requested to be allowed to see W—.

Wondering what a Captain von der Wert could possibly want she consented, and the butler ushered in a German army officer, who clicked his heels together and bowed.

He then addressed W— and said: "Gracious lady, I am a German army officer who fought in the last war and was killed and buried in the churchyard of the village here quite close to your *schloss*. My wife in Germany wishes to re-marry, but she cannot prove my death as there was no record of it. I would be most grateful if you would write and inform her that I am dead and buried in the village church-yard here."

All those present gasped and stared in amazement. They concluded that here was a madman. As he was dressed in uniform, with a big field army grey overcoat and a gun strapped to his shoulder, they were afraid of taking any steps to apprehend him. They all realized he must be placated.

W—, after the first shock of his demand, assured Captain von der Wert that she would be quite willing to write to his wife, but as she had only just arrived at the *schloss* from Warsaw she would do so in two or three days time.

The German replied: "Gracious lady, the matter is urgent and must be attended to at once. Will you ring the bell, and ask your manservant to bring you notepaper and pen and ink?"

W—, whose whole object was to placate a madman, rang the bell as desired, and when writing materials were brought, she sat down and wrote at Captain von der Wert's dictation a letter to his wife. He gave the address of the lady in Germany, and when the letter was finished, he bowed and asked that it should be dispatched at once to the nearest post office.

W—, still under the illusion that here was a madman with whom she must temporize, promised to post the letter when they returned to Warsaw in a few days time. This, however, was not good enough for von der Wert, who again bowed and requested that the letter should be dispatched to the post immediately.

Looking askance at the assembled party, she realized that there was nothing for it but to comply with this strange request, and again, the bell was rung, and instructions given that a special messenger should be sent off to the nearest post office forthwith.

Laskowski told me that giving the letter to the manservant, and arranging that somebody should be sent with it to the post, had caused a certain stir. They had all turned their attention to the manservant who came in to get the letter and arrange for its dispatch, so that they were not paying attention to the German officer. When they turned round after the manservant had left the room, they found that Captain von der Wert had disappeared. He could not have got outside the door, or have climbed through the window, without their seeing him. No, he had vanished completely into thin air!

One can imagine the sensation this caused, and the eerie feeling it produced. W— was frankly terrified, and absolutely refused to remain in such a haunted house any longer. She was afraid to face a night there for fear of what would happen. If ghosts could materialize during the daytime what might they not do when night fell? Accompanied by her cousin and uncle she returned to Warsaw that evening.

Some days later Laskowski was informed that his cousin had received a letter from Frau von der Wert, who it appears had never been able to prove her husband's death. She was arranging to come to Warsaw, to try and get an order from the authorities to get the bodies of the Germans buried in that churchyard exhumed.

This she did, and after the usual official delays and difficulties, all of which Frau von der Wert managed to overcome, the necessary permission was granted. Otton Laskowski and his uncle both attended the exhumation, and represented W—, who would not approach the place or return to her house, as she had not recovered from the shock she had sustained with this extraordinary happening. As may be seen from Laskowski's statement reproduced below, there were plenty of officials present, as the affair was causing a great sensation. The body of Captain von der Wert was discovered buried there, and his identity disc left no doubt as to who he was. The corpse was dressed in a grey army coat, and a gun was strapped to the holster, exactly as he had appeared at the *schloss* some weeks previously.

Statement of Major Laskowski

"*I hereby state that the story of the German Captain von der Wert really occurred at the chateau G—, and near the railway station of G— I was myself present with my cousin W—, my uncle Otton Myssuna, the land agent and the butler.*

"*My uncle was a judge of the Supreme Court, and therefore a person of the highest integrity. It was I think in October 1922 or 1923. I believe in 1922. When the body was exhumed, not only was I present with my uncle, but representatives from the Ministry of War and Ministry of Foreign Affairs, and the widow Frau von der Wert.*"

(Signed) Otton Laskowski,
2nd April, 1952.

GHOSTS OF THE BATTLEFIELD

Matthew A. Bille

G HOST SIGHTINGS WERE ALSO FREQUENTLY REPORTED DURING World War II. Many ghost stories concerned the British Royal Air Force. According to aviation historian Dale Titler, the most famous RAF ghost was "Old Willie." British night fighters rising to intercept German bombers during the Battle of Britain would sometimes see a World War I Canadian biplane (an SE-5) in their formation, somehow keeping pace with their much faster planes. Willie would fly straight at enemy bombers until they swerved to avoid collision, often hitting each other in the process.

Phantom fighters apparently flew for both sides. The April 1943 issue of *Coronet* magazine told the story of an RAF lieutenant named Grayson who claimed that one night he spotted and chased a German fighter. He got close enough for a clear view in the moonlight. The German craft was a red Fokker triplane from World War I, complete with Iron Cross markings. When Grayson hesitantly told the story to his squadron mates, nobody laughed. They told him they had all seen the Red Baron (or Red Knight, as some called him).

There are some interesting footnotes to this story. First, the triplane was encountered over the coast of southern England, a place Baron Manfred von Richtofen had never been in life. This conflicts with the common theory that ghosts are some kind of psychic filmstrip repeating in locations where they once existed. Second, the encounter was reported in the same year that the RAF got an ironic sort of final vengeance against the Baron when a bombing raid destroyed the German museum housing his rebuilt Fokker. Finally, this was not the only appearance of such a triplane: Martin Caidin, in his book *Ghosts of the Air*, reports that it was seen by a group of German pilots in daylight.

Another ghostly plane sighting was of a Handley-Page bomber. This spectral aircraft, nicknamed the "Hot One," allegedly escorted British bombers into Germany and would dive at German antiaircraft guns, distracting their fire. Unlike the ghost fighters just mentioned, the bomber, an early World War II design, flew with no one in the cockpit.

A different kind of story concerns the "White Angel of Warsaw." In the earliest days of World War II, German bombers flying to attack Warsaw were preceded by a luminous, silent aircraft that would circle the city once at great altitude and then vanish. After Poland fell, no one ever reported seeing this craft again.

Finally, Martin Caidin reports on what has to be the strangest phantom-flier tale of all. After a flight of 12 American-built Boston RAF bombers struck German bases in occupied France, only three crews returned to appear at debriefing. After they'd signed their after-action reports, they left, headed (understandably) to the aircrews' bar for a drink.

They never got there. They couldn't have. All 12 planes had been shot down—before three of the crews appeared at home, in solid enough form to sign a report.

Ghosts—or reports of them—came from the sea as well. The destroyer U.S.S. *Kennison* was patrolling in fog off San Francisco in November 1942 when its lookouts saw and heard a vessel cutting across their wake. The stranger was a two-masted sailing vessel of archaic design. The fantail lookout, who had the closest view, claimed the decrepit-looking vessel seemed empty of life. It left a visible wake, but no trace on the radar screen.

GHOST PLANE OF WORLD WAR II

Elliott O'Donnell

I WAS RETURNING TO MY HOTEL LATE ONE NIGHT IN 1941 AFTER A visit to some friends in Shepperton, England. The night was fine, not a cloud in the sky, the air sweet with the scent of clover and new-mown hay, everywhere so serenely still and peaceful that it was difficult to realize there was a war on. I strode along, filling my lungs with the delicious air. I had just passed a cottage, the windows of which shone with an almost eerie lustre in the moonlight, when I heard the unmistakable humming of a plane.

It sounded to me like one of our planes. Searchlights were sweeping the sky all round but there was no alert. The droning rapidly increased in volume. I looked up into the sky and saw a plane coming, very low, towards me. There were fields on either side of the road and I wondered if it was going to land on one of them. Getting lower as it flew, it passed almost immediately above me.

When it had gone a little way it suddenly nosed downwards, and I realized to my consternation it was out of control and falling. There was a whirring and spluttering as it shot towards the earth, and then a crash, curiously hollow sounding and reverberating. I started running towards the place where it lay but when I was a few yards from it, it vanished—abruptly and inexplicably. I was looking at it one moment, and the next staring in wide-eyed amazement into starlit space. The plane, or whatever it was, was no longer there, and a stillness that was uncanny in its intensity succeeded the terrible crash. Not a little jarred, I lost no time in getting to my destination.

The following day, in answer to my inquiries, I was informed that about 10 years previously a Captain Schofield, when flying towards an airport not very far from Shepperton, had crashed in the very spot where I had seen the phantom plane crash and been killed. Periodically ever since then a ghost plane has haunted the Thames Valley in the neighborhood of Shepperton. Many people have seen it.

CURSED AIRPORT

Elliott O'Donnell

I N AN AIRPORT IN THE SOUTH OF ENGLAND THERE WAS A SPOT where no plane ever was to be seen. Soon after the beginning of the war two young RAF officers were having an argument one morning on the take-off runway. One believed in immortality, the other did not. They became very heated, and the skeptic said:

"Look here, Dick. If I am wrong and there is a life for us beyond the grave I will haunt this very spot on which we are now standing. You may not see me, but I will do all I can to let you and everyone else know I am here."

A week later he was killed in a raid on Germany. Subsequently every plane that took off from the spot which he declared he would haunt met with disaster. One, for some mysterious cause, crashed soon after it had flown, another was destroyed in an aerial collision, a third crashed through its pilot being taken suddenly ill, and several that set out on raids failed to return. It was remarkable, however, that in no instance were there fatal casualties. The spot acquired such a bad reputation that it was tabooed. RAF men avoided it as they would avoid the plague and no plane ever rested on it.

FIFTY YARDS FROM DEATH

Herbert E. Smith

I N THE LATE SUMMER OF 1941 I WAS SERVING WITH SERGEANT FRED Miller in the 31st Infantry in Manila. I received orders to return to the States and we parted, although I tried to get the order revoked. Fred was my best friend.

War came, and I did not hear from Fred again. Years later I found myself in Okinawa, a platoon leader. I was making a patrol of the outer ring of advanced scouts. We were being temporarily held up by intense fire from cleverly concealed enemy machine guns hidden in a slight rise directly in front of our outpost position. I was crawling toward this farthest advanced point when I felt a light hand fall on my shoulder.

"Hold it, Herb!" a well-remembered voice whispered.

I stopped dead in my crawling tracks. I was frankly scared—and not of the Japs or their heavy fire up ahead. I was entirely alone.

Then suddenly a shell hit, directly in front of me, some 50 yards forward. Pieces of shrapnel whistled about me, some glancing sharply off a small boulder at my head. Had I gone forward as I had been doing when that hand touched my shoulder and Fred's whisper had alerted me, I'd have been another casualty in the Pacific war.

I learned, some months after V-J Day, that Fred had been killed in action in March 1942, while helping to repel a Banzai charge by enemy troops on Bataan.

Haunted Airport of England

Elliott O'Donnell

ARLY IN 1942 IN AN AIRPORT IN THE SOUTHWEST OF ENGLAND, an officer of the RAF was in a hospital for some weeks after being wounded in a raid on Germany. The evening of the day of his return to active service was very close and muggy and there was a slight ground mist. He was crossing the airfield, lamenting the sogginess of the turf, when he saw someone in uniform come out of one of the buildings. As the man drew near he saw it was an officer and presently identified him. He was an extremely popular brother officer and old schoolfellow of his named Coles.

Though my informant could not distinguish the man's features at a distance owing to the mist, he knew him by his walk, which was singularly characteristic. Presently, as the man drew nearer, he was able to see his face more clearly and he had not been mistaken—it certainly was Coles.

"Coles," my informant exclaimed, "it's good to see you again, old man!"

But Coles made no answer. Not seeming to hear, he came steadily on, still with the same characteristic walk, his eyes staring straight ahead of him, his expression set and, in the uncertain light, grim. My informant knew that grimness; he had worn it himself during a raid when the enemy's antiaircraft fire was thick and death seemed inevitable.

"Coles," he cried again, "don't you know me?"

Still no answer, and Coles came resolutely on, looking neither right nor left and passing my informant apparently without seeing him.

Much surprised and hurt at such conduct, my informant turned and watched Coles' receding figure. It seemed strangely shadowy and there was an indistinctness and unreality about it that he had not noticed before but which he persuaded himself was due to the mist. It certainly was Coles; he was positive of that.

His superior officer was pleased to see him back again.

"You don't look too well," he remarked. "You seem bothered and agitated. Anything the matter?"

"Not with me, sir," my friend replied, "but what's wrong with Coles? I passed him by just now so close that he couldn't help seeing me, but he didn't appear to, and when I spoke—I spoke twice to him—he didn't answer. I'm sure it was Coles, but he didn't seem himself."

The superior officer paled and gave my friend a strange look.

"You couldn't have seen Coles," he said, "because Coles was killed last night over the Ruhr!"

A Perfect Ghost Story

Author Unknown

WHAT IS DESCRIBED AS "A PERFECT GHOST STORY FROM A scientific point of view" recently was published by John Langston Davies, British psychic researcher, in *The People* newspaper.

During World War II, according to Davies, a boarding house on the South Coast of England was used as a billet for soldiers, who came and went at all hours of the day and night. Early one morning a fair-haired young soldier handed a package wrapped in green paper to the landlady and asked her to mail it to his wife. Only after he had gone did the landlady discover that the package was not addressed.

Hoping to find some sort of identification, she opened the package. She found it contained only some civilian clothes. She placed them in a cupboard, thinking the soldier might write, but he never did.

One day after the war was over the landlady returned to the boarding house from a shopping trip. As she walked upstairs, a fair-haired soldier carrying a package wrapped in green paper strode past her. She questioned her daughter about the soldier, but the daughter said nobody of his description had entered or left the house.

Certain that the soldier was the one who had given her the green package, the landlady went to check on it. She found the package in the cupboard where she had placed it. She opened it again and this time searched carefully through the clothes. In the pocket of a coat she found a photograph of a wedding couple—and she recognized the bridegroom as the fair-haired soldier.

The back of the photo bore the address of the photographer and a number. The landlady wrote for the address of the couple and when she received it she mailed the package. She received a letter of thanks from the soldier's wife, who said she had been puzzled over not having received some money which her husband said he had sent her for their baby. The wife said she had found the money in the toe of one of the shoes in the package. Her husband, she explained, had been killed at Dunkirk.

DEAD MAN'S LANDING

Jack Corinblit

IT WAS A LARGE ALLIED AIRFIELD IN ITALY DURING THE WAR. EN-
glish, Canadian, Anzac, American, and South African planes
were based there.

One afternoon a P-38 came roaring in from the north and was recognized as one long overdue from a strafing and reconnaissance mission. Instead of entering a landing pattern or contacting the tower,
the fighter circled the field in a peculiar manner—not quite out of
control but without apparent purpose. Nor was the control tower
able to raise the pilot. The whole field was alerted as traffic was heavy
and the danger obvious.

Suddenly the plane seemed to disintegrate in the air and plum-
meted to earth. A parachute billowed out and the pilot floated down.
He landed with strange limpness in the center of the main runway
and was soon surrounded by medical personnel and curious onlook-
ers. The medical officer's voice trembled: "This man has been dead
for more than an hour . . ."

Corregidor's Ghostly Troops

Vincent H. Gaddis

AFTER THE PEARL HARBOR ATTACK, THE JAPANESE INVADED THE Philippines. Manila and Cavite were taken on January 2, 1942. With the fall of Bataan on April 8, the Japanese occupied all of the main island. U.S. and Filipino troops made their last stand on the island fortress of Corregidor, guarding Manila Bay. Here, in an elaborate tunnel system, soldiers, nurses, and convalescents lived a molelike existence.

Until the first days of May, the besieged garrison was the target of thousands of shells and bombs. The growing number of wounded taxed the facilities of the underground hospital. Their suffering was intensified by shortages of anesthetics and other pain-relieving drugs. Supply ships were sunk by shore batteries, and dwindling food supplies reduced rations to a bare subsistence level.

Flesh, blood, and sanity could not long endure this merciless day and night pounding, nor could the island's defenses escape destruction. One by one, the pillboxes and gun emplacements were knocked out. The end came on May 6. After five months of resistance, Corregidor surrendered. Then came the brutal death marches to prison camps. Hundreds more perished.

Today, ghosts walk on the tadpole-shaped island's devastated three square miles. Much of it has returned to the jungle. Inside, the tunnel walls are cracked and crumbling. A pall of silence hangs overhead like a giant shroud. The few inhabitants consist of a family of government caretakers, a small Filipino marine detachment, and a group of firewood cutters.

They insist they have heard sounds from out of the past—the marching of troops, the thunder of distant guns, the moans of men in pain. They swear they have observed phantom American soldiers, unsubstantial but distinct. The marines say they have nearly rubbed shoulders with the scouts of many decades ago while on guard duty.

Among the handful of reporters who have visited the island is Lester Bell, military writer for the *San Diego Union.* He tells of several consistent apparitions. According to the caretakers, a nurse in a Red Cross uniform and a red-headed woman have repeatedly appeared and vanished.

At one of the tunnel entrances, a man, apparently an American officer, walks back and forth and occasionally looks up at the sky. Frightened firewood cutters reported that one evening they had seen a group of wounded men standing near a tunnel entrance.

Three nights later, Floren R. Das, supervisor for tourism for Luzon, made an investigation under bright moonlight. He and his wife heard the moans of men in pain. There was the sound of a woman, perhaps a nurse, softly weeping. "The sounds seemed to be moving toward the Malinta Tunnel," he said.

Memories of Corregidor are both bitter with suffering and defeat, and proud with courage and fortitude. As a Philippine defense secretary has said, "It was here in this once-great fortress that the defenders fought almost beyond human endurance, only to have to participate in cruel and vicious death marches, filled with agony. Why shouldn't it be haunted?"

Why, indeed. This bloodstained soil will never dry. Trade winds will never blow away the aura of sorrow that lies like a cloud over this tragic island.

Corregidor will forever be haunted.

❖

RELIVING THE DIEPPE RAID

Edmond P. Gibson

❖

W HILE ON VACATION AT PUYS, NEAR DIEPPE, FRANCE, ON August 4, 1951, two English ladies, Mrs. Dorothy Norton and Miss Agnes Norton, her sister-in-law, shared an amazing auditory experience which lasted for three hours.

The two women shared a bedroom on the second floor of a three-story house, facing the sea. They had chosen the Dieppe area for their vacation because Mrs. Norton, with her husband, spent a pleasurable vacation there the Easter before. Mrs. Norton's two children and their nurse occupied another bedroom on the same floor.

The statements of Mrs. Dorothy Norton and Miss Agnes Norton from which this account is taken, together with additional information collected by G. W. Lambert, C.B., and Kathleen Gay, appeared in the *Journal of the Society for Psychical Research* (British), May–June 1952. The quoted material is published by permission of that society.

The statement made by Mrs. Dorothy Norton is as follows:

"Saturday, August 4, 1951, 4:20 A.M. Agnes got up and went out of the room. I said, 'Would you like to put the light on?' but she didn't. She came back in a few minutes. She said, 'Do you hear that noise?' I had in fact been listening to it for about 20 minutes. I woke up before it started. It started suddenly and sounded like a storm getting up at sea. Agnes said that she had also been listening to it for about 20 minutes. We lay in the dark for a little listening to the sound. It sounded like a roar that ebbed and flowed and we could distinctly hear the sounds of cries and shouts and gunfire. We put the light on and it continued. We went out on the balcony where we could look down towards the beach, though we could not actually see the sea. The noise came from that direction and became very intense; it came in rolls of sound and the separate sounds of cries, guns and dive-bombing were very distinct. Many times we heard the sound of a shell at the same moment. The roaring became very loud. At 4:50 A.M. it suddenly stopped. At 5:05 A.M. it started again and once more became very intense, so much so that as we stood on our balcony we were amazed that it did not awake other people in the house. By now it was getting light, cocks were crowing and birds were singing. We heard a rifle shot on the hill above the beach.

"The sounds became more distinctly those of dive-bombers rather than the cries and shouts we had heard earlier, although we could still hear them. The noise was very loud and came in waves as before. It stopped abruptly at 5:40 A.M.

"At 5:50 A.M. it started again but was not so loud and sounded more like planes. This died away at 6:00 A.M. At 6:20 the sound became audible again but it was fainter than before and I fell asleep as I was very tired.

"I was waked by a similar sound on Monday, July 30, it sounded exactly the same only fainter and not so intense. At the end I seemed to hear a lot of men singing. It ended when the cock started crowing and I went to sleep. My sister-in-law did not waken."

The statement of Miss Agnes Norton is as follows:

"Saturday, August 4, 1951, I woke in what I realized was very early morning although not yet dawn as no birds were singing. I was aware immediately of a most unusual series of sounds coming from the direction of the beach, which were cries of men heard as if above a storm.

"After listening for about 15 minutes I got up to leave the room and Dorothy spoke to me and asked if I would like to put on the light, which I did not in fact do. On my return I asked Dorothy if she heard the noise too, and she said 'yes,' whereupon we put on the light and checked the time at 4:20 A.M. Our next move was out onto the balcony where the sounds intensified and appeared to me to be a mixture of gunfire, shell fire, dive-bombers, landing craft, and men's cries. All the sounds gave the impression of coming from a very long distance, like a broadcast from America in unmistakable waves of sound. At 4:50 A.M. all noise ceased abruptly and recommenced equally abruptly at 5:07 A.M. At 5:50 A.M. planes distinctly heard in large numbers and other fainter sounds dying away at 6:00 A.M. At 6:25 men's cries heard again, growing gradually fainter, and nothing at all heard after 6:55 A.M."

During the occurrence of this auditory phenomenon both women checked their watches with each other. Mrs. Norton's watch was losing time and was slightly behind that of Miss Norton's. The weather was fine and clear during the entire experience.

The very unusual feature of this case is that the noises heard by the two Englishwomen on August 4, 1951, have a very close correspondence to the actual progress of the landings and battle at Dieppe, Puys, Berneval, and Pointe d'Ailly during the British raid of August 19, 1942. The ladies had read of the raid in newspapers at the time but knew nothing of the details of the battle nor the time sequences involved.

Actually the battle opened at sea at 3:47 A.M., August 19, 1942, when the British assault craft ran into a German coastal convoy near Berneval, about three and a half miles east of Puys and four and a quarter miles east of Dieppe. Firing began on both sides at once and the German coastal defenses were alerted. The element of surprise upon which the British had counted was lost, due to the naval action which followed and lasted in the darkness of the morning until after 4:00 A.M. Landings had been planned to take place at Puys, at Berneval, at Pourville, and at Varengeville at 4:50 A.M., to be followed by the main attack at Dieppe at 5:20 A.M. The landings at Pourville and at Varengeville took place on schedule. The fight with the German convoy delayed the landings at Berneval and Puys and the landings actually took place at 5:07 A.M. They met heavy fire from the German coastal defenses, already alerted. The landing at Dieppe took place about 5:15 and air cover arrived about 5:20 A.M. At 5:40 naval bombardment of the coastal defenses ceased but a reinforcement of R.A.F. planes arrived at 5:50 A.M. to replace earlier air cover, which was running short of ammunition and fuel. Air activity reached a maximum at about 5:50 A.M., with German aircraft joining in the action. Intermittent fighting continued well after 6:55 A.M. and the remnant of the Royal Regiment of Canada, which had been pinned to the beach at Puys, surrendered at 8:30 A.M. Twenty-six officers and 528 men took part in the operation at Puys. Two officers and 65 men, half of them wounded, were taken off the beaches by British ships. Eight officers and 199 men were killed in the action. Sixteen officers and 264 men, wounded and not wounded, were taken prisoner by the Germans. The Royal Regiment was practically wiped out.

British and Canadian troops on other objectives fared slightly better but the entire action had ended at all points before 9:00 A.M.

The *Journal of the S.P.R.* presents a comparative table, from which the following is a partial condensation, showing time correspondences existing between the raid and the experience of the two ladies.

TABLE

RAID	TIME	PERCIPIENTS
August 19, 1942		August 4, 1951
Assault vessels in naval action off Berneval.	3:47 A.M.	
	4:00 A.M.	D. Noise started suddenly like storm at sea. Cries. Gunfire.
		A. Unusual series of sounds coming from direction of beach—cries of men.

RAID	TIME	PERCIPIENTS
Zero hour for landing on flanks.	4:50 A.M.	D. Noise suddenly stopped.
Delayed at Puys and Berneval.		A. Noise ceased abruptly.
	5:05 A.M.	D. It started again, more intense.
First wave of landing craft hit beach at Puys under heavy fire.	5:07 A.M.	A. Noise recommenced abruptly.
Destroyers bombard Dieppe.	5:12 A.M.	
Hurricane bombers attack sea front.	5:15 A.M.	D. Sounds like dive-bombers.
Landing under way at Dieppe.	5:20 A.M.	
Naval bombardment ends at Dieppe	5:40 A.M.	D. Noise stopped abruptly.
More R.A.F. aircraft arrived. Noise a constant drone.	5:50 A.M.	A. Heard many planes.
Change in air cover taking place.		D. It started again—sounded like more planes.
Tank landings at Dieppe completed.	6:00 A.M.	D. Sounds died away. A. Sounds died away.
Intermittent fighting.	6:20 A.M.	D. Sounds began again but fainter. D. fell asleep.
Intermittent fighting.	6:25 A.M.	A. Heard cries of men.
	6:55 A.M.	A. All noises ceased at this hour.
Men pinned down at Puys surrendered.	8:30 A.M.	

If there had been an actual, auditory cause for the phenomenon experienced by the two women, other persons in the area would have heard the sounds. However, later during the day of August 4 they made inquiries of several persons as to whether they had been disturbed by noises during the night. One very nervous visitor to Puys was awake during the time the ladies visited the balcony to listen to the "loud" sounds, but the visitor heard nothing.

It would seem from the attention the ladies paid to their watches during the phenomenon that they were aware that their experience was of an hallucinatory character. Mrs. Norton had an incipient and incomplete experience of similar nature on the morning of July 30, five days before the phenomena of August 4, and told her experience to her sister-in-law on August 2, delaying her recounting of the episode as "she was not in the mood to have her holiday interfered with by 'uncanny' happenings." The authors of the S.P.R. article note that Mrs. Norton had earlier psychic experiences, although none of them was purely auditory. Two of her earlier experiences involved apparitions and were not particularly evidential. The third experience, which took place on her Easter vacation at the same spot, might have been a dream and again might have been a veridical scene of part of the occurrences of the Dieppe raid.

Both percipients were impressed sufficiently by their experience to make written records on the day of the occurrence. G. W. Lambert and Miss Gay gathered together the material dealing with the actual events of the raid and correlated the two records. Mr. Lambert and Miss Gay find no normal explanation.

I wrote to the Honorable Secretary of the Society for Psychical Research, W. H. Salter, asking whether he knew when the ladies decided their experience was paranormal, why they paid such close attention to their watches, and whether the sounds they heard differed from normal sounds. This query was turned over to Mrs. Kathleen Gay, coauthor of the original report, who writes:

"I discussed the point which you raised with the percipients. Mrs. Norton informed me that at first the sound of what appeared to be distant gunfire at sea seemed to be entirely objective and she assumed it must be a storm approaching, as gunfire was most improbable. However, she noticed that the curtains in their bedroom remained quite still in spite of the window being wide open, which, in the event of an approaching thunderstorm, would have been unusual. She very soon became aware that there was something unnatural about the sounds as, when her sister-in-law returned to the bedroom and commented on the noise, they went out onto their balcony and realized that no one else was paying any attention to what was occurring.

"Mrs. Norton had had a previous psychic experience, which made it easier for her to believe that the sounds had no objective reality, but Miss Norton, who had never experienced anything of the kind before, told me that she found it very hard to realize that the noises could be hallucinatory—owing to their volume and persistence. Both were completely mystified by the whole affair.

"They had heard no discussion of the raid by the local inhabitants while they were there. The hotel proprietor and his wife were not there during the occupation, and the other hotel guests were tourists who never mentioned the subject.

"Both ladies are unusually sensible, level-headed young women who have no possible motive for concocting an elaborate deception, the exact timing of which would have been extremely difficult for them to know. It is difficult to find any theory which will account for the occurrence."

KEITH'S VISIT WITH GRANDPA

Deda Binton

MY GRANDFATHER HAD BEEN A SONAR TECHNICIAN ON A World War II submarine that had been hit by a Japanese depth charge. Rather than be taken prisoner, he elected to go down with the boat.

My father had been a small boy when this happened and was unable to answer any of my burning questions about my grandfather. Although I would never know him, I felt a close kinship with this long-dead man. In fact, he was the reason that although I was a young nineteen year old from a little town called Redwood, Missouri, I had always dreamed of becoming a sonar technician on a submarine.

I joined the navy right out of high school and became a section head of the sonar team.

One night in 1978, while the boat was undergoing sea trials, I found myself shorthanded and was forced to work a double shift. When my relief finally arrived I staggered to bed, exhausted.

I had barely closed my eyes when I was shaken awake by a strange Chief. "Get out of bed, you lazy young whelp," he ordered, "before this boat blows up!"

Not understanding what was going on, I nevertheless jumped up and followed him. Then I realized he was heading for the torpedo section.

"I'm a sonar tech," I protested, thinking he had meant to get someone else.

But without turning around he barked, "You had to qualify in all sections in order to earn your dolphins. Right?" The "dolphins" was a pin given to those who qualify in every area of the boat and who can call themselves submariners.

"Well, yeah," I answered, still very confused.

"Now get to work and stop spouting off, we don't have much time." He pointed to a torpedo tube.

I obeyed and found a defective mechanism that would have caused a torpedo to explode.

Just then, one of the boat's Chiefs and two technicians came bursting into the area while I was still examining the mechanism.

"How did you know about that?" the Chief asked. "The alarm just went off."

I turned and pointed to the strange Chief, only to find him gone. But to my relief no one was interested in who the man was, just thankful our boat was saved.

Later when I visited my parents, I discovered that my grandmother had moved in with them. While talking with her I picked up a picture she had on her dresser. As I stared in shock, she said, "That's your grandfather, Keith Sr."

"Oh," I said, but couldn't put the picture down, for this was the Chief who ordered me to the torpedo room and saved not only my life but the boat as well.

There is no doubt in my mind it was my grandfather who came from his watery grave to save me from a similar fate.

THE PHANTOM AT PLESKAU AIRFIELD

Bernard-George Meitzel

LTHOUGH I WAS A NEWCOMER IN THE INTERNMENT CAMP, THE colonel in the threadbare uniform of a general staff officer didn't object to me crowding into his "sunny corner," as he called the place. It was at the far end of the camp where some vacant huts in a rectangle formed a kind of windscreen.

I was too tired to walk or to talk or to think, and too hungry to sleep, so I looked over the colonel's shoulder into the book he was reading.

"You haven't anything to read?"

"Sorry, no."

"Well, let's share this story, if you like. It's H. G. Wells' *Men Like Gods*. Do you like Wells?"

I said I did and he halved the worn book and gave me the part he had finished.

Next day, we shared our cigarettes and our ration of black bread . . . that is to say, he got my cigarettes as I am a non-smoker, and I got part of his bread.

The third day he told me his story.

It happened in 1942. The colonel—at that time commanding officer of a reconnaissance battalion—was advancing toward Demjansk to relieve the German garrison which had been surrounded by Russian troops for more than three months.

In Kobylkina, two corporals from C Company arrived at the battalion headquarters bringing with them a civilian with a flattened nose and slanting eyes. The report accompanying them was brief:

"The civilian was taken prisoner in the suburbs of Kobylkina when he was found in possession of a gun. No identity card. No other military equipment. Doesn't understand Russian."

When he was led into the room you could see that he was in great fright, expecting something dreadful. His civilian clothes were worn out and ragged.

The colonel put his questions in Russian first.

"Nix Russian," the prisoner replied.

The colonel repeated his questions in German.

"Nix German."

More questions, threats, all the tricks usually applied to unmask malingerers and deceivers brought the same result.

"Nix Russian. Nix German."

"What sort of a guy was he?" asked the colonel. "An agent of the irregulars? Or had he just picked up one of the guns thrown away by the retreating Russians to barter it for some food and tobacco? I pitied the fellow and racked my brains for a solution to the problem. But as my interpreter knew only Czech and Russian, and the rest of us only German, we could get nothing from the prisoner.

"What was I to do? We were pressed for time and I had to come to a decision at once. We couldn't take him with us. As a potential guerrilla in the rear of my battalion, he couldn't be set free either. Before the operation commenced I had received explicit instructions. I was responsible for a continuous advance and for the continuity of the entire operation.

"I gave the prisoner a piece of bread, a glass of vodka, and a cigarette—and made a sign to the adjutant.

"Afterward, I was told he had kept shouting at the top of his voice:
'Nix German, Nix Russian,' with which he probably tried to express
quite different things, but lacked the words to make himself understood. Then he had stopped shouting and lowered his head to wait
for the deadly bullets.

"When I heard about the execution I was struck with compunc-
tion. Perhaps I should have set him free after all? Perhaps it wouldn't
have been a dereliction of duty? But it was too late then.

"For more than a year, I never thought of the poor chap again, nor
dreamed of him either. Then, in 1943, I had to report myself at Army
H.Q. in Pleskau. Using a courier plane, I alighted on the Pleskau airfield just in time to get an armored car that was on the point of leaving
the airfield for Pleskau.

" 'I'm in a hurry,' said the driver, 'please get in.'

"But just when I stooped to follow the urging driver I discovered a
civilian on the far side of the road, waving to me. I stopped short and
his gestures became more pressing. Though I couldn't hear a sound
over the noise of the car engine, I thought he was shouting something
to me. Ignoring the muttering driver, I went around the armored car
to catch the words the waving man was shouting. From the other
side of the car, I could suddenly make out the face of the civilian, the
flattened nose, slanting eyes. Yes, it was the prisoner of Kobylkina
whom I had ordered killed.

"There was cold sweat on my brow when I entered the control
booth into which he had disappeared. It was pitch-dark in there. I
struck a match only to discover that it was a bare room, empty, and
there was only one door.

"Leaving the booth, I asked a passing soldier:

" 'Did you see a civilian enter that booth?'

" 'No, sir. No civilians are allowed on the airfield, sir.'

"I was completely taken aback and didn't know what to do. As I started to return to the armored car, an ambulance raced past. And when I looked for the armored car, it was gone. A few minutes later the ambulance returned. As he passed me the driver shouted to a medical officer just behind me: 'Dead. All of 'em.'

"I faltered out: 'The car that left the airfield five minutes ago?'

" 'The very same.'

"That happened in 1943. Since then, I've kept asking myself why did it happen? Why was I saved by a man whose execution I had ordered? Was he sent by my guardian angel? Was he my guardian angel? Why was my life spared at all? To get another chance in life? To try to prevent a recurrence of the madness of the last war?

"I don't know the answer yet. But after spending three years in this internment camp I am about to believe that I was only spared to meet a more dreadful fate. Who knows when they are going to turn me over to the Russians or to the Jugoslavs?"

The colonel looked at the sun and his eyes squinted in thought. He inhaled deeply the smoke of the cigarette I had offered him. Then he resumed his reading of *Men Like Gods* and obviously found consolation in Wells' Utopia.

When I got to the sunny corner next day to meet the colonel, I found the place empty. I turned back to his hut to inquire about him and was told by his roommates that he had left the camp under guard the previous night. Nobody knew where he had been transferred.

"To a Soviet concentration camp?" I asked myself on my way to his deserted sunny corner. "To meet an even more dreadful fate?"

STRANGE VISION

Pearl E. Ullrich

BOB WAS A NEIGHBOR BOY WHO ENLISTED IN THE MARINES IN June 1943. He was trained as a communications man and co-pilot of an amphibious tank in the 2nd Marines Division. He was shipped across to Hawaii in May 1944 and from there went by way of the Marshalls to Saipan.

After he left the Marshalls, his parents heard nothing from him for about six weeks. His mother was wild with anxiety and fear, for Bob had last written: "We are getting ready for something big." Meanwhile the Battle of Saipan had been fought and still no word from Bob.

One morning I stood looking across our yard and garden toward our neighbor's mailbox thinking "how grand everything would be here this day if only Bob's mother could get a letter." And I prayed, "Oh God, let her get a letter."

As if in answer to my prayer, there stood Bob, right near the mail-box, dressed in his marine uniform and cap, with his hands straight down at his sides. He and his uniform and cap appeared pale in color and fuzzy in outline. He neither moved nor spoke.

Yet his mind spoke to me just as clearly as though he had spoken the words aloud. This was his message—that he wanted his mother to get the letters he had already written because he could not write anymore.

After Bob stood there for a minute or two impressing his thought on my mind, his "body" started to rise. It stretched out longer and thinner—not straight into the sky, but at an angle of perhaps 30° from the vertical. When the head and shoulders were perhaps 10 feet above where they had been at first they suddenly turned into (or went into) a bright shaft of light, like a very large electrical bolt. The balance of the figure followed the head and shoulders into the light and disappeared.

The bolt appeared about three feet long and four or five inches in diameter. The queer thing was the sparks of blue and green light that appeared to radiate from the lower edge of the three-foot length of the bolt, and the yellow and red sparks that came from the upper end.

That was the end of the vision and I was standing, as I had been, looking across the yard and garden at the mailbox.

Bob's last two letters came that very day, July 3, and had been written June 9 and 11. On September 8 came a "missing in action" telegram, followed 10 days later by a letter adding, "At Saipan, June 15." He has since been declared "officially" dead.

✼✦✧✦✼

UNOFFICIAL NOTIFICATION

Violet Mack

✼✦✧✦✼

DURING THE LAST WAR I WAS LIVING IN LONDON AND MY HUS-band was serving in France with the British infantry. Not receiving any mail from him for several days had made me quite uneasy.

One night as I lay sleepless in bed the figure of my husband suddenly appeared to me. He was wearing army battle dress. He sat on the end of my bed resting his head in his hands. I lay there too startled to move and he looked at me sadly. He said very distinctly, "Oh dear, oh dear!" and disappeared.

The next morning, filled with foreboding, I went to the Foreign Office in Whitehall where official casualty records at that time were kept. I asked one of the clerks if they had any news of my husband and gave him his name and number.

I watched the clerk eye the column of casualty figures from the previous day's fighting. Suddenly his finger stopped halfway down the column and he looked at me with sympathy in his eyes.

Yes, my husband's name was on that list—"killed in action." The British Government would have notified me the next day but my husband chose to come back from the great unknown to communicate with me himself.

LIGHT IN THE NIGHT

Brenda E. Payne

IN MAY 1944 I WAS STATIONED AT A ROYAL AIR FORCE CAMP IN Northwood, Middlesex, England. I was a Women's Auxiliary Air Force teleprinter operator and worked in a signal section which was manned 24 hours a day. My station, for safety and security reasons, was three flights of stairs beneath ground surface.

During night watches, at 3:00 A.M. the activity on the teleprinters would get very slow and we were permitted to go to another room to rest for two hours, leaving half staff to take care of the machines.

The resting room was small and three walls were lined with three-tier bunks. Because it was below ground, the room had no natural light.

One night I lay for the longest time but sleep would not come. Everyone else was sleeping. I could hear the sounds of even breathing against the silence and darkness of the room.

Resigning myself to insomnia, I opened my eyes and stared into the darkness. I was not prepared for what I saw.

Over in the corner of the room was a white filmy "light" which became larger and brighter as I watched, moving along to one particular bunk bed. I stared in disbelief and pinched myself to make sure I was awake.

This continued for quite a few minutes. Then the door burst open and we were called back to duty. I rose from my bunk and looked to see which woman had occupied the one I had seen "visited." It was Margaret Sisson. I decided not to tell her; I did not wish to frighten her.

One evening soon afterwards I saw Margaret in tears. Her fiance, an RAF pilot, was missing and presumed killed. It happened on the night I saw the filmy visitor go to her bunk.

D-Day Echoes in England

John Murphy

O**N A HAZY SUNDAY MORNING IN MAY 1976, AS I WAS WALKING** the dog, I had the strangest experience of my life. It happened as I was standing in a public gardens in Portland, Dorset, England, enjoying the unused air of a new day and looking down onto a now deserted road that had carried many thousands of American troops to a D-Day embarkation point in 1944.

It was 6:30 A.M. and quiet, but suddenly I began to sense clamor and frantic activity screaming out in the silence. Then I saw tanks and lorries halted temporarily in the way they did when United States army road convoys lined up in front of the docks. GIs dressed in olive drab lounged against the waiting vehicles. There were small tents on the grassy area beside the road. Soldiers stood outside them drinking coffee from huge mugs. As I stood there doubting my own sanity, I could hear the raucous shouts and laughter of the servicemen.

The scene ended as abruptly as it had begun and I was alone again with just a shaking, disturbed-looking dog for company. I immediately went home and—choosing my words carefully, in case she thought I'd come off my spool—I told my wife Doreen what I had witnessed. She suggested—and I agreed with her—that I had imagined the scene because I had spent the past several months doing research for a book I was writing about the buildup of American forces in our area just prior to the Normandy invasion.

But in my own mind I was not completely satisfied with that explanation. So the following Sunday morning I went back there with the dog. This time I took a tape recorder with me. Switching it on, I sat and listened to a host of birds chirruping a welcome to spring. I neither saw nor heard anything unusual that morning and at breakfast Doreen and I listened with disappointment to a faithful reproduction of the feathered chorus.

Then, with a click that sounded like a switch, the birds were silent and we sat stunned as the throb of heavy motors roared from the recorder. These were joined by the unmistakable creaking of tank tracks, then an occasional buzz of a lighter, faster vehicle, which I recognized as a jeep dashing past a road convoy.

From among this mixture of noises came a loud human whistle, followed by an American-accented voice shouting, "Now here we go!" The sound of motors and the metallic groan of tank tracks continued for some minutes and we quickly called our only other available witness—our teenage daughter Theresa. She heard the motor noises, the whistle and the shout without any prompting from us.

Several replays later the voice faded. The whistle was next to go but we still had enough tank and truck noises left to baffle the local priest. Then these sounds too vanished from the tape.

In May 1977 I returned to the spot every Sunday morning with my tape recorder but I saw, heard and recorded nothing out of the ordinary.

Her Soldier Came Back

Felipa Errecart

ONE NIGHT IN DECEMBER 1944, I STAYED OVERNIGHT WITH MY best friend Irene. Sympathetically I listened to her whispered memories of her sweetheart who had been killed two months before by a sniper's bullet in the Phillippines.

She told me that the day he was killed she had cried all day long and hadn't known why. The telegram from the War Department hadn't arrived for many days.

I too had a strange memory. On the day she received the fateful telegram I was taking a bath. I stopped drying myself suddenly for I knew that something very sad or terrible had happened to someone I knew. Later I found out how right I had been.

Irene and I finally fell asleep.

Much later I awoke, feeling a peculiar grogginess. I blinked my eyes and, as through a mist, saw a soldier open the door, skirt my bed, walk around Irene's bed and bend over her.

"I must be dreaming," I thought, never having believed in ghosts.

I dimly saw the soldier repass my bed, but I couldn't utter a sound. I couldn't even think clearly.

Irene suddenly gasped, "Felipa! Felipa! Did you see someone?"

I wanted to be sure that we weren't imagining things, so I didn't admit I had seen Joe.

"I saw a soldier!" she said. Then she jumped out of bed and ran through the now open door. I heard her speaking to her mother.

"I know I closed the door. We've never had trouble with the door," she said excitedly.

Then I told her gently, "I saw him. I'm sure it must have been your Joe."

Joe did come back but he wasn't alive.

THE SIGN OF THE
FLAMING HEATHER

Comtesse Madeleine de La Rivière

EARLY IN 1944 DURING "HITLER'S WAR" AND AFTER THE DEFEAT
and invasion of France, a lady, Madame Marguerite, in a castle in Bruz in Brittany had a strange visitor.

She must have dropped off to sleep, in tears and sorrow as always
in those days. Since 1940, for almost four years, when arrogant Nazi
conquerors had invaded her castle as well as the soil of France and
the shores of Brittany, she had been forced to hand over all her possessions, the land, the castle itself, to their dominance. She lived like a
servant, half in hiding, in a tiny old building at the edge of the estate
park with her little son and one aged faithful servant. Half-tolerated,
half-despised, always hiding her face, Madame Marguerite held to
her indomitable instinct, set her teeth and stayed on, braved it out
and refused to become a fugitive. Under any circumstances she was
determined to remain on the ancestral land.

She had no aid, no defender, for her husband, a descendant of the
Seigneurs de Bruz, had disappeared without a trace during those first
nightmare battles four years before when France was overrun by the
enemy. Madame Marguerite had no way of knowing whether he was
dead, a captive, or fighting for France and a dream of victory with the

underground or with comrades and allies overseas. She had no word of him from any source.

Madame Marguerite's husband, who inherited the old castle that is part of this story, proudly boasted a distant kinship with The Bruces or, as they said, with the *Seigneurs de Bruz*. They possessed two proofs of this kinship. Within the castle hung a painting of one of the ancestral *Seigneurs de Bruz*. This portrait showed a man with flaming hair and a craggy chin and tradition gave him a fiery temper as well. Second proof was the garden, for apparently some of the valiant fighters named "Robert" were, in their peaceful moments, tender lovers and great gardeners. One *Seigneur de Bruz* was said to have transplanted, with his own hands and using his sword for a spade, wild heather for his ladylove. And even centuries afterwards, in the 1940s before the occupation, each year the heather bloomed there, tended by reverent hands.

There is an age-long and fierce competition still going on between the French towns of Bruis in Normandy and Bruz in Brittany for the honor of being the birthplace of the famous family called *de Bruc* or *de Bruys*—known in Scotland as "The Bruce."

Any student of history will tell you that Robert the First was a *Compagnon* of William, Duke of Normandy, Conqueror of England, and that for his valiant championship during the conquest this first Robert was given a generous estate in conquered Yorkshire. Robert apparently was a family name with them for the eighth generation of that name was the most famous of them all, "The Bruce," Robert I, King of Scotland.

So it is understandable that both Normandy and Brittany fight for the honor of being his place of origin—Bruis has solid parchments to support its claim; Bruz had a castle, a portrait, and a garden where wild heather grew and bloomed.

It is necessary to remember also that tradition says the coats of arms of both Robert The Bruce of Scotland and the city of Bruz bore the same lovely emblem, a sprig of wild heather—the same heather that grew in the garden Madame Marguerite had been forced to abandon to the German invaders.

It is understandable also that Madame Marguerite felt she and her small son alone remained to uphold the honor of this proud family and so with courage borrowed from her husband's ancestors they remained on the ancestral land.

On this night in 1944, as on many previous nights, Madame Marguerite had kissed her little son good-night, bid the old servant be watchful, and then sat alone watching a pitifully small flickering fire slowly die. And perhaps she dozed as she sat staring into the flames wondering about her husband's fate.

At any rate she suddenly started up, knowing she was no longer alone.

A tall broad-shouldered warrior dressed in armor leaned on his sword before her, watching her. She recognized the figure from the castle portrait and she was not afraid. On the contrary, to the bereft lonely woman his forceful presence brought great comfort and support.

"These are terrible times, Messire Robert," she said, quite naturally as if speaking to a relative and an old friend.

"They are indeed, Dame Marguerite," he replied gravely. "The enemy is within the castle walls. Yet do not be afraid; it is not for long. Aye, soon he will be completely overthrown.

"I have come to warn you," continued the shadowy warrior, "for when this will come to pass, there will be great devastation here. So when you see my sign, quickly gather up your beloved and flee, for destruction is near."

"What sign will you give us, Messire Robert?" asked the lady.

"The sign of The Bruce," was the sonorous answer, "will be the sign of the heather."

The fire flickered and went out. Madame Marguerite choked back a cry and groped for a candle. But when she had succeeded in lighting it with trembling fingers she was alone as she had known she would be. There was no trace of her ancestral visitor.

The brave woman kept the secret locked closely in her breast; yet from that time on she waited hopefully for the sign of The Bruce.

Festung Europa, the fortification, as Hitler boastfully had called Europe, was already surrounded by enemies who now were preparing the last great effort—to be known ever after as D-Day.

The Allied bombardments grew daily heavier and nearer.

Madame Marguerite watched and waited. ·

Then one morning in the first week of May when she went out into the park, early as ever, she was seized by an irresistible impulse. Both fearing and despising the Germans, she had kept away from the castle and the garden as much as she could, but today she walked straight to the ancestral garden. There her eyes were struck by the sight of flaming heather. The Bruce's bushes were in bloom.

The hour was about to strike!

Without losing one second Marguerite walked back to her tiny refuge, and bade her servant prepare herself and her son at once. She gathered up her few remaining belongings, and on foot, a stout stick in her hand, like a pilgrim of old she led her small band to the cathedral city of Rennes, which they reached at sundown. There she applied for refuge in a convent and the good sisters, accustomed by now to seeing weary refugees arrive, took them in.

That very night the city of Bruz was attacked by Allied bombers and almost completely smashed to ruins. It was said that the bombardment was so intense, the flames so high, that my own mother-in-law, in our castle of La Rivière, 30 miles away, was awakened "as if by a terrible earthquake" and saw "that the sky was so red it appeared like a second sunrise."

The proud German officers who had made the conquered castle their home and boasted they would remain forever found their death in its flaming ruins. And after another year of bitter fighting, at last in 1945, World War II came to an end in Europe.

Although now a homeless refugee, Madame Marguerite was happy at last, for among those returning to liberate France was her own husband. And together they have bravely picked up the pieces of their former life and started anew.

The town of Bruz is now rebuilt. Bright new houses line broad streets. The rubble and ruin of old dwellings has been smoothed over and forgotten. The modern church there was planned and built by Canadian contributions, for many sons of Brittany have emigrated to these distant shores.

The castle of the *Seigneurs de Bruz* is counted among the victims of the last war. Ivy now covers what remains of its walls. Gone forever is the portrait of the midnight visitor, the ancestor who came back to sustain and to warn a lonely woman.

Yet, although the forest now claims the garden for its own, the sprig of heather of Robert The Bruce still blooms on the coat of arms of Bruz.

The Galloping Colonel

Rajendra Pathak

I N 1944 MY FATHER WAS POSTED TO THE LARGE GARRISON STA-tioned in the small town of Landsdowne in northern India. From him I learned the strange story of the colonel who first had commanded the garrison. He had been a good polo player and died during a match when his neck was broken in a fall.

A few months after his death the soldiers on guard duty reported having seen the colonel during the night. They were so convinced of his reality that they saluted him. Over a period of time most of the soldiers standing night guard had seen him.

It was always the same. Just after midnight the clattering of hooves would sound and the colonel and his horse would be seen galloping around the polo field. (The guard post commanded a full view of the field.) After a few rounds of the field he would gallop toward the guardhouse end of the field, which overlooked a steep hillside. Here the colonel would continue at breakneck pace over the crest and down the hill. The soldiers always said the sound of the horse sliding downhill was heard clearly.

The officers didn't pay much attention to the troops' stories until the death of a soldier brought things to a head. His mates said he had challenged the colonel during his tour of night duty. The strange thing was that he died suddenly in the morning after coughing up blood. He was known to be healthy and the doctors could find no explanation for his strange death.

The officer ordered to investigate the matter decided to take the bull by the horns. Hiding himself in the guardhouse with the regular guard, he waited. Around midnight came the usual clattering hooves, the circuits of the polo field, and then the sound of the horse approaching.

The officer leaped out, drew his pistol and challenged the intruder to halt. The soldiers who witnessed what followed said the colonel (or his spirit) wheeled his horse and charged the officer. Even bullets didn't stop his onrush. The man on the ground was struck down by the charging horse. The colonel wheeled again and continued pell-mell down the hillside. Every soldier gave the same account.

The soldiers ran to the aid of the officer and found him uninjured but his face was contorted and he seemed in shock. A few hours later, without having spoken a word, he began to cough up blood and soon died.

This time no inquiry was held. After that no soldier in the garrison ever failed to salute—instead of challenging—the galloping colonel.

My Soldier Returned

Joyce DeMerrell

O N NOVEMBER 4, 1944, MATT, MY SOLDIER-HUSBAND LEFT Camp Gruber, Oklahoma, for overseas with the Rainbow Division.

I decided to go to West Virginia to stay with Matt's family at their homestead, which was over 100 years old.

They greeted me warmly and through the severe winter I was content to be where Matt had been born, played as a boy, and lived as a grown man.

I slept in his birth-bed in a room with a big stone fireplace. Every dusk a roaring wood fire would be built in the grate, and chunks of coal laid on. The fire would burn all night with a few rosy coals left when I awoke in the morning.

The war was going badly, and Matt's letters were filled with a longing to be with me. I received one on January 16 that told of preparations for a severe battle.

I thought constantly of my husband, and after going to bed on the night of January 18, I prayed for a long time. Then I drifted off to sleep watching the high flames dancing up the chimney.

Suddenly a feeling of being very cold awoke me. I sat up in bed. Matt was standing near me, his face looking tired and sad in the red glow of the fire. He stared at me intently, leaned over, and taking my hand, he gently removed my wedding ring. I'll always remember how cold his hands were.

Then he vanished.

I looked at the fire. It was very low. It was almost morning. I burrowed under the quilts until I heard the others stirring. Then I hurried out and told them my "dream."

Matt's aunt looked at me strangely. "Dream," she repeated. "No, Matt is dead!"

We went to the bedroom and found my wedding ring under the pillow.

On February 7, my 30th birthday, a telegram arrived from the War Department. Matt had been killed on January 18.

My husband had "come home to me" on January 19.

There is a time lapse of six hours between France and West Virginia.

DEAD SOLDIER ON SENTRY DUTY?

Mercedes Colon

ONE NIGHT IN APRIL 1945 JAY F. RIVERA, THEN A PFC IN THE United States infantry, had an unnerving experience he has been unable to explain to this day. Three days' fighting it had taken to wrest the small sheep town of Amasdorf on the west bank of the Elbe River from the defending Germans. Once the town had been captured Supreme Allied Headquarters sent word that the American troops were to remain there two weeks to await a linkup with the Russian troops.

The small, rather primitive town was much like other European villages with its stone buildings, muddy streets, and encircling trees and shrubbery. A command post was set up in a deserted building in the town and guards were posted at various strategic outposts during the nights. One such outpost was 500 yards from the edge of town and consisted of protective camouflage of clumps of shrubbery and a few logs against a background of trees. On an April night Rivera and his buddy PFC Richard O'Leary were assigned to midnight guard duty at this outpost.

The night was moonless, cool and damp; the sky was dark over the wide, empty terrain. Somber trees behind the pair swayed silently and in seeming rhythm. While there was some element of danger still, guard duty with nothing to do but sit and watch for two hours was extremely dull for young men of 19. They were accustomed to more action.

After 30 minutes O'Leary, no longer able to stand the inactivity, said to Jay, "Say, listen, everything seems pretty much under control. You don't mind if I skip out for a few minutes, do you? If I don't have some coffee I won't be able to stay awake the whole two hours. I'll be right back."

Although it was against orders to leave one's post during guard, Jay assured him it was perfectly all right and he could cover alone. O'Leary disappeared into the trees going toward the town. Once alone, Jay leaned on his 30-caliber machine gun and gazed over the wide expanse, more alert now that he was covering for two. After about five minutes he heard from somewhere behind him a rustling and the sound of light footsteps. Expecting to see O'Leary returning, he turned quickly and was amazed to see PFC Michael Prettyboy, a tall blond soldier from the Second Platoon. The visitor was helmeted and with both hands held his rifle against his chest. He gave Jay a smile and squatted down beside him, laying his rifle carefully on the ground.

"What are you doing here?" whispered Jay, startled.

"I couldn't sleep," whispered Michael, "so I thought I'd take a walk." He relaxed his body against one of the logs and stretched his legs as if he were visiting someone's living room.

"That's a pretty dangerous thing to do," cautioned Jay. "Anybody could pick you off in the dark."

Prettyboy shrugged his shoulders and looked around.

"How come you're on guard alone?"

"I'm not," Jay answered. "O'Leary's with me. He'll be right back."

For the next few minutes the two young men talked about the day's action. They spoke about a tank that had taken a direct hit but kept moving to the rear under its own power with two mortally wounded soldiers sprawled on the top.

"It was a big loss just to capture a hole like this," Jay remarked in disgust.

Michael nodded sadly, his eyes downcast. Suddenly he picked up his rifle and jumped up. "I'll see you, Jay. I'm supposed to be resting and I go on guard in another hour."

"Be careful," admonished Rivera. "Stay in the shadows. You don't want to be mistaken for the enemy." Michael Prettyboy disappeared as abruptly as he had appeared.

Shortly thereafter O'Leary returned and they remained on duty until relieved at 2:00 A.M.

About eight the next morning members of Rivera's platoon were gathered about the chow truck discussing a burst of gunfire they had heard during the night. Investigation showed that one of the GIs had fired into the trees. He insisted he had seen someone playing hide-and-seek among the trees. When the figure stood momentarily in an opening and lifted his rifle, the GI had opened fire. No one was found afterwards but the soldier insisted over and over it was not just his imagination.

Jay immediately thought of his unexpected visitor during the night. "You know," he said, "it could've been Michael Prettyboy. He came over to talk with me for a while when I was on guard last night. Said he couldn't sleep. I warned him to be careful not to get shot by mistake."

An unexpected silence greeted Jay's words and some of the men exchanged questioning glances. Platoon leader Lieutenant Al van Detta, who stood by sipping coffee, then spoke in a somewhat incredulous voice. "Who did you say came to see you last night? Prettyboy?"

"Yes, sir," Jay answered, taken aback by the look on the lieutenant's face.

"Are you sure it was Prettyboy?" Lieutenant van Detta persisted.

"Of course, sir. I know him pretty well." Remembering that he had been alone at the time and fearful that O'Leary might get into trouble, he added, "Ask O'Leary."

"I don't have to ask O'Leary," retorted the platoon leader, shaking his head. "And I can tell you one thing. If you guys saw him then you must have been either drunk or dreaming. PFC Michael Prettyboy was killed in action yesterday about ten o'clock in the morning."

Jay Rivera took a while to accept the lieutenant's words. Had Jay been dreaming? Or had the fallen soldier actually visited him some 15 hours after he died?

MESSAGE IN VERSE

Rose Smith

I N 1945 I LIVED IN A SMALL ARIZONA TOWN. ONE DAY I ARRANGED TO take my ward, Betty, to the state capital the following morning. Because we were taking an early bus, she spent the night with me. About four o'clock in the morning, while it was still dark, I was waked by a voice directing me to turn on the light and get my pad and pencil. I sat up in bed and turned on the bedlamp. I saw my stepson, William, standing at the foot of my bed. He smiled at me and told me to write down what he was going to say. He called me "Mother," although previously he had used the word only in his letters. He could not remember his own mother and through the years had used pet names for me. However, he had called me his mother when speaking to others.

He stood waiting and smiling, dressed in a light-colored navy flier's uniform, without hat or coat. Filled with urgency to do as he directed, I had little time to reflect on the strangeness of his visit.

When I had paper and pencil ready he said:

> *"Don't bury me, Mother, when I am dead*
> *Beneath dark clods of weighty, pressing loam;*
> *No heavy lidded casket be my home.*
> *I want no one to weep, no one to sing,*
> *For mine, the bier of an ancient king.*

A Viking burial they'll give to me,
A great burning ship on the ocean wide,
Giant sails set with the out-going tide,
Deep waters below and the sky above—
For wishes come true at long last, my love!"

As he finished speaking, he moved backward into a thin mist and faded from sight. When he had vanished, Betty raised herself on one elbow and asked, "What are you doing? You look as if you'd seen a ghost."

"I have," I answered. "William is dead."

"What makes you say such a thing?"

"He was just here. Look at the message he gave me."

I trembled as I recalled an incident many years old. William had had difficulty in learning to read. At last he found a book of Norse fairy tales. Fascinated, he spent many hours reading them. One day he came to me and said, "Don't bury me when I'm dead. I want a Viking funeral."

I told Betty I was certain William's ship had burned and that he had been buried at sea. She went to the calendar, marked a circle around the date and said, "There, you can look at that in a few months and realize how silly you were to imagine a dream could be real."

It was May 11.

On May 28 a telegram came telling me William was dead. Later I received the information that he had been killed when Japanese suicide planes hit the deck of his ship, the *U.S.S. Bunker Hill,* setting it on fire. The ship did not sink—but William had his Viking burial.

RETURN FROM LOVE HILL

Edith Rose

ARD YEARS FOLLOWED THE DEATH OF MY FATHER TIMOTHY
Fitch on October 23, 1931, but the troubles of the Depression served to bring my brother Walter and me ever closer—although we were four years apart in age.

It was a blow to me when Walter was drafted in September 1943. He served with the 383rd Infantry at Camp Adair, Oregon, and ultimately became a staff sergeant. The last time we saw him alive was in June 1944 when he came home on a 30-day furlough before embarking for the Pacific Theater.

As he stood on the station platform waiting to board the train back to Camp Adair he turned to me and said softly, "I'll be back, Sis."

He fulfilled his promise on the morning of May 11, 1945. It was daybreak and I was still lying in bed, just about to get up. All at once the edge of my bed sank as if someone had sat down. A strong hand found mine and squeezed it tightly. It was over in an instant and just as silently as he had come he left. The mattress rose as he stood up. No doors opened or closed, no words were spoken—but I knew Walter had come to say good-bye.

The time this happened matched the time of his death in that bloody battle of Love Hill on Okinawa.

MOTHER'S DAY

Ada McCollum

IT WAS MOTHER'S DAY IN 1945. AS I WATERED THE FLOWERS GROWING near the patio wall of my home in El Monte, California, I noted that two red geraniums were the only flowers blooming in the yard. There were dead roses on the bushes but no new buds.

During that afternoon two bouquets, one of peonies and another of a dozen red roses, were delivered by messengers to me. These were sent by my two sons who were in the navy.

Of course, I thought of Ross, my other son who had been a bombardier in the Eighth Air Force. He had died over the English Channel in 1944. Ross had always been the first to go to the garden to gather a bouquet for me for Mother's Days in the past.

That night at 12:00 A.M. I was suddenly awakened. I opened my eyes to find Ross standing near my bed. He was dressed in his flight suit and helmet. I could see him plainly as the night light from the hall shone into the bedroom.

He was holding the two red geranium blossoms from my garden in his hand and I heard him say, "Sorry Mom, I'm late. These were the only flowers I could find. I did remember." He smiled sadly and then vanished.

Ross has come at other times also. I always know when I will see him, for the light on my night stand will blink off and on twice. Whenever he is near, the lights in any part of the house where I happen to be will blink on and off twice. I have tried to work the switch in this manner myself but it is impossible.

The next morning when I went into the garden I found the geraniums still there with their stems bent over.

I told Reverend Kingam, of our Spiritualist Church, of Ross's visit on Mother's Day. She said, "My mother too appeared to me with a bouquet of red geraniums."

KEEP MOVING

Marvin W. Goodman

❖❖

URING WORLD WAR II, WHEN I WAS STATIONED IN THE EUROPE-
an Theater of Operations in the quartermaster corps, I
could only attribute my preservation to the presence of
avatars who warned me of disasters of one kind or another. These
saints who walk the Earth are similar to guardian angels, except that
they show up for anyone who also walks their path.

War movies don't adequately display the perils caused by the
ignorance that surrounded soldiers in any operation. Confused
commands and orders often led to deaths from friendly fire. All too
often, orders were too late or non-existent or, worse, muddled. The
constant flow of rumors led to further confusion. The fluid enemy
front lines caused many inaccuracies in reporting enemy troop and
artillery placements. Why someone not connected with our small
unit (actually a detachment) would simply appear at the crucial time
can only be ascribed to avatars. They wore our uniform, but seemed
to have just the right advice. Looking for them later was futile. They
seemed to melt into the background from which they appeared.

One incident that occurred in 1945 involved the driver of a
tarpaulin-covered four-by-four truck and trailer and me. The driver
and I carried small carbine rifles. We were given a map of the Darm-
stadt area of Germany and dispatched to deliver supplies by ourselves.

It was a beautiful, clear day. On various roadsides, signs stated,

"This area is under enemy observation. Keep moving." However, that warning sign was missing from the road we traveled that day and as we approached the top of a hill, a GI appeared on the driver's side of the truck. He was seated on the ground just below the crest of the hill. His appearance so surprised us that we stopped for no reason other than surprise itself.

I believe it was my driver, PFC Cain, who yelled out, "Do you know if we are headed to the tank division of the Twelfth Army Group?" As units changed positions, the code and sign of that unit might be posted on trees and utility poles, but the signs were not reliable.

The GI remained seated and calmly said, "If you try to go over the top of that hill, you probably won't make it. There is a German 88 [an efficient German antitank cannon] blowing everything off of it."

I believe I was more shaken than Cain as I said, "Turn this thing around and get the hell out of here."

As my side of the truck swung around, I wanted to yell out a last "Thank you," but no one was in sight.

Two questions have been posed to me: Did the GI have a place to hide as you turned around? No. The undulating road ran through a field of grass. No bush or tree was near enough. Second: Some German soldiers dressed themselves in American uniforms to infiltrate our lines. Might this have been one? No. He could have captured us and the vehicle or shot us on the spot. We were unaccompanied. There was no one else around.

We All "Come Home"

Doris Bevan

I T WAS 1945. THE WAR AGAINST GERMANY HAD ENDED, AND ALTHOUGH my older brother Phil had been missing in action since October 1944, my parents were confident he would turn up as a prisoner of war.

Phil was a fighter pilot and last seen by his squadron members shortly before the group was scattered by heavy antiaircraft artillery during a dive-bombing mission to Landau, Germany. He was not observed being hit or crashing, so we felt sure he was alive.

His letters always had assured us that he would come home after the war. He loved his home and every chance he had, before he went overseas, he came home. Usually he'd just appear at the front door without warning. So, although we were concerned, we were more than hopeful that he would turn up among the many prisoners being released.

This particular evening in August or September 1945 my mother had gone out to visit a neighbor. Dad was in the living room listening to Jack Benny on the radio so it must have been a Sunday. I was washing the dinner dishes and smiling at Benny's quips. Suddenly I was seized with the feeling that Phil was standing outside the front door, mentally calling me to let him in.

It was a persistent and urgent mental message and it frightened me. At 16 I had never heard of psychic phenomena or any kind of communication other than written or verbal. But something told me that if I opened the door it would mean that my brother was not coming back to us in the flesh, that he was dead.

No matter how much I tried to resist the feeling that my brother was drawing me to that door, I couldn't. I began to cry softly, afraid my father would hear me. I didn't want him to think I had an overactive imagination, nor did I want him to know his son was dead.

Finally the urgency of the mental message was so strong I had no alternative. I walked quietly down the hall and opened the door at which my brother had so often stood when he came home on leave.

Immediately, I had an overwhelming sense of relief. I had responded to Phil's message and it was as though he, too, was relieved. Although I was sad that I would never see him again, I could sense that he was telling me that he did not really die and that he had fulfilled his promise to come back to us. He was at peace.

Shortly after that we received official notification from the War Department that Phil's body had been found buried in a Belgian cemetery.

Human grief is always painful, but that experience convinced me that death has no power over us. I know now we all "come home."

THE HAUNTED AIR BASE

Author Unknown

A NUMBER OF REPORTS OF GHOSTLY ACTIVITIES HAVE ISSUED recently from the Royal Air Force Station at Ouston near Stamfordhaven, England. The *Newcastle Journal* quotes an administrative officer at Ousten as saying: "These rumors exist at nearly all R.A.F. Stations where men have been killed at some time or another."

At Ousten, according to the reports, a door leading from the sick bay to a Roman Catholic Church often was found open, although it was securely locked each night and the key placed in another building. Sick bay attendants have reported that on several occasions lights have been switched on and off with nobody near the switch, or even present in the room.

Airmen billeted near the sick bay state that they have been waked at night by mysterious noises and footsteps. They ascribe the manifestations to a flying officer who was killed near the billets during World War II.

Ghost Army of the Rising Sun

Bob Dunham

HER VOICE TREMBLING IN FEAR, AN OBVIOUSLY DISTRAUGHT woman called the offices of the *Mainichi Daily News,* one of Japan's largest newspapers, one day in the summer of 1979. She told a fantastic story: she had just seen Japanese soldiers, dressed in World War II uniforms, in the compounds of the Inari Shrine in Tokyo's Shinagawa district.

Mrs. Ikeda, the 46-year-old proprietress of a local restaurant, said that on her way home from work she was taking a shortcut through the dark compounds of the famous Inari Shrine when she saw soldiers coming toward her. "They quickly vanished into thin air," she claimed. "All of them were wearing combat uniforms and had Rising Sun flags and rifles in their hands!"

The terrified woman added, "I screamed at a man passing by but he ignored my pleas and ran off into the night."

Several minutes after the woman called the newspaper, an unidentified man dialed 110, Tokyo's police hotline, from a public telephone booth which was later traced to a location near the Inari Shrine. The caller breathlessly related, "There are some Japanese soldiers walking around in the compounds of the shrine. No, I am not drunk . . . I am positive they're Japanese Imperial Army soldiers. I should know—I was in the army once." Then he hung up abruptly.

The Inari Shrine was a place where young soldiers who were

being ordered overseas gathered for a rousing send-off and then final prayers at the altar.

If they were killed in action their souls were said to return to yet another noted shrine in Tokyo—Yasukuni, the place where all Japanese war heroes are enshrined and worshiped for their courageous acts in battle.

Several days later when one of the caretakers of Inari Shrine was starting his summer cleanup, he found a World War II–era army bayonet inside one of the stone lanterns. Scoffers suggested it was hidden there by some lonely soldier many years ago. But that seems unlikely because there wasn't a speck of rust on it!

THE RESTLESS DEAD OF LONDON

Lorna Gulston

I T WAS THE UNIFORM I NOTICED FIRST. PERHAPS BECAUSE I SERVED as an officer in the Women's Royal Army Corps in the 1950s and '60s, uniforms always catch my eye. The girl on the platform at London's Charing Cross Underground Station that October evening in 1979 wore the smart khaki service dress and forage cap of the wartime Auxiliary Territorial Service, complete with gas respirator slung from her shoulder.

The WRAC discarded khaki decades ago in favor of a chic lovat-green jacket and skirt, so this girl's appearance was unusual, to say the least. She was a well-turned-out soldier, brasses gleaming, brown brogues polished to glassy brilliance, dark hair trimmed to the regulation inch above her collar. An actress, I assumed, homeward bound from filming some TV drama set in the 1940s. Her wardrobe department had done a fine job, I thought.

I didn't like to stare but I couldn't help stealing sideways glances at her. She looked to be in her early 20s, slim, a little above medium height, pale-faced and pretty. She stood motionless, her right hand gripping her respirator strap, gazing straight ahead as if lost in thought. There were few people about—it was after all only half an hour before midnight—and none of them seemed to share my curiosity or acknowledge the presence of someone out of the ordinary. That didn't surprise me. Londoners are more blasé about the sight of oddly clad theatrical folk than a fascinated visitor from Belfast like me.

In a few minutes I heard the rumble of the tube train and the hiss of its air brakes as it slowed for the station. As it glided alongside the platform, the ATS girl moved forward and, to my shocked disbelief, walked through its still-closed doors. The train traveled 15 or 20 feet before stopping and the compartment the figure had entered came directly opposite me. When the doors slid open I dashed inside, scanning every seat. A snoring drunk and a giggling teenage couple were the only occupants. Bewildered, I asked the couple if they had seen a young woman in khaki enter the car. They blinked at me, shook their heads and giggled harder than ever. My journey took me to the end of the line. I watched at every stop. No ATS girl left the train.

I shied away from accepting that I had seen a ghost; yet it was the only logical explanation. Many servicemen and women were killed in the London blitz. There were casualties, too, among antiaircraft and searchlight batteries where all but the gunners were ATS personnel. Could this have been one of them reenacting her last journey through the blacked-out city?

I Think There's a Ghost Here That Likes Me

Marge Desormeaux

MY HUSBAND DESI AND I WERE VOLUNTEERS ON THE U.S.S. *Lexington* Aircraft Carrier Museum that is permanently aground on North Beach in the city of Corpus Christi, Texas. We volunteered our time between giving tours and working with schoolchildren teaching Simple Machines, a hands-on workshop. When special groups came aboard at night for a gala dinner dance, we were there as a welcome committee or crowd control or whatever they had us do to help the staff of the World War II carrier.

One very windy night, we walked up the long gangplank to enter through the quarterdeck. As we stepped into the brightly lit area, Desi looked at me and commented that my new name tag was gone. I had just made us some temporary name tags while we awaited our special volunteer tags that were being made up for us. The wind was so strong that night, we figured that the tag must have blown off to be forever lost in the waters of Corpus Christi Bay.

We did our volunteer work that night, which was mainly crowd control for several hundred teenagers attending a Christian music concert. We left late, only to return the next day when we again did some work—Desi with tours and I with a junior high school group.

We reenacted a war-time tragedy in which a Japanese plane dropped a torpedo that struck the rudder of the ship and also blew a hole in its side large enough for a Jeep to drive through. Using the old ship phones and a script, we reenacted the phone dialog between officers and crew.

It was late in the day when we checked in again with the volunteer coordinator, who asked us, if we again planned to be on board two days in a row, whether we knew that there were quarters available for us to use overnight. Since we did not know of this offer beforehand, we showed some surprise, and Tami, our coordinator, offered to show us the quarters.

Taking a key from her desk drawer, she led us down to the deck below, one that neither of us had visited before. Unlocking a door and turning on a light, we stepped into a comfortable-looking room with adjoining "head" (bathroom). She then led us out and down the passageway to the next room. As we stepped into the second room, we saw a chair in the middle of the room. I stepped up to the chair when I noticed something lying on its seat. It was my name tag!

All of us experienced the hair raising on the back of our necks then. Did the regular ghost of a young sailor bring back my name tag? How else did it get there?

The *Lexington* has its share of ghost stories. The most common story is that of a tall, very blond and blue-eyed sailor who roams the ship and talks with the visitors, sharing information and answering questions. This attractive and amiable young sailor is dressed in his white uniform. Many visitors have asked the staff about him after talking with him. But there is no such person on board the ship to help with tours.

Many of the staff have also sighted someone just ahead of them walking the passageways where no one but staff are allowed, but when they try to catch up to the person, he mysteriously disappears. A volunteer friend of ours has related a time when someone tapped him on the shoulder, and when he turned around, there was no one there.

Whether it was the blond sailor or another of the ship's ghosts who found my tag, I can't say. At least 35 men died aboard that ship during World War II. I believe one of them was very helpful to me.

THE GHOST THAT HATED HITLER

Charlotte Richards

THE HOUSE AT NO. 2 MUNGELTERWEG WAS JUST AN ORDINARY house—or so it seemed at first. It wasn't even old, as houses go, having been built only a few years before World War II. An imposing structure of cream-colored stucco, it was located on a quiet street in Speicher, a picturesque farm village in the state of Rheinland-Pfalz, not far from the borders of France, Belgium, and Luxembourg.

I first saw the house in November 1964. My husband, Fred, who was in the United States Air Force, had left Arizona in September, having been assigned to Spangdahlem Air Base, an American fighter base a few miles from Speicher. Because of an acute housing shortage in the Spangdahlem area, I stayed behind with our five children until Fred could find off-base quarters and send for us.

After much searching, he found the house at No. 2 Mungelterweg and what a lucky find it was! The rent was only $100 a month for a huge three-story dwelling with plenty of room for the children (who ranged in age from almost 18 months to 12 years). It was also in an ideal location—within two blocks of the bank, *Polizei* (police), *Konditorei* (pastry shop), and the bus stop on Bahnhofstrasse where the children could catch the bus to the air base school. In the other direction the short street led to a lookout point and a breathtaking view of the Kyll River Valley, hundreds of feet below.

We congratulated ourselves on our good fortune and began to set-
tle in. For the first few months we were busy exploring the village,
making new friends and beginning to learn a little German. It wasn't
until spring arrived that the first upsetting event occurred.

One Monday in April I spent the morning washing clothes in the
old-fashioned wringer machine in the basement. After lunch I put
Lori down for a nap in the upstairs bedroom which she shared with
her 12-year-old sister Pam, then decided to relax with a cup of tea. As
I sat at the kitchen table, I suddenly heard a man's footsteps going up
the open staircase from the entry hall to the second floor.

That's strange, I thought. Fred didn't tell me he was coming home
early. I opened the kitchen door and called, "Fred, what are you
doing home so early?"

The footsteps kept sounding on the stairs but Fred didn't answer. I
climbed the stairs to the second floor and went into our bedroom,
repeating, "Why are you home so early?"

I stopped short. No one was there. I pushed open the door to the
girls' room. Except for the sleeping Lori no one was in the room. I
looked into the room shared by Keith and Kevin. Empty.

From the doorway to the boys' room I could see directly into the
large old-fashioned bathroom at the opposite end of the wide hall.
Fred wasn't there, either. At one end of the bathroom a door opened
onto a stairway to the third floor. Most of the third floor was attic
space we used for storage but at the far end, an area had been walled
off to make a small bedroom. Our 10-year-old son Kerry had claimed
it as his own because it was quiet up there and he could build rocket
models without being disturbed by his younger brothers. I climbed
up the steep stairs and emerged into the gloomy half-light of the attic.

Almost squarely in the center of the attic a huge fireplace reached
from floor to ceiling. From the hooks in its cavernous interior I sur-
mised it had been used to smoke hams and bacon. I picked my way
around it and through the boxes and trunks looming out of the shad-

ows and opened the door to Kerry's room. No one was there but the window was open slightly and a cold breeze was coming in. As I walked over to shut it, my attention was drawn to an open book on Kerry's desk—a book about World War II. To my surprise, the pages suddenly riffled as if turned by an unseen finger, opening slowly to a picture of Adolph Hitler. I marched hastily to the window and slammed it down. Merely the wind, I told myself. Back downstairs, I searched the remaining rooms, the basement and the garage, finding nothing unusual.

That night I said to Fred casually, "You didn't come home earlier today for any reason, did you?"

He looked up in surprise. "No, why?"

"I thought I heard footsteps but I guess it was just the house creaking." I decided not to say anything more about what had happened that afternoon.

After several uneventful weeks, I had almost forgotten the incident when I heard footsteps again while I was ironing. Hastily snatching up the hot iron, I ran out into the hall, determined to frighten off any prowler who might have broken into the house. I heard the footsteps go up to the landing, turn and continue to the second floor. In hot pursuit I took the steps two at a time. The upper hall was empty. Again I searched the house from top to bottom without finding a trace of an intruder.

Back in the kitchen I poured myself a stiff swig of German cognac (which I don't even like). "In the words of Alice in Wonderland," I said aloud, "this is becoming 'curiouser and curiouser.' " It wasn't Fred or a prowler, the children were in school and I didn't believe in ghosts. It had to be the house creaking.

The house soon found other ways of attracting my attention. On a sunny day in May I began to think idly about the footsteps on the stairs. After mulling over all the possibilities, again I rejected the idea of a "ghost." Lost in thought, I was suddenly startled by a rattling sound. Glancing at the kitchen door, I saw to my horror that the handle was moving up and down. Absolutely convinced that this time a prowler was in the hall, I snatched up a butcher knife. With a combination of fear and anger pumping adrenalin through my veins, I ran to the door, threw it open with a crash, and came to an abrupt halt. No one was in the hall. I had a clear view of the open staircase and as I stood there, perplexed, I could hear the footsteps of an invisible presence walking up the stairs. This time I didn't even bother searching the house. I lay down on the living-room couch and tried to calm my nerves.

That evening I told Fred about the strange things that had been happening.

"Do you think I'm losing my mind?" I asked him. "Nobody hears the footsteps except me."

Fred, rational and levelheaded as always, tried to soothe me. "No, I don't think you're going crazy. There must be a perfectly natural explanation. Maybe it's some trick of acoustics. Perhaps the footsteps of someone walking along the sidewalk sound as if they're going up the stairs."

"Then what caused the kitchen door handle to move up and down?"

"Well, you said the kitchen window was open. Maybe a draft rattled the door."

I protested, "But there wasn't a bit of wind this afternoon."

"How about a sonic boom?" Fred said. "The F-105s from Spangdahlem shake the house when they break the sound barrier."

I shook my head. "I'd have to be deaf not to recognize a sonic boom."

Fred hugged me reassuringly. "Well, I still don't think you're going crazy. Tomorrow I'll ask some of the villagers if they've ever heard anything about the house."

All he could learn was that the house had been the headquarters of a Nazi labor organization during World War II. No one had ever heard of any unusual happenings at No. 2 Mungelterweg.

The house now produced new tactics from its repertoire of tricks. One day Pam and her friend Deby decided to sneak up to Kerry's room while he was out hiking, although his bedroom was strictly off limits. I was downstairs sewing when I heard piercing shrieks and the sounds of the two girls bolting down the stairs as if the devil were after them. I ran into the hall and found them blubbering incoherently.

"What in heaven's name is the matter? I told you girls not to go into Kerry's room. What did he do—set a booby trap for you?"

Deby shook her head fearfully. "No, Mrs. Richards, we didn't even go into his room. We had just gotten to the top of the stairs when all of a sudden the whole attic was filled with music. It was coming from that old radio in the corner near Kerry's room."

Pam chimed in, "It sounded like German military music and it was so loud it hurt our ears."

Leaving the girls huddled together, I went to the attic and inspected the dusty old radio; obviously it hadn't been played for years. I opened the window in Kerry's room but could hear no music coming from anywhere outside the house. A close investigation failed to reveal any device Kerry could have used to turn on the music by remote control. When questioned later about the incident, Kerry indignantly denied making any attempt to harass Deby and Pam.

Another frightening occurrence came a few weeks later. One evening Fred and I left Pam at home to baby-sit the younger children while we went to see a horror movie at the base theater. When we returned, the light in the entry hall was off. As I opened the front door and stepped into total darkness, I was startled to hear an ominous rustling sound directly overhead. Before I could move, the flapping wings of some dreadful "thing" began to beat me about the head and shoulders. I screamed in sheer panic. The frightened children rushed into the hall as Fred hurriedly turned on the light.

"Something attacked me!" I shrieked.

Fred pointed to the floor. Lying open on the black-and-white tiles was the book I had seen in Kerry's room. Again it lay open to the same page—the picture of Adolph Hitler.

"Here's your attacker," he said. "It must have fallen from the railing upstairs. Kerry probably set it there and the draft from the opening door dislodged it."

Hesitantly I agreed. It was certainly preferable to thinking some mysterious entity was deliberately dropping books on my head.

Except for the music that frightened Pam and Deby, all of the incidents seemed directed at me. Although I continued to hear the footsteps occasionally, no one else ever heard them—that is, until the summer of 1966. That year a friend of ours, Ed Deardurff, came to visit us from Wheelus Air Base in Libya where he was stationed.

One evening at dinner I casually mentioned that the builder of the house had constructed a smokehouse in the attic. Ed showed immediate interest.

"Smokehouse? In the attic? That's unusual. May I see it?"

Surprised at his interest, I led him up the stairs to the third floor. Ed walked all the way around the smokehouse, inspecting it closely, then said, "I wonder—"

I replied, "I know what you're thinking and the answer is no. The house was headquarters for a Nazi organization during the war but there's no evidence that the attic was used for any sinister activities."

As we started back to the stairs, we both heard a strange noise coming from deep inside the dark attic. I tried to laugh it off. "Oh, that was probably our ghost. He makes an appearance every now and then."

"Ghost?" Ed exclaimed. "Do you really have a ghost? Tell me about it." He sat down on a packing crate and listened intently as I related some of the strange things that had happened, concluding with the footsteps on the stairs.

He snapped his fingers excitedly and said, "So that's what I heard. After you all left for church last Sunday I heard somebody walking around upstairs. I went up to see who it was but nobody was there. I finally decided it was the house creaking so I didn't say anything about it."

I smiled with relief. "Ed, I'm so glad to hear you say that." At least I knew I wasn't losing my mind. "But there must be a natural explanation for the footsteps."

"Well," Ed said, "if you've ruled out everything else, that leaves only one possibility—the house really is haunted."

"But I don't believe in ghosts."

"Maybe you don't but whatever it is you're hearing seems to be trying to lead you upstairs for some reason. Once you find out why, the footsteps will probably stop."

A search of the attic revealed nothing unusual except an old license plate and several old clocks, none of which worked. Ed returned to Libya disappointed that the mystery hadn't been solved and I resigned myself to hearing the mysterious footsteps for the rest of our stay in Speicher.

One Saturday afternoon Kerry decided to climb up to the attic rafters to look out of a small window near the peak of the roof. I was dusting the living room when I heard him calling, "Mother, Mother, come and see what I found!"

I reached the top of the attic stairs as Kerry swung down from the rafters. He handed me a large flat object which was covered with a thick coating of dust. Wiping it off, I saw that it was a framed picture of Hitler—the same portrait I had seen in the book which fell on my head.

I stared at the picture. Was this image of the malevolent dictator the reason the footsteps trudged up the stairs time after time? Had the house been trying to purge itself of the unwelcome Nazi association? Or had the happenings that had plagued us for more than a year and a half been merely the result of coincidence, atmospheric conditions, or overactive imagination?

A year later we reluctantly left Germany for a new assignment in the States. To this day, all I can say with any degree of certainty about the whole affair is this: After the picture of Hitler was removed from its dusty hiding place, the mysterious footsteps were never heard again.

THE LEGEND OF
SCREAMING CHARLIE

Lawrence W. Carmon

NOW, I NEVER CONSIDERED MYSELF TO BE A DUMB GREENHORN troop, even when I was only a week out of air force training. So when I arrived at Andersen Air Force Base on the island of Guam and first heard the legend of Screaming Charlie, I simply didn't believe it. Ghosts? That was too much, even for the newest airman to swallow!

I was in an old maintenance hangar when I first heard the tale. I had a weeklong orientation to complete, including an official tour of the flight line. Along with about a dozen other new arrivals, I was waiting in a hangar for the tour to begin.

An old civilian mechanic worked alone in a secluded corner of the structure, near a piece of aircraft wreckage that caught my eye.

A couple of others had noticed the wreckage, too. Actually, it was pretty hard to miss. It was easily the size of a large office desk, and judging from the burn marks on it, the crash had been deadly. The metal was so twisted that none of us could even guess what part of a plane it might have been.

I stepped closer to the object, but not too close. I really didn't know much about aircraft, but my dad had been a pilot and I remember him once showing me a picture of a North American P51D Mustang, the fighter plane of choice for the Americans during the tail end of World War II. Upon close inspection, I immediately recognized the style and construction of the piece. It was the rear tail fin of a Mustang.

"Feel free to take a closer look, son," the mechanic said, without looking up from his work.

I was surprised. He hadn't seemed to notice me—I hadn't made any noise—but some sixth sense had told him I was interested.

I stepped up to the wing and reached out my hand. Just before my fingers could touch it, I wondered if I was being too presumptuous.

"Go on . . . ," the mechanic told me, again without looking up. "Touch it."

I put my hand on the tail fin. There was certainly nothing special about it. Once it had been a piece of equipment used in defense of freedom, but that was in the past. Now it was just a hunk of rusting and useless metal.

And yet . . .

"My buddy flew the plane that piece came off of," the mechanic said, finally looking up from his work. "His name was Charlie."

"It was right toward the end of World War II," he continued. "Our planes were still flying patrols over the Pacific, and there were still the Japanese to contend with.

"It was the end of an uneventful air patrol, and Charlie was on his way back to base along with his squadron. As it turned out, one of Charlie's engines blew just before landing, and he went crashing down to the runway and was killed."

What do you say after somebody describes the death of a friend? How do you make sure that your response doesn't sound ignorant, condescending, or just plain stupid?

I said nothing.

The mechanic stood up, stepped over to me, and extended his hand in greeting.

"Name's Mike," he said, introducing himself to the others as well.

He had more to tell us about Charlie. It seemed that Charlie's spirit never departed this world for whatever might be waiting on the other side. Over the years, his ghost had been seen on the flight line by many enlisted personnel. Most encounters were accompanied by unearthly screams.

Just then, our guide for the tour arrived. I thanked Mike, joined the group, and gave no further thought to the legend of Screaming Charlie.

For a short time, anyway.

I finished my base orientation and an orientation as a military police officer. As new troop, I got stuck with bottom-of-the-roster assignments, like baby-sitting aircraft that stopped on Guam only to refuel.

One night I was working the graveyard shift on a remote part of the flight line. I was so far away from the hangars that all I could see was the aircraft I was guarding and the thick jungle. It had rained earlier, and the skies were still heavy with clouds. I'd been alone for well over two hours, and I was starting to feel as though I just might be the only person on Earth. It was an uneasy sensation.

I looked out into the foggy night. An ominous silence did nothing to relieve the eerie feeling. Just as I was about to turn back toward the plane, I heard a piercing, crying sound.

Quickly, I unslung my M-16 from my shoulder and strained my eyes to see into the foggy night. Then I spotted the shape of a solitary figure not far away. The stranger moved with a slow and steady gait, as though he were unaware that he was an intruder here. With my weapon ready, I issued the standard military challenge.

"HALT!" I called.

But he didn't stop. I reached for my radio to call for backup. The batteries were dead.

The figure came to within just a few feet of me. I once more ordered him to stop, and this time he did as he was told.

He was wearing a tattered and filthy olive flight suit. His hands were covered with grime. His face was dirty, too, but it seemed to glow with an unearthly light.

It occurred to me that this might be a prank staged by my fellow troops. As the new guy in the squadron, I had already been the butt of several practical jokes.

I brought my rifle to port arms. "Just what do you think you're doing way out here, mister?" I asked, mustering an authoritative tone.

The stranger smiled, "I'm surprised you haven't heard about me. Didn't they tell you about the pilot who crashed and died here over 35 years ago?"

"Charlie?" I asked.

"Screaming Charlie," the stranger said, "is the name that seems to have stuck with me in recent years."

He extended his hand in a cordial greeting.

I couldn't believe this. Just how stupid did the other guys think I was?

"All right!" I said in righteous indignation. "You can stop right now. This is the most damned stupid joke I ever saw!"

Screaming Charlie just stood until I was finished venting my frustration.

"Look, troop," he finally said, "Why don't we just talk a little while. There's not much else to be done out here."

I looked at him disbelievingly. "I don't have any idea what I'd have to say to a ghost!"

"Nobody ever reacts quite the same," Screaming Charlie said with a shrug. "Most guys ask for proof that I am indeed a ghost."

Now here was a truly irresistible proposition.

"Sure!" I enthusiastically replied.

Raising his right arm, Charlie smiled slyly as his limb began to change into a white, smoke-like substance. It rose into the air and shifted, just as real smoke would have done. A few seconds later, the arm changed back into its original shape.

"Now," Charlie asked, "do you believe?"

I choked and tried to say, "Yeah."

Before I could embarrass myself any further, Charlie brought up his buttered and scorched flight bag, opening it wide for me to look inside.

"This old sack has been with me ever since I crashed here."

He reached inside, dug around, and brought out an old-style military flare pistol. Immediately, I again brought up my M-16, ready to defend myself and my pilot from what had so obviously turned out to be some kind of clever terrorist attack.

"Oh, calm down!" Charlie said, as though he were dealing with a small and somewhat dull child.

Taking his flare gun by the muzzle, he offered it to me handle first.

"Go on," he said.

I hesitatingly reached out and took the pistol. I saw that there was rust on all the metal workings and the trigger itself was gone. It was completely unserviceable.

"I heard about you from the old mechanic, Mike," I told him. Then I repeated the tale Mike had relayed in the hangar.

Charlie gave a quiet nod.

"That's pretty much my whole story," he confirmed.

We continued talking for a few minutes more. Mostly, we discussed the various changes that Andersen and Guam had gone through over the years. Of course, he had seen it all.

"Well," Charlie said finally, "The time has come for me to leave."

I felt disappointed. After all, how many chances do you get to talk with a real ghost? I tried not to show it.

"It's been a pleasure, sir," I said.

About to turn away, he suddenly remembered something important and looked back toward me.

"I've got something that I want you to give to old Mike."

He reached into his flight bag once more and brought out a small flyers' wings insignia.

"Sure," I said, "I'll do it."

A day later, I returned to the old maintenance hangar. Mike was a little surprised to see me again.

"Hello," he said. "What brings you back here?"

Without saying anything, I reached into my pocket, brought out the wings, and held them out to him.

Mike did not ask how I'd gotten them. Slowly, almost reverently, he simply reached out and took them.

"Thank you," he said quietly, and then he turned and left.

The remainder of my tour on Guam was uneventful. No further sightings of Screaming Charlie were ever reported after that night. In the years that have followed, I have spoken with others who were stationed at Andersen after I left the island, and they have no reports of Charlie, either.

I still don't fully believe in ghosts or the paranormal, and I don't consider what I experienced out there on the Andersen flight line to be definite evidence of the supernatural. These days, however, I try to keep a more open mind on the subject. I'm sure that sooner or later I'll learn the truth.

After all, nobody lives forever.

OLD SOLDIERS DON'T FADE AWAY

Raymond B. Padgett

W HEN UNITED STATES ARMY SPECIALIST MARY MEMFI AGREED to moonlight as night cook at the Officers' Club in Katterbach, Germany, she did not anticipate entering the realm of the supernatural. But during her first stint of duty at Katterbach, she encountered the spirits of Hitler's elite Condor Legion—Luftwaffe pilots who do not choose to fade away.

Mary reported for work on a Wednesday evening in June 1976. After the last officer left the club at 11:00 P.M. and the building had been secured, Mary was surprised to see a crowd of men still lingering at the main bar with Juan Perez, an assistant manager. Approaching Robert John, a reporter for the *Stars and Stripes,* Mary asked about the regulation-busting gathering.

"These are gentlemen from the German press," John told her. "This club is haunted and we want the story. The ghosts are said to appear regularly at about 3:00 A.M. on Thursdays. We'll wait for them."

And wait the newsmen did—until four o'clock in the morning. Her work was finished but Mary, who shared the reporters' curiosity, waited with them. The ghosts apparently were publicity shy. They failed to appear.

The Katterbach ghosts were not publicized until about a year later when reporters interviewed Captain Louis Howard, the club manager. He told them that the Officers' Club had been built about 1938 at the Katterbach Air Base, headquarters for German Bomber Wing 53, the Condor Legion, which was recognized as Hitler's elite. These veteran pilots, who got their initial training during the Spanish civil war, flew missions over Poland, France, England, and Russia during World War II. Between missions they retreated to the Katterbach club to mourn their dead comrades and to bolster their courage for the next day with bottled spirits and camaraderie.

Captain Howard told of hearing hob-nailed boots on wooden floors and the sound of windows opening and closing. He mentioned mysterious lights and music and loud parties in the Keller Bar and in the empty ballroom after the club had been locked for the night. He reported that the temperature dropped considerably when the ghosts were on hand and that glasses of wine left on the bar were found empty the next morning.

One night, when he was living in quarters in the club, Captain Howard listened on the intercom for 15 minutes to sounds of revelry in the Keller Bar. When he shut off the intercom and went downstairs to investigate, he found the premises dark and deserted.

Captain Howard went on to describe some of Mary Memfi's experiences but he didn't have the whole story. He had heard and witnessed only some of the supernatural phenomena but his observations had convinced him that the dead Condor Legion pilots still frequented his club.

When the disappointed reporters left the Katterbach Officers' Club that first night of Mary Memfi's employment, she retired to a couch in the Ladies' Suite (quarters for wives and female guests), seeking a few hours' sleep before she returned to her regular job at Ansbach. After lying on the couch for 15 minutes Mary felt chilled. The temperature in the room seemed to have dropped suddenly. She got up, took a blanket from a closet, and wrapped it around herself.

A few minutes later, before Mary fell asleep, the drapes covering double windows in the room fell to the floor. She thought this extremely odd: they fell straight downward to the floor. This is apparently impossible, for the drapes were hung on a T-bar cut to window width and secured with screws through flanges in the middle. Rings to hold the drapery are slipped over the bars from each end. Yet the drapes had fallen straight down before Mary's eyes.

She got up again, climbed onto a radiator cover, and rehung the drapes. An hour later they fell to the floor again—straight down. At this point Mary paused just long enough to determine that the T-bar was still in place. She knew that something beyond her human experience was going on. She was frightened and her fright increased to near hysteria when she rushed into the corridor and realized it was much warmer there than in the Ladies' Suite.

Determined to desert the haunted club, Mary hurried to the front door. When she paused to open it, she heard someone walking in heavy boots down the hallway toward her. They accelerated, as if trying to catch up with her. Mary's hands were trembling; she could hardly sort out the right key on her ring. It was her duty to turn off the ground-floor lights but she lacked the presence of mind to do it.

Once outside the club, Mary rushed to her Spitfire two-seater, happy for the lack of speed limits in Germany. She wanted the security of her comfortable apartment in Ansbach and the company of her tenant, June Bryant. Unfortunately, June was no help at all. She became hysterical and insisted that she herself would never work in a haunted environment. She encouraged Mary to quit.

The next morning Mary told Captain Howard that she would not work in the haunted club unless someone stayed with her. Completely understanding her demand, the captain authorized overtime pay for his assistant Juan Perez, who agreed to stay with Mary. Everything went well for the next five nights—until the regularly scheduled time for the ghosts' appearance.

At 3:00 A.M. on Thursday morning, the Condor Legion held a

spectacular ball. Lights went on in the Keller Bar after the club had been locked for the night. Mary and Juan heard music, male conversation, and the scuffling of heavy boots. The men seemed to be dancing together; no female voices were heard. (It has been conjectured since that females probably were excluded from the club on duty nights.)

When Mary Memfi and Juan Perez timorously descended the stairs to the Keller Bar, the lights went out and all sound ceased. They were aware only of a chill in the air and the sound of heavy footsteps receding. Then, after cook and bodyguard returned to their duties in the kitchen, the revelry resumed in the Keller Bar. Mary and Juan did not venture downstairs again. When they left the club, the party was in full progress.

The following Thursday morning the Condor Legion held another noisy party and when Mary left the club one of the spirits went home with her. Driving to Ansbach, Mary noticed that her car was unusually cold but it didn't occur to her that the ghosts would stray from the club. Then, when she had driven about halfway between Katterbach and Ansbach, she heard a voice behind her speaking in German, a language she does not understand. Terrified, Mary wheeled her speeding Spitfire into a gasoline station where attendants helped her search the car thoroughly. When they found nothing she was somewhat reassured and continued on her way to Ansbach.

Once in her bed, she felt a chill come over her bedroom. Alarmed and wide-awake, she gradually became aware of a male presence near her bed. She sprang to the floor on the opposite side, rushed to fling the door wide open, then shouted hysterically, "Whoever you are, get out of here this instant!"

This outburst brought June Bryant running from her room. June was already almost hysterical because Puff, Mary's huge yellow cat, had hidden beneath June's bed, then pounced on her when she was deep in sleep. This was Puff's favorite game but his subsequent behavior proved that the cat had sensed the occult presence. Instead of his usual defiant attitude ("I got you that time!") the giant cat hid in a heating vent and refused to come out even at mealtime.

During the scene between Mary and June which Puff had set off, the Condor Legion ghost made off, doubtless intimidated. The temperature in Mary's room returned to normal and she no longer felt the male presence.

A week later the Katterbach Officers' Club suffered a severe loss. The dishwasher, a hard-to-find specialist, felt ghostly hands on her shoulders and immediately resigned. She had survived some 20 Condor Legion parties but this physical contact was too much for her nervous system.

For Mary Memfi and Juan Perez the weekly Condor Legion parties soon became routine. They remained alert and a little apprehensive but not overly excited. They even grew accustomed to finding the empty glasses on Thursday mornings. A day waiter was careful to leave three glasses of Rhine wine on the Keller Bar every Wednesday night. In the morning they were always mysteriously empty.

Perhaps because this obliging waiter forgot his weekly duty, the next encounter was climactic. It happened near Christmastime in 1976 when Mary and Juan were struggling with the complex front doors, trying to secure the Katterbach Officers' Club for the night.

They negotiated the first pair of 10-foot-high double doors and relocked them. Advancing four feet, Mary unlocked the outside doors and opened the free one. At this point Juan suddenly panicked. He screamed, rudely pushed Mary out of his path, and ran for his car. Meanwhile, Mary could hear a low-pitched male voice speaking in German.

Later Perez explained, "I felt something icy on my neck, like a cold hand. Then a voice, speaking German, ordered that three glasses of Christmas wine be left on the Keller bar. My panic was a natural reaction."

After this experience Perez resigned from the Katterbach Club and soon thereafter Mary Memfi was ordered back to the United States. She doesn't know whether Condor Legion parties are still held at three o'clock on Thursday mornings—but it seems likely. Such old soldiers as these hearty pilots just don't fade away.

GHOST ON THE HIGH SEAS

Hal D. Browning

D URING THE 1950S I WORKED FOR THE MSTS (MILITARY SEA Transportation Service). We were under the jurisdiction of the United States Navy and hauled troops, dependents, and cargo to the various United States bases scattered around the globe. MSTS hired civilian crews.

On one of these voyages we sailed from Seattle on February 26, 1952, bound for Yokohama. I sailed as maintenance plumber on the U.S.S. *Marine Adder,* a ship not too long out of mothballs and in need of considerable repair. So there was plenty of work to be done.

Some four or five days outbound from Seattle, I lay down on my bunk after supper somewhat tired from a hard day's work. I fell asleep almost immediately. What woke me up I do not know but a man was sitting on the edge of my bunk—bent over me as if trying to tell me something. One thing about the situation that was distinctly unusual was that I knew the man and he had been dead for at least a week.

I had known James Mason for a number of years. We had sailed on the same ship from Seattle to Yokohama and to New Orleans; he was a chief electrician. There were rumors that he had died from acute alcoholism only a week or so after a voyage to the Far East.

The moment Jim saw that I was awake he got up, went to the center of the room, and started to spin like a top. He whirled faster and faster and then vanished. He made no sound whatsoever at any time!

I was rooming with Machinist Clarence Albeck so I hunted him up and told him what I had witnessed. He was not surprised—it seems he had James Mason's ashes in our clothes locker. They had been there all the while, but he never had told me.

We crossed the international date line the next day and apparently according to plan Clarence threw Jim's ashes overboard from the fantail of the *Adder*. He said a few appropriate words as I stood by and then went below.

The few people I have told this story to usually accuse me of coming off a drunk with hallucinations or of dreaming. None of these allegations is true. I was wide-awake and hadn't had a drink in days. But I do not have an alternate explanation—other than that there must be a spirit world.

THE PHANTOM NON-COM

Author Unknown

EARLY IN JANUARY 1953, MEN OF THE ROYAL AIR FORCE AT BULawayo Station reported that the station sick quarters appeared to be haunted by a restless spirit. Most of the staff of the station sick quarters insisted they had heard the ghost.

L. A. C. Kirby related that he was in the kitchen at the sick quarters one night when he heard the handle of the door turn and saw it open. He saw no one but distinctly heard footsteps cross the floor toward another room. He later heard the same footsteps walking the station offices.

Corporal Wragg was on night duty at the sick quarters when he heard a door open. He then heard footsteps pass him and go down a hall. He followed them into the crash room where they were no longer audible.

Corporal Jackson reported a similar experience and offered an explanation of the restless ghost. A few years before, according to Corporal Jackson, a senior non-commissioned officer fell ill at the station and was placed in a sick quarters ward now used as an office. He tried to give a message to a man in the next bed but collapsed before he could do so. He died after being taken to the crash room for an operation. But Corporal Jackson believes that the N.C.O. is still trying to pass on his message.

DAVID CAME HOME

Gloria Gray
as told to Gene Spinks

THE LITTLE BLUE-AND-WHITE CLOCK ON THE KITCHEN SHELF pointed to 4:30. I glanced out of the window as I had done at frequent intervals all that day, Christmas Eve 1949, peering up the snow-covered road, which now was splashed with crimson and purple from the fading sunset.

Countless times during the past three months I had stood at this window of our farm home near Mena, Arkansas, watching for the mail carrier, and hoping for a letter from our only son, David, who was stationed in Korea. His last letter said he had been ill, but as soon as he was well enough he was going to try to get a furlough so that he could come home.

Now it was Christmas Eve. Since we had not heard further from David, I had the feeling he might be on his way home. I had worked in the kitchen since sunup, preparing for our Christmas dinner. Will, my husband, had gone to town that morning to do some shopping.

The thought that David might be home at any minute kept running through my mind as I put the finishing touches to the tree in the living room, prepared the dressing, and mixed the biscuits that David was so fond of.

I looked out of the window again. It was now a little past sundown.

There was not a car in sight, but somehow I felt that David was going to surprise me.

Shep lay stretched behind the range, his eyes fastened on me. He seemed to sense that I was waiting for David, and he too waited.

I lit the lamps as the twilight deepened. I was beginning to feel sick with disappointment. I wanted to cry.

Shep got up, shook himself and trotted to the back door, wagging his bushy tail. He sniffed at the crack, barked and then bounded eagerly at the door.

My heart seemed to come up into my throat as I heard footsteps on the back porch. I opened the door. There stood David, tall and immaculate in his air force uniform, holding out his arms to me. The purple light outside had deepened to a dark gray and seemed to encircle him like a shroud.

My feet refused to move and I was unable to speak. I somehow felt afraid—afraid of my own son. Finally I said, "I knew that you were coming home, Son. You look different. The war has changed you."

He seemed to float rather than walk into the kitchen, where he dropped into a chair by the window. I saw him pet Shep. Shep acted strangely, although he always had adored David.

"I've come home to stay forever, Mom, with you and Dad and Shep." David's voice sounded weak and distant.

From the road came the chugging of Will's old pick-up truck. "That's your dad coming home," I told David. "He'll be happy to see you, Son." As I spoke I was aware that my voice sounded shaky.

Will's truck turned into our driveway. As I went to the kitchen door to let Will in, I heard a strange noise. I turned and saw David floating out of the kitchen, down the back hall and up the stairway toward his old room. Shep followed him to the foot of the stairs and stood looking up as if bewildered.

Just then Will entered the kitchen. He put down his bundles and handed me a yellow envelope. "I hate to bring home news like this on

Christmas Eve—but remember lots of other parents get the same news," he said, placing his hand on my shoulder as if to steady me.

I pulled out the contents of the envelope and read: "We regret to inform you of the death of your son, David Gray, who died from injury—." The words on the sheet blurred and I could read no further.

"I don't understand, Will. David came home just a few minutes ago. He went upstairs to his room. Go and look if you don't believe me."

To satisfy me, Will walked upstairs with Shep at his heels. It seemed ages before he came back down. He put his arms around me and tried to comfort me. But I knew that David had come home. I looked down at Shep and saw an understanding look in his brown eyes, as if assuring me that he knew too.

Shep and I have seen David many times since we moved to California. He always looks happy and it is comforting to know that he is near.

My Life Was Saved by a Dead Soldier

Herman Kane

THE FIVE SENSES ARE VERY IMPORTANT TO THE FOOT SOLDIER, who must see the enemy in the dark, must smell his presence, and must sense his unheard movement; the foot soldier has to be supersensitive to survive. On my last combat assignment I felt I needed much more than my five senses.

I had been transferred to a rifle company in the Yonchon sector just north of Ui-Jong-Bu in the late fall of 1951. I had been in Korea for several months prior to that time, with other units, so infantry patrol duty and I were closely acquainted.

The men of Company C took me in quickly. Most of them were rather young but already battle hardened and very dependable in the firefights that went along with almost every night patrol. Our positions, or rather our bunkers, overlooked a branch of the Imjin River and faced a series of mountain peaks. One tall bare peak, which we called "Old Baldy," rose above the smaller ones just 2,000 yards north of us.

It was the ideal place for the Chinese to send patrols, and it seemed to me at the time that the whole war must have moved to that one hill.

Night after night we moved out, either in force to push them back off the hill, or in small patrols to listen and gather information.

As winter settled down and the shallow river began to freeze, pieces of discarded equipment, along with other debris, lodged against the rocks and froze in place. It made our patrol path easy to locate and follow on dark nights, even when the searchlight companies failed to locate a low cloud to direct their light into the valley. A piece of canvas, a broken rifle, even a small stick became a landmark to us.

Then one night just before the ice became solid, a young Chinese soldier's body lodged in the rocks a few feet from the far shore. There he was frozen solidly into the ice a few inches below the surface. Someone labeled him "Dink," and he became well known in our sector. Some of the other company patrols moving back and forth across the river used him to find the beginning of their path across the ice.

I wondered about him a lot; he must have been near 16, with just a trace of beard on his face. He lay there a few inches under the surface of the ice, his eyes wide, his one arm raised almost as if in salute. Each time I passed the spot a feeling of compassion came over me. I would silently pass the time with him and say a little prayer, always moving just a bit to the side to keep from stepping directly on him.

The bushes started just at the water line; so after passing him I would grasp a handful of bush and climb up the bank to get on with the serious business of a very real war. Some of the fellows kidded me a lot about walking around him, but everything has humor for the combat soldier.

The afternoon of February 6, 1952, was an eventful one for me. I received my orders to report to Division H.Q. at 8:00 A.M., the morning of the 7th, for rotation to the States and reassignment. Then to complete the standard operating procedure of the army, I was assigned to patrol duty that night.

At 10:00 that night we moved out—just a four-man patrol. We

were to cross the river and climb the face of "Old Baldy" to set up an all-night listening post. My feet led off automatically; the icy trail was familiar and a bright moon lighted the rocks below the ice. My mind rambled to the far-off other world. I wondered how it would seem to me after all the long months I had been away. Even the river seemed narrow tonight; we were almost across when my mind returned to business. I thought, this will be the last time I'll see my old friend "Dink."

Suddenly I was upon him, my right foot going down almost in his face! His raised arm waved wildly! I threw myself violently to the side.

Brruupp-p! A full clip of ammo went through a burp gun almost in my face.

The men behind me—Miller and Carmon—were killed. Johnson was badly wounded.

Sergeant Hal Johnson's report said, "Kane heard something and made a noise to warn us, but we weren't quick enough."

I said nothing. I did not say I was warned by a dead friend. I left for the States February 7, 1952.

A SOLDIER RETURNS

Don Worley

ON THE NIGHT OF AUGUST 27, 1951, I LAY SLEEPING IN THE second-story back bedroom of my father's home in Connersville, Indiana. My brother Jack was off in Korea with the Indian Head army division at the battle of Heartbreak Ridge. The back bedroom had been his when he was a happy high schooler.

Sometime after midnight the hall adjoining the room was illuminated, causing me to awaken. I discovered that the spotlight beam from Jack's beloved 1949 Pontiac was coming through the window from the driveway below.

I hurried down to the car, unlocked the door, and switched off the light. I stood there in the still darkness wondering what had happened. No one was around, and even if they had been, why would they have unlocked the car and turned on the light?

I had just lain down in bed when the hall was again full of light. This time my parents woke up and wanted to know what was going on. I went down again and shut off the light, puzzled as to why it had again come on and had been aimed to illuminate the hall. We were greatly worried, for my father had been sure that Jack would not survive the war.

About a week later a Western Union man delivered a terrible telegram: Jack and some of his squad had been blown up when they encountered a mine while going around the end of a downed tree.

The time and date of this awful event corresponded with the time and date of the mysterious night over here. Jack had left his earthly form, but he came home to his loved ones one last time to let us know that he now lives in a fair land and will be waiting to greet us one day.

THE DISAPPEARING HERO

From an AP report with the Second Division

C OMPANY A OF THE 9TH INFANTRY REGIMENT, SECOND DIVISION, was pinned down by Chinese machine guns near Wonju on the Central Korean Front one day a few months ago. Then a stranger with a Browning automatic rifle appeared with an A Company grenadier. The company man tossed a grenade and the stranger stood up to fire. His rifle jammed. This happened three times and each time the stranger was able to fire only once. Then he tossed aside his rifle and picked up an M-1 rifle and bayonet from a dead GI lying face down nearby.

The grenadier tossed a grenade again, and it landed squarely atop the Chinese machine-gun nest. The stranger dashed ahead, right behind the explosion. He fired one shot, then slashed away with his bayonet. When A Company came up the hill four Chinese lay dead—three of them of bayonet wounds. But the stranger had vanished, and he was never seen again.

✽❧❦❧✽

SOLDIER'S RETURN

Ruth Arnold

✽❧❦❧✽

MY PARENTS RECEIVED A TELEGRAM FROM THE WAR DEPART-
ment informing them of the death of my brother, P.F.C.
Howard Gutzman, a day before I had this unusual experience. Howard was killed during the Korean War, by a mortar shell
explosion in Japan.

I couldn't sleep, so I stayed up to watch television after my husband and two children had gone to bed. I watched program after
program, until television finally went off the air. I turned off the TV,
glanced at the clock, and was amazed to see it was 2:30 A.M., and I
still wasn't sleepy.

Nevertheless, I turned off all the lights and went into the bedroom,
deciding to read in bed until I could sleep. I undressed, climbed into
bed, and had just opened my book when there was a knock on the
door. I was sure it was my cousin again. She had been having trouble
at home and, regardless of time, loaded her two little girls into the car
and invariably came to my house.

Grabbing my robe I went to the door. I always turned on my porch
light and looked out my dinette window, which overlooked the
porch, before opening the door. This time I was surprised! There
was no one there.

I started back to bed but hadn't taken more than six steps when there was another knock. I went back to the door, but there still was no one there.

Why I did what I did I'll never understand. I opened the door a wee bit and glanced out. There in the corner, between the window and the door stood Howard, who had been reported dead. He was in uniform. And, strangest of all, he seemed to be floating. Where his feet should have been was a cloud. Howard just stood and looked at me and he looked so sad. Then, in less than a second, he turned and floated off and upward into the night.

I was so shaken I slammed the door, locked it, and leaned against it gasping. I tried to walk but my legs wouldn't move. After what seemed an eternity I ran to the bedroom to wake up my husband.

Harold is the type of person who doesn't believe in anything supernatural. I guess I expected him to laugh at me, but he believed me! He asked me to describe again how my brother looked.

Then Harold said that when he was overseas, during World War II, his buddy, Elton Perry, was burned to death by a flare back-firing. That night my husband had gone to his bunk earlier than usual and just had lain down when there was a knock on the door. He yelled out, "Come in," and in came his buddy who had just been killed. Harold described Elton as looking the same as Howard had looked to me—no feet, floating, and in uniform. Elton had floated to the foot of my husband's bunk, spoke, asking him to promise to go to see his mom, who lived in Glendale, when he was released from the army. The dead soldier asked Harold to tell her he was with him when he died, but not to tell her how he had suffered. My husband said he even answered him, telling him he would.

The soldier then had turned and floated through the door, and off into the night.

Harold said he did take the message to Elton's mother. He also said he never would have told me of the incident if I had not just had the same experience.

WITH HIS HEAD TUCKED UNDERNEATH HIS ARM

Lawrence Stevens

APPROXIMATELY EIGHT YEARS AGO, DURING THE KOREAN CON-
flict, I was stationed with the United States Eighth Army,
just south of Seoul, Korea, near the roaring Han River.

This was a time when Korea still suffered the ravages of past battles. They had been bloody battles and had left the once beautiful
and historic city of Seoul almost completely annihilated. After them
had come famine, poverty, and widespread housing problems.

People were living in every conceivable crude shelter. Some shelters were no more than a few broken bricks stacked up with a large
piece of tin or paper over the top, to keep out rain and snow. The
less-fortunate ones, usually the very old and feeble or the very young,
lived in the very gutters of Seoul. It was not uncommon to see very
old women sitting with their feet in the gutters, resting wrinkled and
gray old heads on their tired and bony knees. Neither was it unusual
to see a child, parentless and hungry, roaming the streets like a wild,
scared animal in search of food. Perhaps he also searched for a spark
of love.

However, Uncle Sam moved my group, a small army postal unit of
16 men, into some old bombed-out Japanese Imperial Army bar-

racks. These old barracks had been patched into halfway decent living quarters and partitioned off into very small rooms. One man per room was quite an unusual luxury in the army.

It was in one of these small rooms that I saw the ghost of Seoul.

June 12, 1953, had been a hot and humid day in Seoul, Korea. I had made my two regular mail runs from Seoul, across the Han River, to Yong-dong-po. This, like most work in Korea during the war, was a seven-day-a-week detail. Later that evening when someone yelled chow I was quite ready.

After dinner and a two-hour card game I was ready to retire for the night. Tomorrow would be another hard day. Besides, during the day I had managed to get hold of a good book—in Korea a book of any kind was a rarity.

I went to my room and sat down on the narrow canvas cot, placing my precious book on top of a small box containing my other, rather meager possessions. Turning on a light at the head of my bed, I lit a cigarette and lay back, closing my eyes. I thought of Shelbyville, Indiana, my home. I would be there in a few weeks. My discharge was due soon. I would be eating Mother's delicious home-cooked dinners. I could almost smell that Indiana pumpkin pie. These were the thoughts drifting through my mind when I heard my door open and shut.

When I opened my eyes what I saw nearly knocked me from my cot. In that instant an impression was stamped on my mind that never has faded.

Standing just inside my door was a United States marine in full battle dress, including an M-1 rifle slung over his left shoulder. Where his head should have been I saw the bloody stump of a neck, sticking up out of the green battle jacket. Bubbles of blood oozed from that gruesome stump and ran down his thick chest. Nestled in the crook of his right arm was a big, bloody, blond head. Blood from it fell to the floor.

Slowly this headless marine moved toward me. He sat down on the box that held my book. After seating himself, he lifted his bloody blond head and accurately placed it squarely on that gruesome stump. Then, with his right hand, he wiped away beads of perspiration from his forehead.

I never shall forget his words or the way he looked at me. "Chinese have broken through everywhere. I sure will be glad when these three months are up."

He mopped at his brow again. There was dried blood on the back of his hand.

I didn't wait for more. I'm sure I set a speed record getting out of that room and down the dimly-lit hall to my friend's room.

Leo Brandenberg answered my knock, rubbing the sleep from his big German face. He asked me what the devil was wrong.

I hesitated. I didn't want my best friend to think me a fool or an idiot. But tell him I did. And I didn't cut any corners! I was shocked when Leo put his hand on my shoulder and a faint smile crossed his lips.

"Steve," Leo said, solemnly, "I'm glad you told me this. It clears up a lot of my troubles. Now, I know that what I saw in there was not a hallucination. You, my friend," he added, with a look of relief on his big face, "have just seen what I call the Ghost of Seoul."

I didn't return to my room that night despite Leo's suggestion that we both go for a look. I shrugged the suggestion away and went to the night guard's room to spend the night. Actually, I was afraid to return. Even the mighty United States Army doesn't train or prepare a man for the situation I had faced that night.

Next morning, with a steaming cup of black coffee under my ribs, my courage returned, and I returned to my room. I wanted to look at the floor. I had seen those blood droplets splashed onto the floor and I thought they would still be there. I was wrong. Not a single spot remained, although I carefully inspected the whole floor.

A few weeks after this I was at home in Shelbyville, Indiana, discharged from the army. Only recently have I realized that from June until September is three months. Everybody knows the Korean War ended in September 1953. The headless United States marine was predicting the end of the Korean War, three months in advance, when he said, "I sure will be glad when these three months are up."

SAY GOOD-BYE

Gerry Sherman

MY MEMORY IS DECLINING NOW, YET SOMETHING HAPPENED 28 years ago which I'll never forget. I was sleeping soundly one night when I awoke with a start. Was it a noise, or did someone whisper my name? My eyes flew open as I tried to grasp the elusive memory.

I turned over on my side to see a figure standing by the foot of my bed.

It was a marine dressed in combat clothes. I didn't recognize him, yet I wasn't afraid. He stretched out a hand toward me, and as I reached out for his hand, he disappeared. It was a long time before I could fall asleep again.

The next morning my cousin called from across the United States to say that her son, Tom, a marine, had died in Vietnam. I hung up the phone in shock. I hadn't seen Tom in 17 years. During his childhood I had visited his family quite often and envisioned how he used to climb into my lap, his chubby little arms squeezing my neck. After a short story, he'd mumble, "I love you," and fall asleep.

My visitor could have been a mature, thinned-down version of the child I had once known, with the same wavy, oatmeal-colored hair and tilted-up nose. Was it Tom who came to bid me good-bye?

Jimmy, Is That You?

Roy Matsuda
as told to Corliss Chan

❖❖❖

IN THE SUMMER OF 1966, WHEN I WAS 17, MY 19-YEAR-OLD COUSIN James Kajiwara and I spent endless hours discussing our plans for the future. Then Jimmy was drafted into the army. His eventual destination was Vietnam. Before leaving for advanced infantry training at Fort Benning, Georgia, he gave me my Christmas, birthday, and graduation presents.

"Roy," he said, "I have a feeling I won't be back."

"Don't say that!" I pleaded. "Promise me you'll be back for my graduation next June."

"Okay, I promise. I'll be back."

But four months later, on March 11, 1967, he was killed in action. I tried to deny his death. At first I felt empty, then angry; finally I felt nothing. Graduation day came and thoughts of Jimmy welled up inside me. The graduating students sat up in the hot bleachers of the Tennyson High School gym while the parents were seated on the main floor. Wiping the sweat off my face, I watched the setting sun cast an eerie light through the doors.

Suddenly a chill swept through my whole body as if someone had dumped a bucket of ice water on my head. I began to shiver uncontrollably. I looked for Mom down in the audience and then I saw him.

Standing in the doorway 200 feet away was Jimmy. A wave of heat engulfed my body. Quickly I looked away in fear.

The student sitting next to me said, "What's the matter? Looks like you just saw a ghost."

Though panic-stricken I summoned my courage and looked at Jimmy again. He was wearing his favorite red Pendleton shirt, carrying his camera as usual, and smiling directly at me.

"Do you see that guy standing over there at the door?" I asked my neighbor.

"What guy? Are you all right?" he replied.

But it wasn't a dream. All I could manage was to smile at Jimmy and then he was gone. My heart sank. Who would ever believe me?

Several days later, when I couldn't hold it inside any longer, I confided in Mom.

"Tell me when and where you saw him," she said. "What did he look like?"

Slowly I repeated the details of my experience to her. "I thought it was a dream but I know it wasn't."

"It was no dream," Mom said, "because you're describing exactly what I saw too."

I was relieved and stunned all at once. Heretofore I had never had any feelings about life after death. Jimmy came back to show me the truth.

LAST PLANE OUT

William Clifton Lewis

WHILE I WAS A SOLDIER IN VIETNAM FROM 1967 TO 1969, I WAS attached to the Ninth Infantry Division, located in the Mekong Delta region. At the 24th Evacuation Hospital at Long Bien, doctors found I had a kidney and bladder infection. They started treatment and told me to return for a follow-up exam on July 5.

On the morning of July 4, I reminded the company clerk of my appointment the next day. I knew I had to leave that afternoon and go to the military transport terminal airstrip at Tan An to catch the last plane out at 3:00 P.M.

That morning, however, word came down that we were on alert. I had to go through many changes to get my platoon sergeant to release me from duty. By noon it was established that the alert was a sham. I got my stuff together and headed back to the company's orderly room.

When I got there the clerk said he hadn't heard anything about my medical appointment from the medical aid station. So I walked over the station to find out what was up. It was closed for the day when I got there, because of the holiday.

I said, "Screw this!" The last mail truck of the day was parked out front. The driver was about to pull away. I got into the back and he drove off.

As the truck moved out of the company compound onto the road to the main gate, the clerk came out of the orderly room and began waving his arms and yelling at me. The driver didn't see him and I ignored him. But at the same time there was something surreal about the scene. It was as if I was watching the event unfold in slow motion. I felt that something wasn't quite right.

The 45-minute trip to the military transit terminal was uneventful. I left the truck and went to the airstrip's depot, where I signed the transport manifest. The plane was an aging, dark green DC-3. As I stood there, a black GI walked up and started talking to me. He knew my name, and he seemed to know who I was, where I was from, and what I did as a soldier in Nam.

I, on the other hand, felt like I was in a haze during our conversation.

He said that he was also going to Long Bien, but via a truck convoy the next morning. He then told me there was a Fourth of July party going on at the terminal personnel's compound. He suggested I come along with him.

It was just minutes before my flight was to leave. I was totally spaced out, as if I was high on something, but I wasn't. I had a strange feeling that I should go to the party, but I was equally determined to get on the plane so I'd be certain to make my appointment.

As if reading my mind, he added, "They're serving tenderloin steaks, as many as you can eat." I would have done just about anything to get those in Nam. He told me, "You can party tonight, catch a ride on the morning convoy, and still get where you have to be."

I gathered up my stuff and left with him. I didn't even bother to inform the depot clerk that I wasn't boarding.

At the party I ate four steaks and all the fixings, drank, and lost track of the GI. I partied until I passed out. In the morning, I went looking for the GI but I couldn't find him. Nobody seemed to know him or his whereabouts. There was, however, a convoy going where I wanted to go. So I found a driver who needed a shotgun rider and moved out with him. I never saw the black GI again.

I got to my appointment on time but ended up waiting a week to see the doctor, who was on R&R. When I finally got back to my unit, I went to see the CO. When the clerk first saw me, he nearly fainted. "You can't be here," he said. "You're dead!"

The plane I'd missed had been shot down, and it had crashed and completely burned a mile from its destination. Everyone aboard had been killed.

MISSING IN ACTION

Leon W. Laframboise

⁂⁂⁂

O N THE NIGHT OF FEBRUARY 29, 1968, I WAS SLEEPING IN THE Air Defense Command Post's ready room in Los Angeles, California. This was not unusual during our 24-hour shift, because the operations room was continually manned by members of my crew servicing the Nike-Hercules units.

Around 3:00 A.M. I awoke with a start and on my right saw my brother Phil crouched facing away from me. I recognized his short haircut and reached out to touch the top of his head, saying, "Gee, it's good to see you." Then he faded away.

As groggy as I was, I knew something strange had happened, for Phil was a staff sergeant serving in Vietnam with the 101st Airborne Division. When I awoke fully I was choking on vomit and I had an overwhelming urge to go outside for some fresh air. I knew something odd was going on but could not face up to the implications.

The next night when I returned home from a local theater I received a telephone call from my father. Hysterically he told me that Phil was reported missing in action. I tried to calm him by assuring him that many men are reported missing, but later turn up alive and well. This calmed him down and I promised to call him back the next morning. That night all I could hear was a bugle sounding taps over and over again; I became convinced Phil was dead.

Two days later we were notified that indeed he had been killed in action.

When Phil was alive he had a habit of continually tapping his fingers on the table as if playing drums as he had when he was younger. We often admonished him: the noise drove us buggy. On the day of his funeral as I was getting into uniform I was startled to hear that same rhythmic tapping on the wall. I asked my parents if anyone was making this unusual noise and they said no. I felt then that Phil was letting me know he was there.

For months we wondered where and how Phil had been killed. The army said only that he was killed on a secret war mission. About a year after his death I was in a pizzeria across from Fort MacArthur's army hospital when a medic came up to me. He had noticed my name tag and asked if I had a relative who had died in Vietnam. When I said yes, he explained that he had evacuated Phil's body from Hue. Phil's entire platoon had been killed in an ambush on their way into that "secure city." My God, I thought, what a coincidence to run into this particular medic! Perhaps Phil had chosen that way to answer our questions.

"I Was Killed Instantly . . ."

Lawrence LaRocco

I N AUGUST 1968 BOB WALSH UNEXPECTEDLY VISITED ME. WE HAD been inseparable friends in high school but had drifted apart after graduation. We hadn't seen each other in over two years when he arrived that sultry summer evening.

I don't remember the doorbell ringing as I was cramming for an exam, but my mother walked into my room saying, "Larry, Bob Walsh is here to see you." Elated, I bounded down the stairs to the kitchen and we just stood there staring at each other for a full minute before Bob broke the silence.

"Aren't you going to ask me if I want a beer?" Bob asked with a grin. I did just that and we spent the next three hours catching up on old times and filling each other in on the last two years. We had a terrific time, but just before he left Bob became serious. I was completely surprised when he said he was leaving for combat duty in Vietnam the next day.

"I wanted to be sure I saw you one last time before I left," Bob explained.

"You make it sound like you're not coming back," I replied.

Deadly serious, he answered, "I don't think I am coming back." Bob went on to explain that the night before he'd had an unusually vivid dream in which he was ambushed and killed in the Vietnam jungle. But Bob quickly changed the subject and we parted on a less somber note.

I wrote to Bob twice while he was in Vietnam but never received a reply. Approximately four months later Bob appeared to me in a vivid dream. He was wearing his combat uniform and it was covered with blood.

"I'm sorry I didn't answer your letters but I never had the time," Bob explained. "The Viet Cong ambushed our patrol and I was caught in the cross fire. I was killed instantly; there wasn't any pain."

Three weeks later I got a letter from Bob's mother informing me that Bob had been killed in Vietnam when his platoon was ambushed by the Viet Cong. Was Bob's own dream prophetic? Did he actually appear to me in my dream? To this day I believe the answer to these questions is yes.

A BROTHER'S LOVE

Teresa Lingerfelt

THERE WAS NEVER ANYONE MORE LOVED THAN MY BROTHER William. Though William was nine years older than us, he always made time for my younger sister, Gloria, and me, making us feel important and very loved.

When he joined the army we were very proud. My father served during World War II, so it seemed only natural for William to fight for his country in Vietnam. It never entered my 12-year-old mind that I might never see him again.

On July 16, 1969, he was on scout duty in Chu Chi when his dog stepped on a land mine. My darling brother was gone.

Several days after we received the news, I lay in bed silently grieving, when suddenly I felt a presence and opened my eyes. There was William, standing beside my bed and smiling. "Don't worry about me, I'll be okay," he said.

I closed my eyes, and when I opened them, he was gone. I never told anyone what happened, and over the years convinced myself I was just dreaming or had imagined it. Then, 20 years later, I told my sister.

Gloria and I were sitting at her kitchen table reminiscing about our childhood. I began to tell her of our brother's visit and she looked at me with surprise. "I saw him, too."

"He said, 'Don't worry about me, I'll be okay,' " she whispered.

I nodded my head and we began to cry. We both knew that had been our final gift of love from William.

John's GI Guardian

Marti Sisto

⟡⟡⟡

MY CHILDREN AND I HAVE ALWAYS BEEN IN TUNE WITH EACH other and most of the time we are able to sense one another's pains, anxieties, and emotions. Even I was amazed, however, at one incident which occurred when my oldest son John was in Vietnam.

My heart was breaking that one of my children should be far away in a foreign country, fighting a senseless war which I felt didn't even concern us. Every evening before retiring I would sit at my desk, stare at the map of Vietnam which was tacked on the wall, and write a page or two of our daily news to John. I would cry a few tears, then kneel down and pray for his safe return.

One evening in September 1972, as I was staring at the map, a picture came into focus. As it materialized right before my eyes, I saw my son and another GI standing beside a burned-out helicopter. The GI had his arm across John's shoulder, buddy style. The picture seemed to move closer and focused on the GI. He was a bit older than John, a bit shorter, with a light complexion, dark hair and full mustache. He looked directly at me and said, "You don't need to cry anymore. He will be coming home safe and sound."

Then the picture faded away, but from that night on I knew I had nothing to worry about and need not shed anymore tears.

The following January John did come home, safe and sound.

When I described to him the vision I had in September, he said, "Mom, describe the GI to me again." Then he brought out a sack of pictures he had taken during his service in Vietnam. He spread the pictures out on the table and asked, "Do you see the GI here in any of these photos?"

There on my kitchen table were several pictures of the soldier I had seen in my vision. I picked them out and handed them to John. A strange look came over his face and tears welled up in his eyes as he said, "Mom, that was my buddy who was shot down last April."

The GI had been killed in April 1972, five months before I saw him with my son in the vision. He and John had shared a part of their lives together and now I felt he had shared part of his afterlife with me.

I will always be grateful to that guardian GI.